P9-DHJ-786

Your Life

Why It Is the Way It Is

and

What You Can Do

About It

Your Life

Why It Is the Way It Is

and

What You Can Do

About It

Understanding the

Universal Laws

by Bruce McArthur

A.R.E. Press • Virginia Beach • Virginia

Copyright © 1993

by Bruce McArthur

1st Printing, May 1993

Printed in the U.S.A.

All rights reserved. No part of this book may be reproduced or transmitted in any form or by any means, electronic or mechanical,
including photocopying, recording or by any information storage
and retrieval system, without permission in writing from the Publisher.

A.R.E. Press
Sixty-Eighth & Atlantic Avenue
P.O. Box 656
Virginia Beach, VA 23451-0656

Library of Congress Cataloging-in-Publication Data
McArthur, Bruce, 1918-
    Your life : why it is the way it is and what you can do about it / by
Bruce McArthur.
        p.   cm.
    Includes bibliographical references and index.
    ISBN 0-87604-300-7
    1. Spiritual life—Miscellanea. 2. Conduct of life—Miscellanea. 3.
Cayce, Edgar, 1877-1945.   I. Title
BF 1999.M452   1993
131—dc20   92-21229

Edgar Cayce Readings © 1971 by the Edgar Cayce Foundation.
All rights reserved.

Cover Design by Rick Britton, Studio 55 Associates

DEDICATION

This book is dedicated to our grandchildren, Mary Elizabeth, Amy, Aaron Isaac, Peter, Elisha, and Anna, and to all grandchildren, for in them, through their understanding and use of the Universal Laws, lies the hope of the world.

CONTENTS

Chapter 4:

Chapter 5

Foreword

Bruce McArthur reminds me of a country lawyer I once knew who never attended law school but ended up as a distinguished lawmaker in the United States Senate. He simply "read law," as they used to call it, in the office of a practicing attorney in the little Oregon logging town where he grew up, and when he had learned enough to qualify he began to practice law. I believe Abraham Lincoln entered the legal profession by a similar route.

That's how the author of this fine book became a universal lawyer. An engineer by profession, he nonetheless "read law" for many years in the A.R.E. Library at Virginia Beach. His sources were neither Blackstone nor Gladstone, but the Edgar Cayce readings. From these documents, packed with the wisdom of the spheres, he derived a fascinating perspective on how the universe works.

Specifically, Mr. McArthur discovered these laws by studying the profound recommendations that Edgar Cayce gave to thousands of people who came to him with all sorts of personal problems. Of the 14,000 and some readings Mr. Cayce gave, over 8,000 were for physical conditions. Time and time again, he offered his clients wise and compassionate counsel; but he also put their problems into the context of the cosmic order to suggest how they might avoid repeating them. When giving a physical reading, for example, he often began by inviting the individual to look at his or her own attitude. As he put it in reading 3312-1, " . . . if one would correct physical or mental disturbances, it is necessary to change the attitude and to let the life forces become constructive and not destructive. Hate, malice and jealousy only create poisons within the minds, souls and bodies of people."

As Bruce McArthur began collecting these cosmic truisms one by one, he found patterns that we could all apply in our own lives.

Here were the laws which govern the Universe and its movements — and ours in it. Thus, he was able to see why our lives turn out the way they do — and to suggest what we might do to improve them.

Next thing we knew, he had codified these metaphysical laws just as more celebrated personages, Hammurabi and Napoleon, had codified the civil laws of ancient Babylon and 18th-century France.

There is, of course, a significant difference, in what Mr. McArthur has accomplished. The cosmic laws are not made by us. They can't be repealed or modified, so far as we know, except by the Almighty Lawmaker. These laws are not punitive but descriptive. Like the law of gravity, they describe how things work. But, if you believe as I do that the Universe cares about us, you will discover that the Universal Laws are not a threat to our pursuit of happiness if we are on the spiritual path. As the author puts it, they "always work for the highest good of all" and are "just and beneficial for everyone at all times and in all places." We stand to be punished, or instructed, by them only as we ignore and transgress them.

Mr. McArthur began telling us about Universal Laws from the lecture platform and in articles published in *The A.R.E. Journal* years ago, so that he is recognized as the resident specialist in this metaphysical field. Now at last he has given us his magnum opus on the subject, compiling and illuminating the Universal Laws in a handy, instructive text that offers us much-needed guidance for the years of change that lie ahead.

Serious attention to his wise findings offers rich rewards.

A. Robert Smith
Editor, *Venture Inward*
Virginia Beach, Virginia

Acknowledgments

My wonderful wife of the past fifty years has been deeply involved with me in the preparation of this book. She is my spiritual teacher as well. Charlotte's ever-loving, encouraging, and discerning spirit has truly made it all possible. Her patience, her thorough understanding, research, and organization of material, coupled with her willingness to give completely of her time, talents, energy, and ideas have made this book a co-creation—indeed, it is our fourth "child."

The teachings and sharings of another of my family of spiritual teachers, my son David McArthur, who is a Unity minister in Spokane, Washington, have been particularly valuable and helpful. The others of that family, my daughter Sue Clemans and my son Thomas, have been wonderfully encouraging and helpful; each has made his or her own unique and important contribution to this work.

This book owes its existence to the dedicated life and work of Edgar Cayce and those who, through the years, have recognized the great value and stature of his readings, preserved them, and made them available to all. In particular, some who have been the greatest help to me include Everett Irion, Hugh Lynn Cayce, Mae St. Clair, Gladys Davis, Eula Allen, Elsie Sechrist, and Charles Thomas Cayce. There are many others whose lectures, books, and personal sharing have been invaluable. Dr. Robert Jeffries' review and encouragement of my first efforts in writing this book were very helpful and much appreciated.

The contributions made by Al Miner, Joshua Setliff, and Mary-Margaret Moore through their published and unpublished works have been of great value in providing additional viewpoints and information on Universal Laws.

I have greatly appreciated the contributions of those who have edited this book for me: Bea Morton, Ph.D., Associate Professor Emeritus of the English Department, Bowling Green State University of Ohio; Annita Harlan, Ph.D., Research Associate, Department of Ecology and Evolutionary Biology, University of Arizona; and A. Robert Smith, author of several books and editor of *Venture Inward,* the magazine of the Association for Research and Enlightenment, Inc. Each, through his or her unique talents, has made an outstanding contribution to this work.

Joe Dunn, Editor-in-Chief, A.R.E. Press, through his diligent work has helped me greatly to clarify and enhance the theme and subjects of this book to a far greater degree than I would ever have thought possible. His cooperation, encouragement, and inspiring guidance are deeply appreciated.

Kay Kennedy's ideas, suggestions, examples, enthusiasm, and great spirit have been deeply appreciated and were of major importance.

"Bear" Albrecht, computer genius, has added years to my life!

In production of the manuscript, Marie Allen's cheerful attitude, commitment, dedication, top quality work, and patience through countless drafts and changes made it an enjoyable process. Liz Winslow's talents were of great help. Nancy Martinez added to that with her willingness to do whatever was needed carefully, effectively, and always with a smile.

Thank you one and all!
Bruce McArthur

Introduction

Many years ago as an electrical engineering student, I found it very satisfying to learn that there are specific principles or laws of electricity that are taught and accepted by all—no controversies over them, no differing schools of thought. They are clear and precise and they work. When I learned them and how to use them, I could design a circuit on paper, then go into the laboratory, connect the components, and the circuit would work precisely as the laws had predicted.

I found there were precise and workable laws in other areas of science, areas like mechanical and civil engineering, physics, and chemistry. The basic laws of each are taught and demonstrated as a part of university curricula throughout the world.

I soon learned, however, that in areas outside the scientific fields, like psychology and social studies and those that deal with humans, an entirely different situation existed. There were no universally accepted laws or principles. There were theories and beliefs, most of them controversial. While teachers, leaders, and experts in these fields assured us that certain theories and beliefs were correct, I observed over many years that they were continually changed and disputed; most proved to be erroneous in the long run. In those areas dealing with humans there seemed to be no solid base on which to build or operate with assurance. A sad situation!

As I went on to a career as an executive, I found that the same lack of reliable laws existed in the practice of management and also in dealing with individuals or groups, whether at home, in business, in the community, nation, or world. This did not seem reasonable to me. I always had the feeling that there must be reliable laws that applied in the affairs of individuals as well as in science.

It was many years before I learned of a very unusual source of knowledge which explained that there really are laws that apply in our relationships, in business, and in our everyday lives. That source was the Edgar Cayce readings. Edgar Cayce was, in most respects, an ordinary person, but he had an amazing gift. He was a psychic, perhaps the most famous and most carefully documented psychic of our time. He began to use his unusual abilities when he was a young man. For over forty years, he would, usually twice a day, lie on a couch, go into a sleeplike state, and respond to questions. He gave over 14,000 of these discourses, called readings. They were carefully transcribed by his secretary and have been preserved by the Edgar Cayce Foundation in Virginia Beach, Virginia.

The Edgar Cayce readings, given for thousands of individuals who asked for help and guidance in their lives, cover a vast array of conditions and situations. To a great extent the readings deal with relationships among individuals, and individuals and their world, their inner selves, and their Creator. The readings frequently explain these relationships in terms of the basic laws by which life operates and referred to them as "Universal Laws." The readings are a gold mine of information and guidance for understanding how the laws apply to every aspect of life. They explain how, by our use of the laws, we create our lives, our relationships with others, and the quality of both. They explain how, through our use of the laws, we unknowingly create the conditions we experience in our lives: financial, social, mental, and spiritual.

Upon investigation, I found that when Edgar Cayce's readings were correctly utilized, they had indeed helped most of those for whom they had been given. This fact was attested to by the hundreds of letters of appreciation that are in the files.

I found that not only had thousands of people been helped by their readings, but the advice given continues to provide inspiration, insight, and physical help to countless others who choose to apply it in their lives. This led me to try the advice for myself.

I found that when I judiciously selected from the information given and applied it correctly, it worked for me. I found it gave me new tools with which to deal with life. It helped me to understand and gave practical answers for problems at work, at home, with my children, with others. Most important of all, the Cayce material gave me an understanding of why my life was the way it was, why certain situations were happening to me, and what I could do to change them.

In short, information on the Universal Laws, derived from the Cayce readings, changed my life. Instead of facing the problems that came to me with a sense of helplessness, I found a sense of understanding and a knowing of how to deal with the difficulties and being certain of what I was doing. Life became not only understandable, but enjoyable. I learned that I was indeed subject to Universal Laws in every phase of my life and that these laws are the keys by which we can transform our lives.

You do not need to accept the Edgar Cayce readings as a reliable source of information in order to derive full benefit from the Universal Laws. In fact, the readings were only a window which highlighted these principles. The laws stand on their own. They need no further authority for they are so basic and fundamental you can check them out for yourself. You will realize their true magnificence as you come to know and apply them in your life. You will learn for yourself that, through their application, you can gain a fuller understanding of existence, of your relationships with others, and with your Creator. You can not only create a far better life for yourself, but also help others to do the same. Based on more than twenty-five years of experience, I can assure you these Universal Laws have done this for me and for many others, and they can do the same for you.

The readings speak of many kinds of law: God's law, divine law, spiritual laws, natural laws, nature's laws, laws of mind, of body, of spirit, law of force, law of creative forces. All of these are often referred to collectively as God's laws or as universal laws. All of the principles which humanity divides into laws of science, mathematics, biology, Newton's laws, spiritual laws, and the like are laws set by the Creator and considered by the readings to be universal laws.

It might seem that there must be an infinite number of universal laws. However, in researching the Edgar Cayce readings, I have found only about sixty laws that apply to our lives. Of the sixty, about a dozen of them were referred to far more frequently than others. These are the master laws that are most important for us, the laws which you and I can easily study and understand. These are the Universal Laws which are vital to our lives.

When I write about these mental, spiritual, and physical laws that apply to our lives, I will refer to them with first letters capitalized: "Universal Laws." (I will also capitalize the word "Universe" when it refers to the source of these laws.) When all universal laws is meant, including the laws of science, I will use lower-case letters: "universal laws."

As noted, there are many Universal Laws. Occasionally, however, I shall refer in the singular to all of them as a body of law; for example: the path of Universal Law.

By the Universal Laws we unknowingly make or break our relationships, our careers, our finances, and our lives. If we become aware of them and use them effectively, we can create joy in our relationships, success in our careers, and abundance in many forms in our lives. These master mental and spiritual laws are the basic ones this book will present to you as the keys to help you transform your life.

Once I had become aware of what Universal Laws were like, I began to find them in other literature—sacred texts like the Bible and the Bhagavad Gita—and in writings of the ancient mystery schools. Universal Laws may also be referred to in other literature as "principle," "universal principles," "laws of consciousness," "timeless laws of the universe," or similar terminolgy.

The most exciting and rewarding aspect of my study of the Universal Laws was the realization that these are guideposts to an absolutely basic path of spiritual development. That path can lead all people from their present state to the highest state of consciousness—one which will enable them to fulfill the purpose for which they came into the earth.

Bruce McArthur

Usage of the Edgar Cayce Readings

The Association for Research and Enlightenment, Inc. (A.R.E.), is a membership organization for those interested in the study and use of the Cayce readings.

For reference purposes and to preserve anonymity, each person who received a reading was given a number, and the reading carries that number instead of the name of the person. For example, reading number 3902-2 was given for the person assigned number 3902. This particular reading was the second one that person obtained from Cayce, as indicated by the "-2" following the reading number.

I used the readings in this volume in several ways.

They are quoted verbatim, paraphrased, or used as a reference source. Used as a reference source, the reading excerpt may be included in the chapter notes or the reference number may be given so that the seeker can research the subject further, if desired.

In giving readings, Cayce sometimes used archaic biblical language. In order to make these easier to understand, I have received A.R.E. approval to substitute modern English language equivalents for the archaic words. These substitutions do not change the meaning of the message. In these cases the reference reading number is followed by the designation AR for "Archaic Revised."

In some cases I have, for clarity, paraphrased a reading. The reading number in this case is followed by P for "paraphrased."

Part 1

Universal Laws:

Keys to Your Life

Chapter 1

How the Universal Laws Affect Your Life

Imagine with me for a moment that every aspect of this world is operated by laws—laws that are created out of kindness and love; laws that result in your having exactly what you need when you need it, that always work for the highest good of all; laws that are completely impartial, that apply to everyone equally everywhere throughout our world; laws that work without prejudice, without bias, without judges and courts and trials and lawyers, without bribery; laws that are just and beneficial for everyone at all times and in all places.

What a wonderful world that would be!

The great and exciting news is that this vision is a true one—this is the way our world is right now. There are such laws in operation in our lives—each day, each hour, and each minute. They are the Universal Laws, the vital laws of life!

You are probably asking yourself, "How can this be? My life is chaotic, unpredictable, filled with uncertainties, problems, and difficulties. When I watch the nightly news, I see a parade of the world's failures and problems. I see no good answers and few satisfactory solutions. How can we claim that the laws of the universe are just and beneficial for everyone?"

It is indeed a strange and disturbing world because both conditions exist and co-exist. This paradox of a world of law, beauty, and order co-existing with an ugly world of chaos and suffering can be confusing if we don't understand how and why such conditions exist.

The great joy, the great hope, the answer to this paradox lies in coming to an understanding of the Universal Laws, for they produce both conditions. They create chaos and suffering when we misapply them. They create beauty and harmony in our lives when we use them in the highest way. Therefore, these laws are the keys by which you and I can make our lives and our world what we would like it to be.

We can make this transition by coming to know and understand the Universal Laws and then by constructively applying them in our lives. As we do this, we will transform our own personal world from the uncertain, chaotic, and traumatic one we have been living in to one of understanding, peace, and constructive growth—no matter what may be going on in the world around us. This is the great potential that the Universal Laws offer each of us. In addition, when we begin to understand these laws, we begin to realize why our life is the way it is, why the world is the way it is, and how we have helped to make them so.

The Universal Laws are fundamental laws of mind and of spirit, of which most of us are not aware. They are not mind-control or positive-thinking techniques. They are, rather, the basic principles by which life operates. You and I experience daily—minute by minute, hour by hour—the results of the operation of universal laws in our lives. We normally don't associate these experiences with laws or realize they are governed by law. So, for a moment let's consider a few examples of the operation of universal law in the physical aspects of our lives.

Join me for a while as I sit here by the window. Notice the prism on the ledge which breaks the rays of the sun into the beautiful array of colors, which move across the ceiling of my room as the sun moves from east to west. The universal laws of optics and of light are operating right here. A jet trail, like a finger, traces across the sky; the plane flying by its use of the laws of aerodynamics. Minutes later a cloud moves in from behind the mountains, and snow starts falling. The moisture in the clouds precipitates into snow at a precise temperature and condition, by law, and the snow falls in accord with the law of gravity. Trees and a meadow in the distance display their autumn and winter colors through the operation of the laws of nature.

Night falls, and we see the stars and planets in their stately movement across the heavens, their positions governed by the laws of planetary motion. A satellite, following the same laws, is on its way to an empty point of space millions of miles away. When it arrives in that particular area, a planet will be passing through at that precise time in accord with the laws. The satellite will transmit pictures and data back to us over these millions of miles, all possible because we know and use the laws of radio transmission.

We come back into the room, flip the light switch, and light fills the room as the laws of electricity operate precisely and predictably. The laws of hydraulics provide water for our showers at the turn of a spigot, water that is heated according to the laws of thermodynamics.

Our cars, our telephones, our television sets—everything operates in accord with the universal laws that apply to each. If it were not so, these instruments could not be designed to function reliably. Realize that the universal laws by which these devices operate have been in existence from the beginning of time. Humankind has only recently discovered them and learned how to put them to use.

For the purpose of this book we are interested in these laws of the physical plane only to realize that they truly are laws and that they are evidence of the fact that "Everything in the earth is ruled by law." (3902-2)* We are included in that "everything," for the universal laws are operating in every experience of our lives, no matter who we are or where we are or what we are doing.

THE PURPOSE OF UNIVERSAL LAWS

You may have a negative reaction to the thought that you are subject to Universal Laws; most of us prefer to be completely free of any sort of restriction. There is no need for concern. These laws are not restrictive. They are truly laws created out of love which will produce every good in your life, if you choose to work with them in the right way. Not only are there laws governing everything at all levels—spiritual, mental, and physical—but they are guided, guarded, watched over, and kept in accord with divine love.[1]

The essence and purpose of all universal laws and the reason for their existence is to manifest the infinite love of the Universe to you and to me.

(Universe here is synonymous with God and Creator and Creative Forces.)

Consider the comprehensive nature, the extent, and the importance to us of the physical universal laws, such as laws of electricity, chemistry, hydraulics, atomic physics, radio transmission, planetary motion, nature's laws of growth and reproduction, and many others. It seems only reasonable that the Creative Force which pro-

---

*The statement quoted is from an Edgar Cayce reading given for the person assigned number 3902 for anonymous identification. See "Introduction" and "Usage of the Edgar Cayce Readings" for more information on the readings and their numerical classification.

vided those laws for us would likewise provide laws of mind and spirit that we could equally rely on to effectively function in our lives. Many sources, ancient and modern, including the Bible, other sacred texts, and seers throughout the ages from Hermes to today's psychics, assure us that that is the case. It would not have been logical or consistent for the Creator to provide precise laws for the physical world and to have left the functioning of the mental/spiritual world of humankind to chance or worse.

YOUR GROWTH THROUGH UNIVERSAL LAW

As you first begin to work with the Universal Laws of mind and spirit, you will learn how to meet and resolve the problems or traumatic conditions that you face.

Second, as you come to know these Universal Principles of mind and spirit and effectively apply them, you begin to live so as to create more peace, joy, and understanding in your life. Others see the change in you. As a result, you become an example to them.

Third, you come to realize that the Universal Laws are vital to your life, for you see how they determine the conditions you experience. You come to understand how through these laws you make or break your relationships, your career, your finances, your life.

Fourth, as you become aware of the Universal Laws and use them effectively, you transform yourself and your life; you create joy in your relationships, success in your career, and abundance in many forms in your experience.

Fifth and most important, your life becomes a fulfilling one because your actions will be in accord with the purpose of the Universe.

For the above reasons, the Universal Laws of life are as important to us as the air we breathe or the food we eat. Yet these laws are little recognized or understood in today's world. Relatively few people know them, and even fewer try to apply them in their lives. The laws are rarely taught in our educational systems. Where they are set forth in the world's literature, they are seldom seen in their true significance and even less understood in their relation to life.

To try to live without understanding the Universal Laws is like your trying to drive a car without knowing how to control it. The results can be disastrous even though you may be trying hard to drive correctly. Likewise, if you do not understand the Universal Laws by which your life operates, you can end up in difficulty, chaos, pain, and confusion without understanding the reasons.

Therefore, it is vital to your happiness and that of others that you learn these laws of our lives and how to constructively use them.[2]

BASIC NATURE OF UNIVERSAL LAW

There is a missing link in the world today: a true, clear, basic understanding of how our lives operate. Understanding of Universal Law is that missing link! It is the fundamental means through which we can consciously take charge of and redirect our lives with the awareness of what we are truly creating.

A key to the great advances in the material world was the understanding of Newton's laws and quantum physics. In the mental/spiritual world the equivalent to that discovery is the realization and understanding of Universal Law as the fundamental fabric of our lives.

To begin to learn and apply these laws beneficially, we need to come to an understanding of their basic nature. A universal law is not like the laws of a city, state, or nation. A universal law applies throughout the world and the universe. Most important, it applies to each one of us, to everyone we know and don't know, without exception and regardless of place, economic condition, color, or creed.

An example of a universal law in the physical world is the law of gravity. It applies everywhere on earth. Whether you jump off a cliff in California or Peru, the result is the same—down you go! The law applies equally to all human beings. When you jump off that cliff, the effect is equally certain whether you are a son or a daughter, a janitor or the president—down you go! It even applies to things. If you toss out a rock from the cliff—down it goes!

The law of gravity is in operation night and day, winter and summer, this century as well as the last one. It never rests and never changes! It shows no partiality for anyone. It is available to all. We can use it as we choose. It is completely reliable, always there, and does not change.[3]

The law of gravity demonstrates some of the basic characteristics of all universal laws, including those of the mental and spiritual. Using these characteristics and my understanding of the universal laws gained from the Cayce readings and other sources, I have formulated this simple definition:[4]

A Universal law is an unbreakable, unchangeable principle of life that operates inevitably, all the time.

We can define the universal laws as a group as follows:

The universal laws are unbreakable, unchangeable principles of life that operate inevitably, in all phases of our life and existence, for all human beings and all things, everywhere, all the time.

This definition makes clear the universality of the laws and the all-encompassing nature of them in our lives. It also reveals to us, if we think about it, a deep sense of the impartiality, the equality, and the fairness to all as well as the perfection that is inherent in them.

The universal laws are also referred to by others as principles or universal principles, as laws of consciousness or laws of mind action.

We need to recognize that there are multiple universal laws which interact. For example, you know from experience that, if you are in a swimming pool, gravity will cause you to sink. If, however, you apply the law of flotation by using a float of some sort, the pull of gravity can be counteracted. Both the law of gravity and the law of flotation are in full operation. We have not changed the laws, only the results. By effectively employing the laws, results can be dramatically changed.

The great importance of our coming to know and effectively live the Universal Laws in our lives is further emphasized by a beautiful statement from the Cayce readings. It tells us how you and I may use the laws to a greater purpose:

> To Spirit, to Spirit's Universal Laws, must all come; the nearer we apply those laws in keeping with divine love, the greater blessings to self, the greater may be the blessings of self upon others. (2906-1)P[5]

Each of us has the opportunity to bring "greater blessings to self . . . greater . . . blessings *of* self upon others." To achieve this goal, we need to understand the meaning of the above statement. Some of us will think of "Spirit" and "divine love" in terms of God, Jesus, the Christ, the Christ within, the Father, or the One. Others may think in terms of the Universe, the Buddha, the Infinite, Krishna, the Universal Consciousness, the Source, the Force, the Creator, Creative Force, Energy, Universal Forces, or some other name. The readings are open to the acceptance of any concept based on the existence of one supreme being, force, power, or spirit regardless of name or concept. We are invited to use the understanding which best fits our particular background, concepts, and spiritual orientation, based on the highest ideal which we individually can comprehend.

Because the power or force or nature of Spirit is not limited to a name, we can feel free to use any name for it or for aspects of it with which we feel comfortable. With that understanding, the above quotation from the Cayce readings explains that as we apply the Universal Laws from the highest consciousness which we individually can achieve at this point, regardless of how we identify it, we can bring greater blessings to ourselves and to others.

The "others" who are recipients of these benefits are far more extensive than we realize. The Cayce readings explain that one reason we are here in the earth plane is to learn and understand the Universal Laws.[6] As we do, we not only bring about our own development, but by our growth we also raise the consciousness of the world. What a challenge to know that our individual efforts to grow in understanding and application of the laws can actually benefit the whole world!

TRANSFORMATION THROUGH
THE UNIVERSAL LAWS

Each one of the Universal Laws is a law of transformation!

All of the Universal Laws are guideposts to your path of transformation. They give the basic principles involved so that you know what is required of you if you choose to transform your life. Regardless of where you are in your development, they will map the steps you need to take. The laws provide a clear path to follow by which you can progress from one stage to another as you grow in understanding and practice. They are not only the guideposts, but together they form an overall picture—a complete path for your transformation.

Let's consider for a moment that overall picture of the Universal Laws. Each one of the Universal Laws is like a piece of a jigsaw puzzle, each contributing to a portion of the picture. Taken together, they form a complete mosaic showing how life can be lived to make it more meaningful and to bring peace, contentment, and joy.

There is a right way to put the puzzle together. Four major phases or levels are involved on your path to transformation with the Universal Laws. These can best be represented by imagining that you are building a pyramid (see Figure 1). Each level represents a state of consciousness with the laws related to that level. Higher levels are higher states of consciousness.

Remember, however, that only you can complete these phases for yourself.

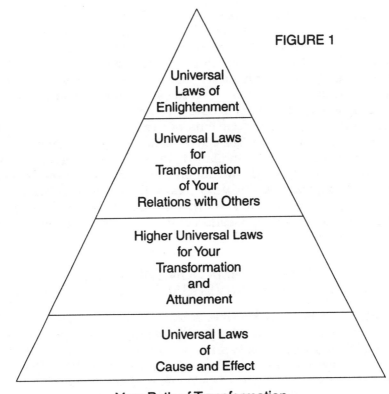

FIGURE 1

Universal
Laws of
Enlightenment

Universal Laws
for
Transformation
of Your
Relations with Others

Higher Universal Laws
for Your
Transformation
and
Attunement

Universal Laws
of
Cause and Effect

Your Path of Transformation
with Universal Laws

Start at the bottom with the laws that form the base of the pyramid, the foundation-stone laws. These are the simple but extremely important "Universal Laws of Cause and Effect." These laws provide a logical basis for understanding why our life is the way it is and who is responsible. These are the laws by which the world, to a great degree, unknowingly operates.

You build the second level of the pyramid with the "Higher Universal Laws for Your Transformation and Attunement." These are the laws by which you begin to change the nature of your life from what it is today to what you hope it can be. With these laws, you can begin to heal and to transform yourself as you learn:

1. What transformation is, the laws that govern it, and the basic steps to achieve transformation of yourself;

2. Your relation to and the nature of your Creator;

3. Your purpose on the earth and ways to achieve your purpose through the Universal Laws;

4. The master law of manifestation and how you continually build your life with it;

5. The laws of attunement, keys to effective transformation;

6. The laws of guidance and how you can obtain guidance for any condition you face;

7. The laws of self and your true relation to others;

8. The law of balance for your life; and

9. Ways to apply the laws effectively to achieve the highest good for yourself and others.

The third level, "Universal Laws for Transformation of Your Relations with Others," enables the seeker to heal relationships with others through the master laws of relationships and the laws of forgiveness, mercy, and grace. These will enable you to move from karmic conditions to grace through the Universal Laws.

The capstone of the pyramid consists of the "Universal Laws of Enlightenment." These represent the crowning achievement of life through which you are able to develop your full potential, which is far greater than you can conceive from any other levels. These Universal Laws lead to the ultimate goal in transformation. This achievement is described in various ways, such as samadhi, God realization, Cosmic Consciousness, or the Christ Consciousness.

In this volume we will work to build the necessary foundation, primarily the first two levels shown in Figure 1.

Most of us will discover that we know little about the laws, even on the first level. We may have heard of them. We may have considered them only as trite sayings, without ever having understood their significance. It is here that we start our work—at the foundation-stone level with the "Universal Laws of Cause and Effect."

Part 2

Why Your Life

Is the Way It Is

Chapter 2

Like Begets

THE LAW OF CAUSE AND EFFECT

The law of cause and effect is a master law encompassing several sublaws as shown in Figure 2. The first of the laws of cause and effect we'll work with is "like begets like." It is itself a master law with two sublaws: the law of increase and the law of attraction. We shall consider them after we have studied "like begets like."

One of the most important, basic, and helpful of the Universal Laws that is so vital to our lives is the law:

LIKE BEGETS LIKE

We can readily see the application of this law in nature, by reflecting on the following examples of its operation:

dogs	beget	dogs
cats	beget	cats
pine trees	beget	pine trees
apples	beget	apples
humans	beget	humans

This law is basic to our existence. Imagine the chaos that would result if dogs were to beget other creatures at random or if we had no idea what would come up when an acorn fell upon fertile soil.

This law, "like begets like," also operates in our lives and relationships in many important ways, as one Cayce reading states:

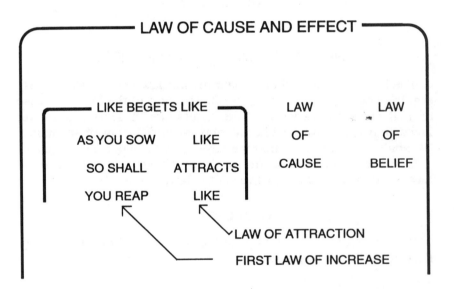

FIGURE 2

This is the law, for like begets like; and [you] do not gather olives from thistles, neither apples from bramble bushes, neither [do you] find love in hate. (349-17)

The last phrase clearly links the law to our lives. Hundreds of readings emphasize that our attitudes, feelings, and actions—by this law—determine the attitudes, feelings, and actions of others toward us.

A woman who was having trouble at home and with her relatives asked how she might overcome her difficulties. Cayce, from his trance condition in which he saw her deeper nature and its need, told her that if she wanted to have friends, she must be friendly. If she wanted peace with her neighbor, her relatives, her family, she would need to be peaceful in herself and toward others. She was assured that if she adopted these attitudes, the conditions and circumstances she faced would change and she would come to the real joys in life. What a simple prescription for a complex and disturbing situation and what a wonderful result promised with its resolution![1]

The critical point that is evident in this case is that the law, **"like begets like," makes each one of us individually responsible for the kind of relations we have with others!** Whether or not you have a friend depends on you, not the other person. It depends on your attitude and approach: you must first be friendly. Likewise, having peaceful relations with your family depends on you: you must be peaceful *in yourself* regarding them. The law is simple and unchanging: "like begets like." Your inner peace and outward peaceful attitude will bring a similar response from others. Some of us might view this law as a great responsibility, for we can't blame the other person for an unsatisfactory relationship. If we look at this from a positive viewpoint, however, we see what wonderful possibilities it opens to us. For if it is true, we are the masters of our lives and we can create the kinds of relationships with others we truly want to have. To achieve such relationships we must first manifest what we want in ourselves. If we don't have the kinds of relationships we want, we know we have to do some work on ourselves.

We can intellectually debate whether or not this law is valid, but this seldom resolves the question. To try to apply this law is the only way to settle the question. Many experiences in my life and the lives of others have proven for me the law's validity. I suggest that you, too, prove it for yourself—try it and see if it works. We need, of course, to be aware that the results sometimes take a long time to manifest and at other times they appear quickly.

APPLICATION OF THE LAW

You can write your own version of this law for whatever you wish to have in your life. Let's consider how you can apply this law to a particular problem. For example, are you sometimes impatient with others? With the waitress who seems to avoid you? With a slow-moving checkout line? With a seemingly never-changing red light? With a child who has no sense of urgency? Or with the slow pace of an older adult? If so, the Universe is trying to tell you, through the feelings that you experience in these situations, that you are impatient. It is giving you these situations as opportunities to develop your patience. The Cayce readings point out that most of us are here to learn greater patience. You may also wish that others would be more patient with you. They will be if you apply the law.

So, applied to the examples above or to a similar situation in your life, "like begets like" becomes: "patience begets patience." This can be stated as a personal law to apply such as: **"If I am to have patience shown to me I must show patience to others."** (1587-1)P

Patience is an attitude of mind; it is not passive submission. In order for patience to beget patience, your patience must be an active growing force within you.

One of the best ways to show patience is by really listening to other people, to what they are saying without at the same moment thinking about how to reply or how to end the conversation. This applies whether we are talking to an older, slower person or to a child or to our spouse or a friend. Patience requires us to shift our focus from our own thoughts, desires, and concerns to those of the other person for a period of time, whether it be moments or hours.[2]

The following, based on "like begets like," are typical of other personal laws you could create and apply to resolve specific problems in your life:

If you do not seem to have joy in your life:
If I would have joy, I must make joy in the lives of others.
If others do not seem to cooperate with you:
If I would have cooperation from others, I must cooperate.
If you feel you do not have enough good in your life:
If I would have good in my life, I must do good to others.

The law, "like begets like," not only applies in all of our relation-ships, it also makes us responsible for the ways we are treated by others, as this reading states:

Remember, **others will never mistreat you if you never mistreat someone else.** It isn't the nature [of the law], for like begets like. (5354-1) [Author's emphasis]

A powerful concept! We see that we—each one of us—can deter-mine what happens to us by the way we treat others. For example:
If we dislike others—others will dislike us!
If we are kind to others—others will be kind to us!
If we are considerate of others—others will be considerate of us!
If we are hateful of others—others will be hateful of us!
We could extend this list indefinitely. Let's be practical now—does it really work? Some years ago I wrote a series of articles on Universal Laws for *The A.R.E. Journal.*[3] Later many readers wrote me about their experiences with these laws. A good example of the operation of "like begets like" came from a woman who wrote:

"I got into my car in a parking lot and, as I was in a hurry, I pulled out quickly without noticing that the car parked next to me was pulled in awfully close. As a result of my impa-tience, I scraped a thin line, about six inches long, along the door of the car (a Buick). However, since it was not a new car and had a few other small scratches on it, I rationalized in my mind that no one would notice, and drove on.

"Two weeks later, much to my chagrin, our brand-new Opel received a two-inch round *dent* in the door, which is there to this day. I knew immediately why and that I must mentally forgive the one who did it. Furthermore, I resolved to remem-ber the lesson of the incident.

"It was a year later that I got my 'opportunity' to practice the lesson, in the very same parking lot. In a hurry again (we Aries never quit!), as someone was impatiently waiting to take my space, I pulled out at too narrow an angle and put a two-inch double scrape and small dent in a newly painted 1957 Thunderbird! A split-second thought went through my mind to forget it and just go on, until I suddenly remembered the previous incident of the year before. I pulled over, took out a pen and a scrap of paper from my purse, and left a note of

apology (I could see it was a well-loved and cared-for car!),
plus my name and phone number.

   "A few days later, a lady phoned me, absolutely amazed to
have received the note. ('It's so *gracious* of you,' she said!) We
arranged for her to have the fender touched up and for the
garage to send me the bill. Know what? The bill never came,
and I never heard from her again. Perhaps it was enough 'pay-
ment' to have recognized the situation for what it was and to
have acted upon it. Interestingly, her name was Mrs. Kaiser,
which means 'king' in German. Perhaps it was symbolic of my
having had power of dominion over my situation, instead of
having let it rule me."

As we gain control over our lower motives, like selfishness and
fear, and begin to manifest from a higher purpose—such as this
woman did with her concern and thoughtfulness for others—our
experiences begin to change for the better. By this simple shift of
motives we move to a higher consciousness.

   We could attribute the woman's series of incidents to chance or
luck, good or bad. I prefer to see these, as she did, as a series of
incidents brought on by a loving Universe to provide an opportunity to learn a lesson and, thereby, to grow in spirit. She flunked
the first test by thinking only of herself. The Universe always gives
us a "grade"—the dent in her Opel. When she changed the spirit of
her approach from "I can get away with it" to "I will take responsibility for my action," she was given another chance and passed
with flying colors. Her grade was no need to pay. She had learned
her lesson!

   As we look at the Cayce readings and personal examples, we can
see that the responsibility for what exists or occurs in our lives is
entirely ours. The kind of a life we are living begets (creates) the life
we will have, because "like begets like" is one of the Universal Laws
by which we create our destiny.[4] It applies in all aspects of our
lives, and, as a result, the Universe brings to us actions, situations,
emotions that reflect what we have expressed or held in mind toward others. For example:

Our motives beget like motives.
Our emotions beget like emotions.
Our attitudes beget like attitudes.
Our thoughts beget like thoughts.
Our approach begets a like approach.

Our acts beget like acts.
Our spirit begets a like spirit.

In other words, what you are "like" is what your life is "like." You beget your life! **Therefore, you can tell, by watching what is happening to you in your life, what you are really like.** If you don't like what is happening to you, it is a signal to you that you need to make a change.

For greater understanding in deciding what to change, we need to be aware that we may harbor conflicting emotions. Consider this statement from a reading: "For, in the application of love is love begotten: In the application of hate is hate begotten." (347-2)

If we do both, hate some and love others, we will experience both.

Some of us may have sincere doubts about the validity of the first statement in reading 347-2 above, when we recall instances in which we loved another but the love was not returned. The law does not specify when, where, or from whom the love will come. In such a case, there may have been other factors (laws) involved that created that particular result. But according to the law, the love you put into that relationship is not lost but comes back to you at some other time, possibly through someone else. The law makes no exceptions. A friend's experience during and after her divorce vividly portrayed this principle.

Louise was involved in a divorce action. Her husband became obstructive and vindictive, continually harassing her through their children. Instead of reciprocating, she remained understanding and supportive of him toward the children, even though she had had difficulties in making the transition from housewife to breadwinner. Eventually she met a man who was very understanding and supportive of her through her period of readjustment. They later married. It was exciting to see the law working in this case, to bring back to Louise—when she was in such need—the understanding and support she had so wisely manifested in her relationship toward her husband during the period of divorce.

There is no deviation from the law, as I discovered one day with my granddaughter Elisha, who was four.

It was my day to take her to meet the school bus for her preschool class. We were late. I asked Elisha to fasten her seat belt. Nothing happened. Polite requests and pleading were to no avail. Being slightly larger and stronger, I fastened it forcefully. She struggled against my effort. "Force begets force!" Grandpa was definitely in the doghouse—not a pleasant way to learn a lesson from someone you love! Two days later the Universe gave me the opportunity to try again. This time we were going outside, again in a hurry. It was cold. She needed to wear her snowsuit. She rebelled and resisted as I tried to help her with it. This time Grandpa, a mite wiser, said, "Honey, I am not going to fight with you about it. I love you," and I fully meant every word of it; it was not a psychological ploy. I started to move away and go on with something else. She looked at me, her frown changed to a smile, her resistance disappeared, and she said simply, "O.K., Grandpa, you can help me"—and she held out the snowsuit to me. "Love begets love." Our children and grandchildren can be our finest teachers if we will be aware that they, too, are manifesting the Universal Laws, reflecting to us as clearly as a mirror our own spirit, our attitudes, and our emotions.

Many people who have never heard of Universal Laws or of "like begets like" have an inherent feel or understanding for this law and express it in various ways. One particular form I have heard used in different locales is that "what goes around comes around," a very apt statement of the law.

It has been my experience over many years that whenever I become cognizant of a law and start to use it or apply it or teach it or study it, the results from my use of the law come rapidly back to me and are very evident in daily happenings in my life. The experiences are as though the Universe, like a good teacher, is quickly returning the answers to my experiment to make the point clear that the law works and to encourage me to learn the lesson it has for me.

In the Unity movement the law of "like begets like" is referred to as the law of thinking or the law of mind action. It is defined as "that held in mind produces after its kind." [5] Ernest Holmes in his book, *Science of Mind,* refers to it as the "law of correspondence."[6] These or similar titles are also often applied to other laws addressed in this book. What you title the law is not important, as long as you understand the law, realize that it works, that it applies to you, and that you are using it continually through your thoughts, words, and acts toward your fellow beings. Here are examples of how completely our lives are conditioned by this law:

When you are tempted to say or think this:	Remember the law works this way:[7]
"She has a nasty wagging tongue!"	If in your thoughts or speech you condemn another, you will bring condemnation upon yourself.
"Look, if you don't do it this way, I'll . . . "	If you choose to use force, there will be just as strong opposition against you.
"He is so careless!"	If you find fault with others, others will find fault with you.
"Well, they are thoughtless and selfish!"	If you speak ill of everyone else, then everyone will look and find that in you to speak ill of.
"I just don't trust you!"	There must be trust given if you would have others trust and believe in you.
"I'll never forgive you for that!"	If you would be forgiven, you must first forgive.

THE RIPPLE EFFECT

Another important aspect of the law of "like begets like" is the "ripple effect," beautifully described in *A Search for God*[8] in this way: "As a pebble tossed into a lake sends out ripples that finally reach the farthest shore, just so do our acts, whether good or bad, affect others."

Violet Shelley, former editor of *The A.R.E. Journal,*[9] told me a true story of a sales manager that illustrates this ripple effect.

"Part of Joe's job as a sales manager was to work with the salesmen, helping them with problems. Joe had flown into a territory and was met at the airport by a young salesman, Bob, who shortly thereafter, while driving Joe to his hotel, ran out of gas. Joe turned choleric, subjected Bob to a roaring tirade, and Bob hiked for gasoline. During the rest of his stay in the territory, Joe mentioned his outrage more than once. Soon after Joe returned to the home office, he had to go to the airport to pick up Mr. Aaron, vice president of the company. Leaving the airport, Joe all of a sudden ran out of gas. He was terribly embarrassed and expected a dose of his own medicine; however, Mr. Aaron said, 'Never mind, Joe. I have plenty of paper work to do.' The next time Joe went into Bob's territory, Bob again ran out of gas. Horror-stricken, he waited for the tongue-lashing. Imagine his surprise when Joe calmly said, 'That's all right, Bob. I have plenty of paper work to do.' "

In that series of incidents we see "ripples" in the situation of running out of gas and in the mature response of Mr. Aaron (which carries through to Joe, then from Joe to Bob). Clearly, through the law of "like begets like," we can set up a "ripple" effect that moves on to others we do not even know. We can be sure it will also eventually bring back to us that which we created, just as Joe had to face the same situation for which he had criticized another.

THE LAW IS IMPARTIAL

The law is impartial about emotions and attitudes. Whether you express love or hate, the law will bring it back to you. The law works for all attitudes and emotions—negative or positive, pleasant or unpleasant. It is up to us to choose what we will manifest in our lives, but whatever we choose, the law will bring it back to us. When people were questioned or complained about what had happened to them, Cayce often responded, "You are meeting yourself!" In other words, this is what you did to someone, so when someone does it to you, you are truly "meeting yourself."

THE SPIRIT IS THE KEY

We find the law's effect on us difficult to accept when our experience is an unpleasant one. If someone were to cheat us out of $100, we might vehemently proclaim that we never cheated anyone in our lives. We need to analyze each incident carefully. We forget that we may have cheated others out of something more valuable than money by treating them unfairly, by withholding help when they needed it, or in failing to give them encouragement, understanding, or love at a critical time in their lives. "Like begets like" does not mean that the specific act will be the same. The Universe operates on spirit; the spirit involved will be the same. We can learn some valuable lessons if we study carefully what happens to us in order to discover the spirit involved. "Like begets like" could be translated as follows:

The spirit in which I act will create and return to me in the same spirit.

If I cheat someone out of money or love, what is the spirit involved? Isn't it the spirit of self-first or selfishness? This can come back to me in many forms, such as others acting in a selfish manner by ignoring me or leaving me out or thinking of themselves first. The acts are different, but all result from the same spirit.

Also, when we are selfish, we are cheating or taking from another. At a deep level, we recognize the nature of our act and realize that we have set in operation the law that will eventually create conditions in which we will be cheated or deprived or robbed in some way. The result is doubt and fear that grow in us.

However, because we know the law is impartial, we also should consider the good situations that happen in our lives: being loved, praised or appreciated; others sharing with us, giving us recognition, or including us in happy occasions. The spirit that comes to us in these situations is of sharing, of love, and of thinking of others. For this spirit to come in any form, it must have been created by us sometime in the past. Be thankful and keep living, being, and doing in that spirit!

In his book *Universal Law, Natural Science, and Philosophy,* Walter Russell, a talented composer, artist, architect, and author in science and philosophy, shows one way to make the law work for you. He writes:

If you do not like your work, it gives back to you what you give to it; you become fatigued and devitalized. There is no task which manifests God which is not beautiful—if you make it so—for beauty is not in any task; it is in you. If you have to sweep the floor, do it gloriously; the floor must be swept. If it falls to you to do it, do it perfectly—with love—and it will bless you.[10]

UNWISE USE OF THE LAW

There are many ways we can use the law to our own detriment. Two unwise uses frequently cited in the readings are: being judgmental and faultfinding. These create a dilemma for us in application of this law because we all have developed, for very good reasons, the ability to judge and to detect faults. We, therefore, need to explore further how, when, and where we can use these abilities without creating difficulties for ourselves through this law.

WHEN IT IS APPROPRIATE
TO JUDGE OR FIND FAULT

Are there times we should find fault—say, in business? Supervisors of employees have a responsibility to make certain that standards of quality and efficiency are upheld. This requires that errors or faults be called to the attention of the employees. The following excerpt from the readings acknowledges this fact, but cautions against doing it too often. The excerpt also suggests that it be done in a loving manner—that is, in the right spirit.

An office supervisor was given advice by Cayce about better methods of handling her work and was told: " . . . don't find fault so often . . . Be sincere. Be patient. Be gentle, be kind." (254-115)

This is not a discrepancy in the law; such faultfinding will come back to us, as every supervisor knows, most probably from the boss! But as long as you are dealing with your employees in the right spirit and for the right purpose, the criticism will come back to you in that spirit and for that purpose. The key is that you have agreed to a responsibility which requires that you exercise judgment and correct faults for the mutual good. This is far different than taking on faultfinding of others for whom you have no responsibility and aiming to straighten them out "for their own good."

Dealing with employees in business is somewhat similar to parents dealing with children. Parents have a responsibility to guide and correct children, always in a loving manner, and to practice what they preach because "like begets like."

In our dealings with others—as people together in business, as families, or friends, or any one of many possible relationships—we may need, in the course of affairs, to analyze, evaluate, and discern what others do based on the effect with regard to the purpose of the relationship. So far so good—as long as we accept them as they are without judging or finding fault with them as individuals; that is, without deciding that they are guilty, deficient, or less than we are. We do not have to agree with them. Each one of us sees truth differently; some in very strange ways, I'll admit! But the way they see it is indeed their truth, and by that consciousness they live and act and have a perfect right to that understanding as we do to the way we see the truth.

The Bible also warns against judgments on our part and affirms the operation of "like begets like": "Pass no judgment, and you will not be judged. For as you judge others, so you will yourselves be judged . . . "[11]

We should not, however, suspend judgment entirely. It can be beneficial to judge or find fault with *things*; it is detrimental to judge people. We need to judge possessions and other items to make certain they are serving us well, so we have a wide range for use of our abilities to judge.[12]

We have the right and responsibility to keep our own creations in decency and in order, and to decide when they are right or wrong or effective for us in accord with our purpose. To put it more specifically, if you have a washing machine, its purpose is to wash clothes. If it is broken, that is contrary to its purpose. Get it fixed.

WHEN IT IS DETRIMENTAL
TO JUDGE OR FIND FAULT

Modern psychology today recognizes our need to analyze and evaluate, discern and compare, but it also verifies how destructive certain judgments and faultfinding can be when we make what it terms "value judgments." Dr. Robert Anthony explains this in his statement on "The Destructive Power of Value Judging":

> The basic cause of most inharmonious human relationships is the tendency to impose our values on other people. We want them to live by what we have decided is "right," "fair," "good," "bad," etc. If they do not conform, we become resentful and angry . . . There is nothing we can do to alter other people's values, concepts, or beliefs if their awareness is not ready to accept change. No one is obligated to change just to make the world a better place for you to live in. People may disturb or anger you, but the fact that not everyone objects to their behavior indicates that the problem is yours. You are resisting their reality and desiring to see things, not as they are, but as you would like them to be. This is the point at which you start

value-judging. Nothing can destroy a relationship or break off communications faster than value-judging. If you wish to develop a positive self-esteem, it is imperative that you *stop all value-judging*. This begins with the right motivation: the motivation that all forms of value-judging are disastrous to your well-being. Just discontinuing verbalized value-judgments is not sufficient. If you say one thing and think another, your words are meaningless for your thoughts are equally as powerful. The Scriptures remind us that, "As a man thinketh in his heart, so is he."[13]

SEEING FAULTS IN OTHERS

What about our friends, spouses, or other relatives whose faults become obvious to us? Sometimes we are tempted to help them by pointing out their faults. The law of "like begets like" tells us that if we point out others' faults, the same will happen to us—and most of us do not like to hear about our faults from someone else, particularly our friends or close associates!

Consider one aspect of "like begets like": like sees like. For example, what you see and dislike in someone else is a reflection of a part of your own nature.

Fortunately this reflective principle applies not only for our negative characteristics but also for our positive, loving attitudes which others reflect to us as well. We readily accept and enjoy these reflections. But when we see a disturbing fault in someone else, we are not apt to agree or even consider that we also have that flaw in ourselves. However, the fault in another would not disturb or upset us if we did not have that same defect. This is a concept most of us find hard to deal with and accept.

But stop and consider. You are aware that a particular flaw in someone else may be upsetting to you but others may not notice it at all, or if they do it may not disturb them. Or vice versa, what troubles someone else may not bother you at all. Obviously there must be some reason within you for your reaction to a particular fault in another. It may be that you have repressed the fault in yourself so effectively that you do not recognize it at all on the conscious level, so you strongly reject the idea that you have that failing. But it can still be there. Many readings pointed out to individuals who were complaining about others: **"Know that the fault you find in others is a reflection of a fault in yourself."** (1688-9)P

This reflective action of the law "like begets like" is sometimes referred to as the mirror principle.

THERE IS A BETTER WAY

The reflective nature of "like begets like" tells us that when you judge another, the only person you are being judgmental of is yourself. There is a better way as suggested in this reading: " . . . **you cast judgments upon others. By whose standard are you measuring your brother? By God's love for you?**" (3660-1)AR

The individual who received that reading was obviously measuring others by his own standard and not by God's love for him. God's standard eliminates judging and faultfinding; there is no "guilty" or "not guilty" involved in love. When we truly love, we do not judge. We accept others just as they are. If we can do that, we have no need to judge. More wonderful is the fact that others then accept us just as we are—without judgment, for "like begets like."

A first step in accepting others without judgment is to stop judging ourselves. We need only apply the standard set out in the above reading: "God's love for you." Know that God loves you and accepts you just as you are. Therefore, it's O.K. to love yourself just as you are. To love yourself is to help eliminate the guilt and fear that pushes you to judge yourself and others. The acceptance of God's unconditional love as your standard is, therefore, a wonderfully freeing experience.[14]

Jesus well knew and understood the fundamental laws of our beings. He knew that the faults we see in others are our own faults and that we hide this fact from ourselves. He spoke of it graphically:

> Why do you look at the speck of sawdust in your brother's eye, with never a thought for the great plank in your own? Or how can you say to your brother, "Let me take the speck out of your eye," when all the time there is that plank in your own? You hypocrite! First take the plank out of your own eye, and then you will see clearly to take the speck out of your brother's.[15]

I have found that getting the plank out of my own eye is not easy, but it can be done. When something that someone is doing is disturbing or upsetting me, I write down as clearly as I can what is affecting me, what it is that I don't like about that individual or what he or she is doing. I am usually absolutely sure that I am in no way like that or doing that. But since I know that "like begets like," I know it must be there somewhere, so I sit down and carefully examine all phases of my life to see where it is. If I am truly honest with myself, I find it.

Tom, a co-worker of mine, seemed to completely ignore my ideas. When I needed something for my project, he did nothing about it until I really pressured him. This irritated me. I, of course, was certain that I was never like Tom, that I was very considerate of others and always promptly responded to their needs! However, in desperation one day, after he ignored an urgent request of mine and after I reminded myself that like does beget like, I sat down to seriously analyze why I had to put up with the situation. After considerable time and effort, I was still completely baffled and was ready to give up. Finally the thought suddenly came to me that I should do something about the washing machine which my wife had been telling me for two months was not working properly. Then it hit me! I had been doing to her exactly what Tom was doing to me. I had been completely ignoring her ideas and her needs for her projects. "Like begets like!" That washing machine got fixed fast!

I wish I could report that the next day Tom happily cooperated on my project. He didn't. It took months of my working on my relationships with others—not only with my wife—and their needs until I truly began to really care and listen and try to help others. Over this period of time Tom's attitude toward me changed gradually, but I knew I had finally made it when one day he came in and asked, "What can I help you with today?" This example illustrates the following facts:

1. I can never change the attitude I dislike in another person unless I change myself.

2. This is so because "like begets like"; therefore, life mirrors back to me what I am like.

3. So if I do not like what I see, I must change. When I do, what I see will change.

4. But when I change myself, that person will seem to change (because I see only my reflection)!

5. Be careful now, for I do not change the other person. He or she does not make any change. The person may still have the same characteristic which I disliked. But since I have changed, I am different from what I was before.

6. Therefore, I no longer beget the same result from that individual, or no longer see it, or no longer react to it. To me,

therefore, that person is different—a changed individual.

7. But the other person is only a mirror for me. **What I am really seeing in him or her as change is the change I have made in myself!**

USING "LIKE BEGETS LIKE" TO CHANGE YOUR LIFE

Our relationships with others give us great opportunities for utilizing this law and the above-listed concepts in life-changing ways. You can make your life much happier. For example, regarding the marriage situation and the temptation to judge and find fault with our spouse, the readings offer excellent advice:

> . . . the peculiarities, the oddities, the errors are to be minimized, *not* dwelt upon and increased! *Minimize* rather than crystallize or magnify any faults in the other. *Know* that your associations are to be on a fifty-fifty basis, not forty-sixty nor twenty-eighty but *fifty-fifty*! and that you must adjust yourselves to each *other's* idiosyncrasies or peculiarities. (1722-1)AR

To me that is a classic statement for the application of the law "like begets like" in the finest way to any marriage or close relationship. Try it. The results will amaze you.

The following reading gives another clue as to how to overcome our negative attitudes toward others and thereby apply "like begets like" in a higher way:

> Quit finding fault with others and others will quit finding fault with you . . . And let this be a new experience for you—to recognize the abilities as well as the faults. (3544-1)

This suggests a shift in focus—for a very good reason. We know that nature abhors a vacuum. It is not enough to stop a bad habit. Better to substitute a positive and constructive act or thought to take its place. For example, when I was working as an engineer, a supervisor seemed to check up on my work more often than necessary and that irritated me. When I recognized my reaction, I realized that I could choose a different one. So I chose to use his checkups as opportunities to clarify any questions I had about the project. This gave me an entirely different feel about his visits, for I then saw them as a help to me. I was surprised to find I began to look forward to his coming. We eventually became good friends.

Anyone can find fault. The wise person finds ways to encourage others in the turmoils and problems of life. A smile, a word of praise, a hope, a sharing of an uplifting thought, or a bit of humor are great alternatives to faultfinding. By use of these suggestions, instead of finding fault we then apply "like begets like" in a totally different way and create rewarding results in our lives.

When we are tempted to find fault, we can consider this concept from the readings: Every one of us has a place. Like trees, we come in a great variety, but we each have our place. The other person may be a pine and you may be an oak. Therefore, you can't expect that one to be or act like an oak, like you. People are different—God bless them. Let each do it his or her way, you do it your way!

In view of the operation of "like begets like," our ideal should be to see the good in others and not judge them or find fault with them. We have an ancient precedent for that view in Jesus' statement, "Love your enemies and pray for your persecutors." (Matthew 5:44) Doing this, we emulate the Creator "who makes his sun rise on the good and bad alike, and sends the rain on the honest and the dishonest." [16] The key here is to treat everyone with love. That's the ideal. You thereby apply "like begets like" in the highest way. Then, by that law only the highest and best will come back to you.

TO ACHIEVE THE IDEAL

So that we can achieve the ideal, all of us need some way to check up on ourselves to determine (1) how we are using this law and (2) whether or not we are improving. To do this checkup, the readings often suggested an interesting process: **Stand aside and watch yourself pass by;** that is, stop and review what you have been saying, doing, and thinking. Review your last contact with someone—why did you say what you did? How did you feel about it? Would you do it the same way again if you had the chance? Does it measure up to what you feel would be the ideal way to act?

Such an analysis of your actions provides a foundation to use in making changes and improvements. By such evaluation you are able to discern how you are unknowingly applying the law. You, then, are able to make any changes required to act more nearly in accord with the ideal.

These steps of analysis, evaluation, discernment, and comparison with the ideal are vital to your growth and to your transformation. The steps do not and should not include at any point a judgment, conclusion, or decision that says you are wrong or deficient or a failure, or suggest anything that implies guilt or a put-down of self or a need for fear or condemnation. It is such criticism or judging that is an unwise use of the law. Don't do it to yourself or to others.[17]

From long experience, I can tell you that the process of standing aside and watching yourself go by is one of the simplest and most effective tools for personal growth I have ever found. The first time I tried it I was appalled at what I saw! As I sat down for lunch that day, I was feeling very stressed and dissatisfied. I began to stand aside and look back at myself as I had lived that morning. I watched myself severely criticize the hotel clerk when I checked out. I felt my anger as I condemned the manager of the repair shop for not having my car ready when promised. I saw myself in the meeting I had attended expressing very judgmental opinions of two of my associates. Then to top it off, I realized I had just been rude to the waitress who was serving me! I found myself trying to rationalize all this, but there was no denying that the picture was not a pleasant one. As a result of this process, I began to try to make changes in the way I dealt with others. I began to watch myself even as I interacted with others. It is a powerful way to begin to know yourself. As you look at what you are actually doing and compare it with your ideal, you have clear and direct evidence of how you need to change.

Opportunities to misuse the law of "like begets like" come by the trainloads—opportunities to judge, gossip, criticize, resent, hate, condemn, be jealous or envious, angry, vicious, contentious, grudging, speak harshly, etc. If we can be alert when these opportunities come, we can tell ourselves, "No, that's not my train. Mine is the train carrying hope, joy, peace, cooperation, understanding, forgiveness, love, confidence, trust, and peace—and that's where I'm going!"

LIKE BEGETS LIKE IN OUR
RELATIONSHIP WITH THE FATHER

Edgar Cayce once gave a reading at the request of the daughter of a man who had disappeared, leaving a suicide note. One of the reassurances Cayce's source gave to her was that if she would put her trust in the Higher Power, she would find that:

. . . the love of the Father will sustain you; and that love, as it will be manifested in the lives, the activities, the hearts, the presence of your fellow man, will bear you up. For, like begets like. (378-29)AR

This case shows us that the law is so important it even operates in our relationship with the Father. It also presents us with a startling requirement: we need to first trust Spirit if we are going to have a relationship with Spirit and derive the benefits of it. This is not to say that at any time God does not trust us. But if we are to be aware of that trust and to bring the fruits of that into our lives, we first need to set the law to work for us by trusting God.

The fact that we must take the first steps in our relationship with our Creator explains why those who follow the intellectual approach alone can't make the breakthrough to understanding the spiritual. "Like begets like" means we must take the first step in spirit if we wish to know, experience, or manifest the spiritual.

THE CHOICE IS YOURS

In using this law, we can dispense love and cooperation and friendliness or faultfinding or judgment or hate. We have the choice. There are many ways in which we apply this law. Which do you choose to create in your life:

tolerance or intolerance

courage or fear

gossip or support

open-mindedness or narrow-mindedness

faith or fear

patience or impatience

joy or sorrow

peace or contention

forgiveness or grudges

condemnation or acceptance

While there are apparently many choices, there is only one fundamental decision required of you about how you apply this law: Will I choose the high road, living in accord with the flow of peace, love, and joy of the Universe? Or will I choose the low road of faultfinding, judgment, condemnation, and selfishness? Whichever road you choose becomes a part of your life and your destiny.

SOME HIGHLIGHTS OF THIS CHAPTER

The law:

LIKE BEGETS LIKE

is irrefutable, unchangeable, immutable, and cannot be avoided.

It operates whether we are aware of it or not.

The law applies in our lives as well as in nature.

It assures that whatever we hold as an attitude or emotion in any situation will at some later time come back to us.

It operates impartially, working for both positive or negative, constructive or destructive, spirit, thoughts, words, or actions.

"Like begets like" puts us in charge. As we use it for good or for ill each day, we are indeed the pilots, the directors of our lives.[18]

Chapter 3

Laws of Increase

The laws that are the topic of this chapter deal with greatly multiplying a particular condition. For that reason I have termed these the laws of increase. They are extremely important and basic to our lives. The first law is:

> ... **AS YOU SOW, SO SHALL YOU REAP.**
> (1529-1)AR (cf. Galatians 6:7)

This is one of the most understandable of the laws because we have clear examples of it in nature. Each time we plant a garden or see new growth from what were barren fields, we see this law in operation. More important, as we work with nature through this law by planting and harvesting, we experience—in the physical realm—the contributions of the Creative Force that enable us to accomplish our goals. As we study and observe what takes place in this growth process, we gain a deeper understanding of how the law works in our lives and how we can best work in accord with it and with the Creative Forces.

THE INCREASE

My wife has a greenhouse and a green thumb.
She plants several tiny seeds.
In a few months we are eating huge, delicious, fresh ripe tomatoes.
She sowed only several tiny seeds.

She was patient.

She gave love, care, consideration, food, water.

She reaps not just a few seeds—but wonderful, nourishing, beautiful fruit and hundreds of new seeds.

The miracle in this law is one of abundance and joy and beauty, wherein you reap not only what you sow, but far, far more—multiplied many times—when the right kind of seed is nurtured with the spirit of love and cooperation. The harvest is abundance.[1]

We reap abundantly in our gardens and in our lives according to the seed we sow. The prosperity comes through the operation of the law of increase. The operative power behind that law is not just our efforts but is explained by the readings as: "God alone gives the increase." (3660-2)AR

THE LAW IN OUR LIVES

We all know or have experienced the pleasure of planting a seed and waiting to see the first green shoots. We have marveled at the growth of the plant, cared for it, and eventually reaped the harvest in the beauty of a flower or food from our garden. We, therefore, can conclude that "as you sow so shall you reap" is a basic, organic law which works in nature. We know that a large part of our food supply is dependent on the operation of this law. We can also conclude that it must indeed be a Universal Law because, under the proper conditions, it works for anyone, anywhere, all the time, and has apparently been an inherent part of our world since the beginning of time.

Equally important, however, is the fact—recognized in ancient literature and teachings—that this law applies in our lives as well as in nature. We, through our words and acts, sow seeds which will grow, and we will reap the results in our lives. Ralph Waldo Emerson put it this way: "Let a man learn that everything in nature goes by law and not by luck and what he sows he reaps."

As with the farmer, it can take some time for those seeds to grow and mature, but they inevitably seem to do so. The Bible speaks of the law in this manner:

Make no mistake about this: God is not to be fooled; a man reaps what he sows. If he sows in the field of his lower nature, he will reap from it a harvest of corruption, but if he sows in the field of the Spirit, the Spirit will bring him a harvest of eternal life. (Galatians 6:7-8, NEB)

Another important point is that we sow these seeds not only by spoken words or acts toward others, but also by thoughts. Our thoughts are basic to our creative power; we use them to direct our energy. We can consider a thought as the seed that carries all the potential of that thought, just as a wheat seed carries all the potential of the plant it will produce. Cayce's source defined thoughts as deeds that may become crimes or miracles![2]

Frank Laubach, in his book *Prayer: The Mightiest Force in the World,* writes:

> If you shout, your voice carries barely fifty yards. But when you think, your thoughts go around the world, as far and as fast as the radio . . . Every thought tends to become true in proportion as it is intense and as it is long dwelt upon. Thoughts result in deeds and deeds make history. Our thoughts leap across space and appear again in other minds, in proportion as they are intense and long dwelt upon. Thoughts are contagious. "What you whisper in secret," said Jesus, "shall be shouted from the housetops." Yes, even your thoughts shout though others may not know it is you who are shouting . . . Our thoughts are the threads weaving the garment which the world tomorrow will wear. You and I created a piece of tomorrow in our thoughts today.[3]

So, you and I with our thoughts are gardeners of the world; we are continually planting seeds. What happens in our lives are the fruits springing from those seeds.

THE NATURE OF THE SEEDS

The character of the seed within the thought is determined by the spirit which we put into it. That spirit determines the fruits that will be produced in our lives, just as the apple seed contains the spirit or nature of apples.[4]

When in the spirit of love you think a loving thought about someone, such as, "She is a wonderful person," you plant a seed of love by the energy of your thought. That seed, planted in the realm of thought, will grow until another person is moved to think a loving thought about you. You will pick up that feeling of love, and it will make your day brighter—all of this without a word being spoken. In fact, many such loving thoughts of you may be generated and come back to you from different persons because, as in the case of planting a physical seed, it is multiplied many times.[5]

LAW OPERATES ON ALL LEVELS

In addition to your original loving thought, let us suppose that you act in a loving way toward the person mentioned above. Perhaps you call or send a gift. You have now planted the seed in both the world of thought and in the world of action. It will grow and come back to you in both forms, as someone is moved to think and to act with a loving nature toward you. Remember:

What we do in the physical we meet in the physical, what we do in the mental we meet in the mental, what we do in the spirit we meet in spirit. "Whatsoever a man soweth, that shall he also reap."[6]

The readings tell an intriguing tale of both deceit and bravery for one individual who, in a previous life, was a member of a tribe about to be driven out of its country. He made an agreement with the opposition leader by which his people could stay, but he did it in a deceitful manner. This, he was told in the reading, was gnawing at his own soul, for "What a fatal net we weave when we first practice to deceive." (3084-1) Deceit, even in an attempt to help others, brings disturbance to one's soul. For the purpose with which we sow is the purpose that we reap.[7]

If we can understand that our purpose is often father or mother to our spirit, then we are helped in determining the kind of seed we are sowing. If we ask ourselves, "What is my true purpose?" and honestly answer the question, we will know what kind of seed we have created. We must, however, be careful not to deceive ourselves! Had the tribe's leader asked himself that question, he might have answered, "My purpose is to save my people," and thus ignored his purpose to deceive. Be skeptical of your own answers; look for any additional, hidden agendas. Your true purpose determines the nature of the seed and of the harvest you will reap.

MEANS AND ENDS

The above example of the tribe member also illustrates the error in thinking that the end justifies the means. It does not. By this law the means (what we sow) determines the end (what we reap).

The reason most of us are not clearly aware of the direct relationship among our thoughts, words, and acts and what is happening to us is because we don't realize that these things carry that seed of spirit and purpose in them. Furthermore, there is usually a delay—just as in nature—between sowing and reaping. In human affairs we don't connect the two, so it seems that many things happen to us without reason.

Also, because the law operates on all three levels, what you hold on the spiritual or the mental level will eventually manifest in the physical. Since we are often not conscious of what we are carrying on those levels, we do not realize that we are the cause of what is happening to us. For example, the deep unconscious beliefs we hold often contribute to our thoughts and actions in ways of which we are not aware.

Not understanding these factors tends to obscure the relationship between the seeds we plant and the harvest we reap. Being aware that there are such factors enables us to more clearly observe the working of the law in our lives.

MANIPULATING THE LAW

We may be tempted to try to manipulate the law for personal advantage by planting seeds of "nice" thoughts and actions for others so that others would do nice deeds for us. That is the right idea, but the wrong purpose. The spirit of that "nice" deed is a selfish desire to receive, rather than to love. The result will be selfish acts toward you by others. The readings warn us that God is not mocked—the true motivation or spirit is always known and the laws operate accordingly.[8]

If you "use," "work," or "manipulate" the Universal Laws for selfish purposes, that spirit, that purpose, will come through and you will reap detrimental results.

THE SPIRIT IN WHICH WE ACT

Since the key to this law is the spirit (seed) with which we sow, let's look at a practical example:

Two people can perform the same act with opposite results. Each could bake a cake to surprise a friend, each one feeling it would be a nice action to do. Their basic spirit (purpose), however, might be quite different. One might act in the spirit of love, wanting to bring the friend joy and happiness. The other might act in the spirit of self, hoping to impress the friend or to gain attention for self.

In each case the same act occurred, but two different seeds were planted. One will return a loving fruit; the other selfish acts. The law is impartial. It works equally to multiply negative or positive seeds. Witness the abundance of weeds in our gardens. If we express (plant) in a spirit of hatred, envy, doubt, or fear, we eventually will have to face these things—in abundance! Seeds of discord and malice will eventually return a harvest of contention and despair.[9] On the other hand, as we feel or express in a spirit of gratitude, kindness, joy, or other positives, we are sowing seeds in that spirit, which—by law—will bring even more of it to us. The law does not judge what should or should not be done. It produces from the seeds sown, just as in your garden the weeds and flowers grow without partiality. The words "as you sow" are simple, clear, and deeply significant without any qualifications and without ifs, ands, or buts. The law will reproduce exactly as you sow.

WHERE DO WE SOW THE SEEDS?

Are we, by the spirit of our thoughts, words, and deeds, sowing the seeds in the other person? That is possible, depending on their interest and perception of us. More important is the fact that the seed—the spirit—in which we think or speak or act is sown in our own inner self; there it grows. The more often we think or act in a particular spirit, the greater the energy given to that seed, and the stronger it becomes in us. Eventually, that energy creates in us the results of that particular seed. There is one point we need to recognize, to repeat, and to emphasize: It is through our attitudes toward others that we sow the seed in ourselves. Consider this example:

Assume that you lack self-confidence and wish to develop it. The way to create it in yourself is to find and have confidence **in others.** As you think and act in that spirit and with that purpose toward others, the seed will gradually grow in you. As it does, by the operation of the law "like begets like," others will come to have confidence in you. This, in turn, will add to your self-confidence.[10]

This procedure works for the development of any attitude. It offers great potential for developing positive, constructive attitudes in ourselves. But be careful; it will also build negative and destructive attitudes when we hold those same attitudes toward others.

TIME AND PATIENCE

Let's assume you have planted a loving spiritual seed. You do something for someone—maybe it's a prayer or a loving thought or you look for and praise the good you see in the other person. Once you've planted the good seed, like a farmer, you wait. Don't dig it up to see if it's growing. These readings explain why:

> . . . man may only sow the seed of life—God *alone* can give it life! *He* gives the increase! (1152-4)AR

> For it is the law that as you sow, so shall you reap. And you are the sower; but leave what may be the results to your Father! (1529-1)AR

These readings set out a requirement for patience. It is during this time—as you are patient—that the Creative Forces do their work. We need to acknowledge that it is not up to us alone, but that we are co-workers with the Creator. Once we have done our part in planting the seeds, the Creative Forces do their part in providing the growth. In whatever we do, there is both a time for action (the sowing) and a time for nonaction (patience or rest and waiting), while the Creator carries out the growth. This, too, can be a time for our own growth in spirit through prayer and meditation, to attune ourselves to the coming changes which we have initiated.

Our only requirement during the time of growth is to be sure that our spirit, our purpose, is right, that it does not change, and to check it each day or each hour, if necessary. If we have planted seeds of love, keep loving; if seeds of peace, stay peaceful. Beyond that, it is up to the Creator. Our worry or anxiety only causes difficulties for us. Knowing that we have put the Creative Forces to work, there is no need for worry or anxiety, and we can wait patiently for the results.

Charles Fillmore, a contemporary of Cayce's, was a prolific writer, a modern mystic, a great spiritual teacher, and a co-founder of Unity. He expresses similar concepts:

> Thoughts are seeds that, when dropped or planted in the subconscious mind, germinate, grow, and bring forth their fruit in due season. The more clearly we understand this truth the greater will be our ability to plant the seeds that bring forth desirable fruits. After sowing, the plants must be tended. After using the law, we must hold to its fulfillment. This is our part. God gives the increase. You must work in divine order and not expect the harvest before the soil has been prepared or the seed sown. You have now the fruits of previous sowings. Change your thought seeds and reap what you desire. Some

bring forth very quickly, others more slowly, but all in divine order.[11]

We have planted seeds, and we patiently wait. When the plants appear—possibly some weeds also—the farmer goes to work again to cultivate and care for the plants and to pull the weeds. So should we. Weeds come from the seeds planted with negative thoughts—like "It won't grow," "I didn't do it right," "It wasn't the right seed," or "I should have done more."
Every negative word, such as one of criticism or of doubt, is a weed seed. In some way it is based on fear or distrust or other destructive attitude. Pull those weeds and throw them out! Better still, don't plant those seeds!

THE SECOND LAW OF INCREASE

There is another reason why the spirit in which you plant the seeds is so important. It is expressed in this second law of increase:

THE SPIRIT OF YOUR ACTIONS
MULTIPLIES THE RESULT.

This is a sublaw of "as you sow so shall you reap" as shown in Figure 3.

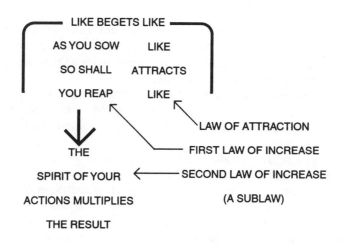

FIGURE 3

That may need some explanation:

The Universal Laws, in many instances, seem similar; yet each contributes uniquely to our life. Some of them, master laws, define an overall principle. Others are subsets of the master and define specific aspects of that principle. For example, the master law we are studying is "like begets like," which deals with a like condition begetting a like condition. The first law of increase—"as you sow so shall you reap"—defines a specific aspect of "like begets like" and is, therefore, a sublaw of it.

The law we will study in the next chapter—the law of attraction—defines another aspect of "like begets like," so it, too, is a sublaw.

The second law of increase—"the spirit of your actions multiplies the result"—defines a specific aspect of the first law of increase and is, therefore, a sublaw of it.

THE AMOUNT OF INCREASE

The following reading gives the keys that determine the "spirit of your actions." These set the amount of increase that occurs after you plant the seed.

> Use then that you have in hand [plant the seed]. For He will multiply it, some to ten, some to twenty, to some sixty, to some an hundredfold; dependent upon that purpose and that sincerity to which you may use that in hand. (1397-2)AR

Thus, there are three areas on which you need to check yourself to insure multiplication by the law of increase. They are:

1) **Your purpose.** How clear is your purpose? How definite? Is it in accord with the Creative Forces?

2) **Your sincerity.** Are you lukewarm or really intent and committed to your purpose? Are you free of hypocrisy, deceit, or duplicity regarding your purpose? Is your dedication to it as pure as you can make it?

3) **Your willingness.** Are you using that which you now have available to you? If you are not willing to use what you have (your talents, gifts, ideas, mind, materials), your purpose and sincerity are questionable. Pie-in-the-sky predictions of what you would do "if" are just that.

Reviewing these requirements, we can see why results are so varied for different individuals. For gardeners this may explain the "green thumb." Those who are clear about their purpose and who work in sincerity with plant life appear to have a "green thumb." Of course, the implications of reading 1397-2 go far beyond gardening and into all of life, as we plant seeds in one way or another. The Creative Forces are aware of our purpose and the sincerity and willingness with which we are doing our sowing. The results vary accordingly. In fact, they vary greatly—some get ten or a hundred times as much as others. As always, the results depend entirely upon us.

SEEDS OF FEAR

If you have a great fear of being robbed or having your house burglarized, you're planting seeds of fear. You're planting the seeds of "I am going to be robbed." You may buy numerous devices, such as alarms and locks to prevent a burglary or to warn you and protect you. These devices are of no value unless they enable you to overcome your fears. If so, then you have destroyed the seeds of fear. If you are still fearful, then the seeds are still present and will bring their fruits: a robbery. The greater your fear, the greater the chance it will happen. The reason you fear is because you have faith it will happen. Your increased fear, in effect, gives the negative seeds increased energy. This is implicit in the biblical commandment: "Thou shalt have no other gods before me." (Exodus 20:3, KJV) You can make "little gods" of fears and unwittingly pray to them.[12]

Denise, a member of our study group, lived in a high crime-rate section of the city. Her car, even though locked, had been broken into several times. Finally, she decided she would not lock her car but would leave it to God to protect her and her possessions, and she would no longer concern herself about it. For several years after that decision, she had no thefts. Then one day a friend from New York, who was staying with her overnight, insisted that she lock her car since she wished to leave some items in the trunk. Denise reluctantly locked it. It was broken into that night. The seeds of fear introduced by a friend brought an immediate response.

The ideal would be to develop and maintain a positive attitude of complete faith in the Creator as our protector in all circumstances. Then we would never need to lock our doors. By planting the seed "I am protected," we can reap that result: we are protected.[13]

I have known people who have not locked their doors for years, even though they live in heavily populated areas. They have had no problems. To do what they do, you must be sure of your faith, certain that your consciousness harbors no hidden fears or doubts about such a course.

My approach is different, but also adheres to the law. I feel that I, as a co-worker, must do my part with what I have. I lock my door, but I do so knowing that with that act I am planting the seed of protection. But I also plant the seed of knowing that the Universe will give the increase to whatever degree of protection is required. The spirit that I sow and that the Creative Forces multiply is protection, even in case the lock is not enough or I forget to lock it. By using the law of increase this way, I am completely protected regardless of circumstances.

COOPERATION

My approach is one of cooperation. It is based on the knowledge that the farmer must not only plant the seeds, but also do what he knows to do—such as cultivating the crop—to cooperate with the Creative Forces in producing the harvest. Cooperation is necessary for us as co-workers. It is all a part of "as you sow."

We must recognize that we can only do so much; we do what we can with what we have. Our powers as humans are limited—but as we cooperate as co-workers with the Divine, there is no limit to the power available to us. The Higher Power has no limits and is totally dependable because its nature is to love and care for us. By turning to that source and away from our fears, we substitute truth for illusion or true power for imagined power. As a result, we can be "in the world," seeing and hearing all its troubles and woes, but "not of it." In recognizing the higher power of our Creator and using the Universal Laws in that spirit, we are freed from our fears and those of the world because we then recognize we have nothing to fear.[14]

APPLYING THE LAWS IN THE BEST WAY

Some of us can make that switch in consciousness in a moment. For others the change comes slowly. All of us have been programmed and trained for many, many years to put our faith in others or in materiality rather than in the Creative Forces and in ourselves as creators of what happens in our lives. Therefore, we need to change those limiting beliefs.

We can begin to move toward faith in the Creative Forces and in ourselves by applying the law in the highest ways through planting positive seeds. There are many wonderful seeds which the readings recommend we sow: faith, hope, patience, gentleness, kindness, and love. These and others—forgiveness, trust, peace, joy, and mercy—are occasionally referred to in the readings as seeds of the spirit of truth. We are assured that "as we sow" them, they will return to us in abundance as fruits of the Spirit and will create harmony in our lives. Obviously, as this law operates through time, such results must come. How wonderful it is to realize such joyous results can be a part of our lives; that it is not up to fate or chance, but is our choice, and as we apply the law the results will, must come![15]

MISAPPLYING THE LAWS

The law, "as you sow so shall you reap," is cited many times in the readings because it applies to so much that we do. Here are two examples of how we can misapply it. A 79-year-old man asked:

(Q) Have personal vices as tobacco and whiskey any influence on one's health or longevity?

(A) . . . you are suffering from the use of some of these in the present; but it is overindulgence. In moderation these are not too bad, but man so seldom will be moderate. Or, as most say, those who even indulge will make themselves pigs, but we naturally are pigs when there is overindulgence. This, of course, makes for conditions which are to be met. For what one sows that must one reap. This is unchangeable law.

(5233-1)

The answer was just a polite way of saying: Yes, it adversely affects your health and decreases your life span, and you will have to meet those conditions.

A woman asked this intriguing question:

(Q) Do you see that it is possible for me to straighten out this tangled affair?

(A) *All* things are possible with God. Though it may bring some heartaches, though there are already many regrets, begin with the *spiritual* activity. Do not expect results in one day, nor one week. Individuals do not sow one day and reap the next. They reap what they have sown in the periods when *that* sown has come to fruitage. For what you sow, so shall you reap. Indiscretions, and the sentiments that are based wholly upon material satisfactions, must bring the tares and the weeds in the experience of the body. Those things sown in mercy, truth, justice, will bring their rewards in the same realm, in the same coin as sown. (971-1)AR

The key to straightening out the affair was to "begin with the *spiritual* activity"—to sow the right seeds of mercy, truth, and justice—no doubt far different than those previously sown.

This reading offers an extremely important precaution to us: "Do not expect results in one day, nor one week. Individuals do not sow one day and reap the next. They reap what they have sown in the periods when *that* sown has come to fruitage." The woman, though she planted new seeds, would still have to face—maybe in her next lifetime—what she had created in the past. The change would come later, when the new seeds would begin to mature. However, her change in consciousness represented by the attitudes of mercy, truth, and justice would enable her to deal with whatever came and prevent planting seeds of less desirable nature as she dealt with it. As we make changes in our lives, we need to have patience to allow the new seeds to grow and mature. We also need to acknowledge at the same time that we will still have to deal with that which we have created in the past. How we do this is an important part of the law.

SEEDS I HAVE ALREADY SOWN

If you have sown some seeds in the past which you now wish you hadn't or you are concerned about their possible manifestations, you can do something about them. There are several possibilities:
1. You may not have to meet them in this lifetime.
2. You are never presented with more than you can handle at any time as long as you put your trust in your Creator.
3. Know that whatever seed you have sown is for a purpose, for your benefit, for your growth, and that you can get help from the Creative Forces in meeting the results. You, of course, need to ask for that help.
4. There are higher laws—such as the law of grace, the law of forgiveness, and others—that enable us to meet the conditions we have created without going through all the chaos and trauma that we ordinarily would.[16]

You are not alone. Every one of us faces difficulties which we created in this or previous lifetimes. Consider these as opportunities and as lessons to be learned. The earth plane is our school of law. Whatever the condition that you are reaping or whatever the seed that you have sown, there is always a way available to you to meet it.

Suppose, for example, you have been resentful and bitter toward others over some situation, and you know that your attitude will only bring more of the same to you. What can you do to change? We often resent others because we have doubts and fears regarding ourselves and others. Turn over that doubt and fear to your Creator by simply saying, "Here are my doubts and fears about this situation. Help me to cast this resentment and bitterness out of my life. I don't want it!" Toss it out of your life and put in something better. Let the love and peace of the Higher Power so fill your mind and your body that there is no place for resentment, doubt, or fear. Whenever you feel resentment, replace it with a constructive thought or affirmation, such as, "The love of God now fills my mind and my body." Repeat it until you feel it or sense it in you. Then manifest it by being of help to others.

JESUS AND THE LAW

The source of the readings points out that our purpose when we were created as souls "in the beginning" was to be companions with the Father-God. They further explain that we, of our own choice, took paths which separated us from our Creator. The reason we are here on this earth plane is to find our way back to the Father. Jesus found the way. The readings explain that when He entered the earth plane nearly 2,000 years ago, He came in as you and I did—with temptations, problems, and difficulties. But He discovered that the Father was within Him, that He and the Father were one: "Believe me when I say that I am in the Father and the Father in me . . . " (John 14:11, NEB)

Jesus attuned Himself so completely to the Father within that He became perfectly spiritualized in body, mind, and spirit and thus eventually became the Christ. The readings express it as Jesus (the man) who became the Christ (christed).

This reading gives us a clue as to His transformation: " . . . whatsoever a man soweth, that must he also reap. This was truly exemplified in the life of the man of Galilee." (5749-12)

The law is the key. Jesus sowed spiritual seeds which spiritualized His spirit, mind, and body, for the law works on all three levels! So, as Jesus sowed the seeds of the spirit of love, joy, peace, patience, kindness, goodness, gentleness, and others, He began to reap these as spiritual fruits.[17] He thus became as the Father within, the spirit of love, of joy, of peace, of patience, and all the others. So, in this way, He became spiritualized. The wonderful part about this is that He said we could do it, too:

> In truth, in very truth I tell you, he who has faith in me will do what I am doing; and he will do greater things still . . .
> John 14:12, NEB

Jesus was applying the law "as you sow so shall you reap." We can do it in a similar way as He did by sowing the same seeds.

Indeed, His life exemplifies this law. He stands as our guide on this path of Universal Law because He has passed this way before and has shown us the way—not the only way, but the highest way to use the Universal Laws.

WHAT SEEDS SHOULD I SOW?

We need to ask this question of ourselves and we need to ask it from the consciousness of "What would I like to do for or give to others?" Possible answers to this can be found in the following list of "seeds of the Spirit" given in the readings plus other "joy" seeds from which you might wish to choose. These seeds are attitudes that express our spirit. We sow them by making that seed our attitude toward self and others. We "be" that attitude, so that then becomes our "Be" Attitude!

Look at this list of wonderful attitudes that you can give first to others and eventually have in your own life:

"Be" Attitudes	*The Fruits*
Sow these seeds of the Spirit in the hearts, in the minds, in the lives of others*	**And harvest this in your life**
be loving	love
be gentle	gentleness
be kind	kindness
be patient	patience
be friendly	friends (fellowship)

*These "seeds of the Spirit" listed here are designated as such in the Edgar Cayce readings.

be merciful	mercy
be truthful	truth
be hopeful	hope
be faithful	faith
be good	goodness
be joyful	joy
be peaceful	peace
be humble	humbleness
be harmonious	harmony
be understanding	understanding
be consistent in acts and speech	consistency

Other Constructive Attitudes

be content	contentment
be honest	honesty
be appreciative	appreciation
be generous	abundance
be cooperative	cooperation
be just	justice
be forgiving	forgiveness

HOW MAY I SOW THE SEEDS?

Pick one or two of the "Be" Attitudes as a start. Work diligently to apply them by thinking, acting, and speaking in that manner in all your dealings with others. Use your ideas, imagination, and creativity. It takes conscious effort and patience. The key is to apply the law: Whatever you want in your life, sow that in your thoughts, words, and acts toward yourself and others. It will grow and return to you. Think what that means to each of us: we can be or have anything in our lives we want by applying this law, provided we are not doing it for a selfish purpose, but to share and to give the same to others.[18]

To sow any one of these seeds, you need to make that attitude a part of your life, make it the spirit in which you act. Believe it, live it, do it, express it, be it—become that attitude—"be" that attitude.

For example, you may choose to "be joyful" in order to bring more joy into the lives of others. The Cayce readings, which spoke frequently about joy, suggested being joyful in all you do. Express that joy with smiles and "Smile often, for *smiling* is catching—but sadness drives away." (518-1) As we bring any of the seeds of the spirit to our associates, we are expressing a portion of the Christ Consciousness. Whenever we do that, we bring joy to others. This is further emphasized in this reading:

> Your body is indeed the temple of the living God. There He has promised to meet you often. Meet Him, in joy, in song, in prayer. Thus you will find your life blossoming—physically, mentally and spiritually—even as the rose. And the very fragrance of your life, the beauty of your life, will make and bring joy to many. (3440-2)AR

To a young man, Cayce offered important advice on sowing seeds and also gave him a unique and meaningful purpose:

> Find each day where you may help someone less fortunate in some way, whether in body, in mind, in opportunity, in circumstance. Help not for pay, not just because you want to help, but because he is your brother, because he is yourself, for as you do unto others you do to your Maker . . .
> In that manner, then, may you . . . find that which will bring the greater help, the greater joy, the greater experiences of life. (5250-1)AR

We can summarize the steps to becoming a channel for joy in our world:
1. Be joyful in all that you do.
2. Smile often.
3. Manifest to others the seeds of the Spirit, such as peace, love, joy, and patience.
4. Pray and sing joyfully.
5. Help someone each day.

You can create a similar program for any one of the seeds of the Spirit you choose to manifest. "As you sow—so shall you reap!"

Whenever we start such a program, our actions are understandably a bit mechanical—like a child first practicing the piano. Practice, however, will make perfect. We should be kind, gentle, and supportive of ourselves while we are learning. I often write notes to myself to remind me of what I'm trying to do. Then I put them in many places so that I will find them as I go through my day. Or I use a timer to jog my memory. I even give myself a reward when I remember without the notes. Such aids can be helpful when we are working to change our consciousness.

In addition to having the mental drive to follow these steps, your heart must be in it as well. It takes Spirit (heart) to give the seed the spark of life that makes it grow and multiply.

To a timid soul Cayce urged making or exerting yourself to be more dominant. This is important because each one of us has much to give. We have the power to give but may lose it all if we hide behind our timidity. On the other hand, if we tend to be domineering, we can easily suppress the wonderful talents of others. We need to express ourselves, but that expression should always be tempered with the seeds of the Spirit. There are good reasons for this as clearly explained in this passage:

> Make or exercise yourself as to be more dominant, but with that dominance tempered with mercy and justice and love and faith and hope as you have desired and do desire to be expressed toward yourself and your relationships.
>
> For remember, there are immutable laws as respecting the mental and spiritual life. And these are they that live *on* and *on*. And in the material associations these are the basis of that manner in which you should act, should express yourself. For it is in so doing, in sowing the seeds that are truth, that are life, that are eternal, that the source of happiness, peace and contentment arises. (1752-1)AR

What a simple prescription for such a wonderful result!

WHAT KIND OF SOIL?

In what kind of soil do you seek to sow? Life is the soil in which we sow. But what is the character of that soil in your life and heart and body? Jesus had much to say about sowing seeds. His parable of the sower may help us understand the character of the soil in our lives.

> He said: "A sower went out to sow. And as he sowed, some seed fell along the footpath; and the birds came and ate it up. Some seed fell on rocky ground, where it had little soil; it sprouted quickly because it had no depth of earth, but when the sun rose the young corn was scorched, and as it had no root it withered away. Some seed fell among thistles; and the

thistles shot up, and choked the corn. And some of the seed fell into good soil, where it bore fruit, yielding a hundredfold or, it might be, sixtyfold or thirtyfold. If you have ears, then hear."

[And Jesus explained the parable in this way:] "You, then, may hear the parable of the sower. When a man hears the word that tells of the Kingdom but fails to understand it, the evil one comes and carries off what has been sown in his heart. There you have the seed sown along the footpath. The seed sown on rocky ground stands for the man who, on hearing the word, accepts it at once with joy; but as it strikes no root in him he has no staying-power, and when there is trouble or persecution on account of the word he falls away at once. The seed sown among thistles represents the man who hears the word, but worldly cares and the false glamour of wealth choke it, and it proves barren. But the seed that fell into good soil is the man who hears the word and understands it, who accordingly bears fruit, and yields a hundredfold or, it may be, sixtyfold or thirtyfold."   Matthew 13:4-9, 18-23, NEB

If our lives are like the "footpath" — so busy that we think we have no time to study, to understand, and to work with these laws in our lives, there is no growth. I often find myself in this position when I have too many books to read or lectures to attend or trips to take or other things to do. My life, then, is like the footpath because I allow unimportant activities to take my time and energy, leaving nothing for the seeds of the Spirit which have been sown. These other activities, in effect, like the birds on the footpath, devour the seeds before they can sprout. To correct that I need to make the choice to care for them and nurture them and give them importance (time and attention) in my schedule.

The "rocky ground" occurs in my life when, though I may be enthusiastic to apply new truth in my life, I fail to make the commitment or discipline myself to study, to work with, and to follow through. In other words, there is no depth to the soil in which I have sown this seed. Therefore, there is no growth.

The "thistles" in my life, as the parable indicates, are the worldly cares about job, family, home, and health. All are valid concerns, but they become thistles if I allow them to choke out the seeds of the Spirit. The thistles of "false glamour of wealth" are ones that grow when we let desire for money, position, or power deprive us of time for nourishment of the seeds of the Spirit.

The "good soil," Jesus says, is the life of a person who hears the word (is awake and listening for truth) and understands it (gives it priority and applies it). To do that, the person keeps life in balance so that "other" aspects do not devour nor choke out nor destroy the seeds of truth. Since there always seems to be more to do than we have time for, such a life requires assigning value to what we consider important and eliminating those items of lower value. At the very least, it requires giving precedence to and adhering to specific periods each day for work on our spiritual growth.

As a practical exercise and a test of the kind of soil your life is, do a good deed for someone each day (as the Boy Scouts, Girl Scouts, and Cayce readings suggest). Make a commitment to yourself to do it consistently over a reasonable period of time and keep a written record. If you can do it consistently, you have good soil. If you cannot do it consistently, you need to revise your life to eliminate the footpaths, rocky ground, and thistles until you develop good soil.

THE LAW APPLIES TO ALL ASPECTS OF LIFE

The application of "as you sow you reap" is evident everywhere— *even* in the business world. Those who prepare themselves by sowing their time, energy, money, etc., in study and education and experience grow to be doctors, secretaries, lawyers, engineers, nurses, managers, and the like. Step by step, they achieve what they have prepared themselves for. This accomplishment is not by chance, but a consequence of the actions they have taken to prepare themselves—to sow the seeds.

If, in your business relations, you seek favors, something for nothing, from others, you have sown a seed. Others will make similar requests of you. If you sow selfishness or strife, you will not reap harmony. If in your business (or your life) you waste money or words or time, you will reap a lack of money or words or time. The law works in all that you do—in all aspects of your life.

THE WISDOM OF THE LAW

The Creative Force, that infinite aspect of the universe which carries out the law once we have set it in operation, has wisdom beyond our comprehension. We can easily fool ourselves as to what seed we are sowing. But the Creative Force knows the truth and grows the true seed we have sown. It also knows the degree to which we have sown. For example, the more we apply ourselves in study or learning or the more responsibility we take, the greater the reward we receive. If we are ready to assume the responsibility for much money, the amount that we are prepared to handle will come to us. If we are willing to assume the responsibility of fame and prepare ourselves (plant the required seeds), fame will come. It is not that some people are lucky and become rich or famous; rather, they have planted the right seeds. Through use of their will power, they have followed through and, as a result, receive their rightful heritage—the fruits of what they have sown. The beauty of this fact is that you and I can do it, too: whatever you desire to achieve you can achieve. If you want to have a perfect home and you are willing to take the responsibility, use your will power to prepare yourself for it and make it your heritage. It will come to you not by luck or chance or good fortune, but by law.

SOME HIGHLIGHTS OF THIS CHAPTER

The first law of increase is:

AS YOU SOW SO SHALL YOU REAP

Through your thoughts, beliefs, words, and acts, you sow seeds. The true seed is the purpose with which you think, speak, and act. It determines the harvest you will reap. You always have the choice of the purpose for which you sow. If the purpose is in the flow with peace and love and the seeds of the Spirit of the Universe, you will reap the high road of life. On that road you will have greater peace and love and understanding with which to face the problems that come to us all. All of us are familiar with the low road on which we live, when our purposes stem from our doubts, fears, guilt, and hate. This law shows us the way to the higher road. Remember that the law operates on all three levels: spiritual, mental, and physical.

The second law of increase is:

THE SPIRIT OF YOUR ACTIONS
MULTIPLIES THE RESULT

You plant the seed, and the Universe gives the increase. The amount of the increase depends upon the spirit in which you sow, upon your dedication to your purpose, and your sincerity and diligence to use what you have. You reap what you sow when the time is right; when you are ready, you will receive.

Chapter 4

Laws of Attraction

The law of attraction is:

LIKE ATTRACTS LIKE

This is the second sublaw of the master law "like begets like." Remember that "like begets like" is a law of creation of a like condition.

"Like attracts like" is a law of attraction, dealing with the attraction between ourselves and other individuals, things, conditions, and places. It, too, deals with like conditions and so is a sublaw of "like begets like."

The readings explain that in the beginning the Creator, through thought, made the universe and us (as souls) and gave us creative power. With that creative power we create our own unique and personal universe.

We accomplish this through our thoughts and beliefs. They bring to us, by attraction, the people who are a part of our universe — friends, enemies, relatives, associates, and all others with whom we come in contact. We realize that we are the creator of our universe and that everyone and everything we see or are involved with or are aware of, in any way, constitute our own universe. It is our life. No one else sees our universe as we do. Through the Universal Laws, we have made it what it is, and the law "like attracts like" has played an important part in that creation.

HOW DOES THE LAW WORK?

All of us are familiar with magnets that attract or cling to a piece of steel or to other magnets. We know that two magnets can be attracted to each other by their electromagnetic fields. It has been scientifically established that these invisible fields exist within and outside the body of the magnets. Two such magnets, properly oriented, even some distance apart, will draw together due to the attracting force of the fields existing between them.[1]

We, too, have some form of a field around us. Many psychics are able to see this field or aura that exists around human bodies. Edgar Cayce could see it and from its shape, size, or color could tell an individual's mental and emotional state and condition of health. Shortly before his death, Cayce wrote:

Ever since I can remember I have seen colors in connection with people. I do not remember a time when the human beings I encountered did not register on my retina with blues and greens and reds gently pouring from their heads and shoulders. It was a long time before I realized that other people did not see these colors; it was a long time before I heard the word aura, and learned to apply it to this phenomenon which to me was commonplace. I do not ever think of people except in connection with their auras; I see them change in my friends and loved ones as time goes by — sickness, dejection, love, fulfillment — these are all reflected in the aura, and for me the aura is the weathervane of the soul. It shows which way the winds of destiny are blowing . . .

A person's aura tells a great deal about him, and when I understood that few people saw it and that it had a spiritual significance, I began to study the colors with an idea of discovering their meaning. Over a period of years I have built up a system which from time to time I have checked with other persons who see auras. It is interesting to note that in almost all interpretations these other people and I agree . . .

An aura is an effect, not a cause. Every atom, every molecule, every group of atoms and molecules, however simple or complex, however large or small, tells the story of itself, its pattern, its purpose, through the vibrations which emanate from it. Colors are the perceptions of these vibrations by the human eye. As the souls of individuals travel through the realms of being, they shift and change their patterns as they use or abuse the opportunities presented to them. Thus at any time, in any world, a soul will give off through vibrations the story of itself and the condition in which it now exists. If another consciousness can apprehend those vibrations and understand them, it will know the state of its fellow being, the plight he is in, or the progress he has made.

So when I see an aura, I see the man as he is . . . [2]

Our auras reflect our nature. Though most of us may not see the auras of others, on some level we are conscious of or aware of the nature of each individual with whom we come in contact. This may be due to a subconscious awareness of his or her aura. Those of like nature are attracted to one another as the result of the attractive force existing between their auras, similar to the attraction of two magnets of like nature. Thus the law of "like attracts like" operates for human beings as well as for magnets.[3]

Charles Fillmore called the field around us a "thought atmosphere":

Every man produces a thought atmosphere that has character and power in proportion to his ability as a thinker. Power increases with expansion; in thought, power is great or small as the ideals are high or low. When you follow narrow ideals, your thought atmosphere is correspondingly contracted; but mental breadth enlarges and strengthens it in all directions.

"How can a man conceal himself?" said Confucius. In the light of the ever-present thought atmosphere with which we surround ourselves, he cannot. Nearly all people have the ability of sensing the thought atmosphere of those they meet; and a man may cultivate this ability to project himself until he becomes an open book and the air about him is filled with his silent yet potent words, ever telling what he has thought.

The thought atmosphere is a real, substantial thing, and has in it all that makes the body. We have a way of considering the things we cannot see as unsubstantial, and although we are told that we cannot conceal ourselves we go right on believing that we can. Hence it is good for us to know that of a truth we do carry about with us this open book of our life, out of which all persons read whether we realize it or not. Some people are good thought readers while others are dull, but all can read a little, and you cannot conceal yourself. Also your thought atmosphere is constantly printing its slowly cooling words on your body, where they are seen of men. But with a little practice we can feel the thought force of this atmosphere that surrounds us and gradually gain a realization of its existence that is as real as that of the outer world.[4]

The Cayce readings suggest that the auric field is a product of our physical, mental, and spiritual condition, and each person's field plays an important part in interactions with others. Since the field around us is related to all three levels, it is reasonable to assume that the attraction between two individuals can be on any one, two, or on all three levels.[5]

LAW OF REPULSION

We can consider the law "like attracts like" as the master law of attraction which operates in a broad context in our lives. It applies in attracting to us that which we are like; for example, boys who like baseball are attracted to boys who like baseball. There is also a corresponding law of repulsion:

OPPOSITES REPEL

When fields of magnets are in a certain position, we know that the magnets are attracted to each other. When the magnets are in the "reversed" or opposite condition, they are repelled from each other. For humans the law of repulsion, as well as the law of attraction, operates through the fields or auras of individuals.[6] These two laws raise some questions: What attracts us and what do we attract? What repels us and what do we repel?

SECOND LAW OF ATTRACTION

To answer these questions, you need to be aware that higher laws are involved, laws which give you the power to bring into your life whatever you choose to seek. One of these laws can be expressed in terms of attraction as:

AS YOU SEEK, YOU ATTRACT
AND ARE ATTRACTED TO
THAT WHICH WILL FULFILL YOUR SEARCH

This second law of attraction applies only when you seek. Your search may be for growth and development or whatever you desire. Another law also applies when you seek:

SECOND LAW OF REPULSION

AS YOU SEEK, YOU REPEL AND ARE REPELLED BY THAT WHICH WILL NOT FULFILL YOUR SEARCH

Figure 4 shows the relationship of these laws.

FIGURE 4

RELATIONSHIP OF THE LAWS

(ARROWS POINT TO SUBLAWS)

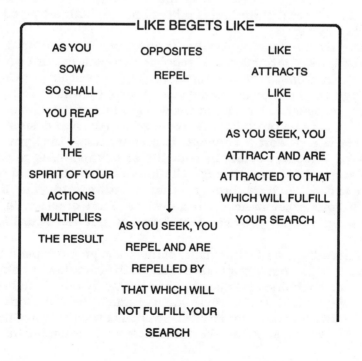

These laws give us one answer to our questions: whatever attracts or repels us and whatever we attract or repel depends upon what we seek in our lives. The universe has given us these laws to aid us in finding that which we seek; these laws, like others, are impartial. They will work whether we seek something beneficial or something detrimental for ourselves or others.

These laws offer one reason why we may immediately like or dislike some individuals when we meet them. There is an attraction or a repulsion, depending upon the positive and negative forces reflected in our auras. Our auras mirror what we truly seek, regardless of what we may say or do. Cayce refers to these auric emanations as vibrations, which always speak louder than our words.

My wife usually does not "see auras," but she has an uncanny ability to sense whether a person we initially meet is sincere and trustworthy or whether such behavior is a front. I don't have her sensitivity, but I've learned to implicitly trust her feelings; it has always proven correct. I am sure we all have this ability—basically being able to sense another's aura. The more we open ourselves to it by accepting it and recognizing it, the greater benefit we can derive from it. We must remember that this is a two-way street—for we can both attract and repel others and are both attracted to or repelled by others.

It is fascinating to realize that through our inherent nature, we set the laws of attraction and repulsion to work in our own lives. The implications of this are mind-boggling: once again our Creator, through His love for us, has given us laws by which we become totally responsible for our lives, laws by which we attract or repel depending upon our particular patterns, needs, and desires.

This is a powerful concept. It means, then, that you have created whatever exists in your life or is happening to you at this time. You have, through the laws of attraction and repulsion and other laws, brought that creation into your life to fulfill your present needs and desires. That creation is what you need now for your greatest development and your highest good!

The readings verify the validity of this concept and explain how it occurs. Each atom of our bodies radiates the vibration to which it is attuned. Each one of us attunes our atoms by our thoughts, beliefs, words, and deeds. These atoms radiate the vibration which puts into action the appropriate Universal Laws that bring into our experience the conditions, the individuals, and the happenings that are necessary for our own development. Isn't that tremendous! Not only are we in school daily, but we plan and establish our curriculum according to our needs. The Creative Forces pick up the vibrations we send out and, through the laws, present us with the lessons we need to learn. You are the student and life is your teacher. Your lessons may come in the form of an accident, a new job, change in an existing relationship, a financial problem, or something as simple and frustrating as a flat tire or as exciting as winning a million dollars. What a school![7]

Two of the most important keys to this school of life are the laws of attraction and the laws of repulsion. You use these laws throughout your entire life. You even used them before you came into the earth plane!

ATTRACTION TO PARENTS

You may or may not believe that you have lived before this lifetime as a man or a woman on the earth. This concept, called reincarnation, is a fascinating one. You do not have to either believe in it or accept it to understand and use the Universal Laws. However, the Cayce readings do consider this concept as a fact of life. They explain that we, as individual souls, return to the earth experience many times as stages in our growth. If this is so—and I believe it is—it helps us to understand why life is the way it is. It also raises interesting questions as to the affect of the law of attraction on the selection of parents by the incoming soul.

We learn from the readings that each soul chooses to enter the earth and is attracted to certain parents by the parents' strengths and weaknesses as well as by their influences and activities during the period of gestation. The parents provide the opportunity for the soul's needs to be fulfilled. It is this opportunity for fulfillment that is the attraction.

The soul still is given the opportunity to choose and is even shown possible results:

. . . each soul is attracted to those influences that may be visioned from above. Thus *there* the turns in the river of life may be viewed. (3128-1)

So, we did not come in blindly or by chance. We knew what we would face. We were attracted to our parents through the operation of the laws of attraction. But we still had the choice, and we chose our parents. Believe it or not!

Some individuals have said to me, "I can't believe I would have chosen my parents!" Yet when looked at from the standpoint of their growth through that choice, most agreed their parents were probably the ones they really needed. When children realize that they actually selected their parents, it can make a great difference in their attitudes and relationship. It gives them an entirely different perspective.

WE ARE RESPONSIBLE

The realization that we, as souls coming to the earth plane, were attracted to and actually chose our parents gives us a different view and greater understanding of some of the difficult family situations that occur. I remember Edgar Cayce's son, Hugh Lynn, telling of a man whom I'll call Harry Adams. Harry came for a reading; Hugh Lynn was present. While Edgar Cayce was in trance, Harry asked why his father had beaten him so. The reply was, as Hugh Lynn told it: "In a previous lifetime you were his father and you beat him unmercifully, so when you arrived he had the old shillelagh out and ready!"

So those whom we now view as victims may well have been abusers in a previous life. They may have chosen abusive parents in order to face the karma they created and, through it, come to realize there must be a better way. This in no way justifies such actions nor relieves us of our responsibility to do all that we can to help the victims of child abuse as well as the abusers. It does, however, offer some reason for such enigmas and a realization that all that happens is for a purpose. Fortunately the Universal Laws not only enable us to understand why such conditions exist, but also are the keys to meet and to deal with them whether we are the abuser or the abused or a concerned observer.

ATTRACTION TO PLACES

When Cayce gave a reading, he entered a trance state and then was given the name and location of the individual. In one case in which he had just been given that information, he seemed to be going back over the years to find the person's birth place and location. He said in an undertone:

Very interesting to notice the difference here in the environment . . . to which the souls of humans may be drawn or attracted by those very conditions which have been experienced by them in their . . . dwelling in such an environ in previous experience . . .(757-8)

His comments suggest that even the earth has an aura, with certain kinds of emanations or vibrations for mountains, farm lands, rivers, or other areas. We may be attracted or repelled by them depending upon our previous experiences in this or similar locations. If we feel the appeal of a particular spot, it may be more than just its natural beauty. Other readings indicate that certain areas or environments may attract us because they hold opportunities for us to live more creatively or to meet ourselves (to face our problems), and thus to experience greater development.[8]

ATTRACTION TO SOURCES

Another important aspect of the Laws of Attraction is:

. . . those who are thinking along the same lines, or who are desirous of individual achievement, are drawn to those sources from which help or stimulating influences may be had. (2410-1)

So you may be drawn to sources that can provide what you need—such as books, people, schools, conferences—or locations that could be the source of stimulating influences. That attraction to such sources may occur in amazing ways. At every seminar on Universal Laws I have heard surprising stories from some participants as to how they came to attend. I remember one such story in particular. A woman told me she had been unhappy and despondent, feeling a great need for change. She was walking down the street on a windy day. A piece of paper blew by; she felt compelled to run after it and pick it up. It was the announcement of the seminar! As it turned out, it was a life-changing experience for her.

How can I explain such a happening? I can't—except I know that the laws work. There was a need, there was an attraction, and the Creative Forces were at work. It's a wondrous combination; how it happened is not important. The fact that it can and it did is the glorious part! This is a typical case of what Carl Jung termed synchronicity, which is actually the effect created by the operation of the laws of attraction in our lives.

Now, there's an important key in applying these laws. The reading quoted above says, "Those . . . who are desirous"—**you need to have the desire.** Years ago I was employed by a firm which built large electrical installations; we ran into a problem on one that was going into a steel mill. I realized that the solution would require specialized equipment. I didn't know if what I needed was even available. A friend said he'd heard of such a device, but he didn't remember where he had read about it or where it could be obtained. My staff and I searched all the usual sources without success. This all came up on a Tuesday. By Thursday we hadn't found a thing. I had a great desire to locate that device because I had either to find it or shut the project down. On Friday on a flight out of Youngstown, Ohio, to Chicago, as I was deep in thought about the situation, a man sat down beside me and we started to talk. He turned out to be the vice president of the only company in the world that manufactured the device I was looking for! His company had just recently put it on the market.

Little wonder I believe in these laws! At that time, I didn't know anything about them. But when that meeting on the plane occurred, I certainly had the feeling it was somehow inevitable and that it had been arranged on a level of which I was not aware. At that time I had an intense desire to find the solution we needed and was searching for such a device. The man I met was involved in marketing those devices, so we were, as the reading indicates, "thinking along the same lines" and each was "desirous of individual achievement": I to solve my difficulty, and he to sell his product. The law worked—we were attracted to each other.

ATTRACTING A NEW ABILITY

As we have noted, the Creative Forces respond to our desires. Through that understanding, we can accomplish other wonders because desire attracts more than people and things. With it we can even develop new abilities, as explained in this excerpt:

> . . . with the innate desire to be a . . . leader . . . there is builded or gradually attracted . . . by the very thought and mental forces (as the mind is ever the builder), the possibilities and innate abilities to become such an influence. (284-1)

This reading holds tremendous potential for each of us; it says that, **by law you can attract the possibility and the ability to**

become that which you innately desire to be.

Your Creator knows your potential and gives you that "innate desire" for fulfillment through use of your talents. As you recognize and accept that desire, you put your mind to work; it will attract and build the possibilities and abilities that you need in order to accomplish your desire. You can do it!

DOING WHAT YOU LOVE TO DO

You recognize and honor that "innate desire" when you devote time and effort in your life to doing what you love to do whether as an avocation or a vocation. What you love to do is an inherent part of you, a part of your purpose in the earth. In doing what you love to do, you are in accord with the purpose of the universe; you are in the flow. Because of this, when you begin to do what you love to do, the law of attraction goes to work for you. Things really begin to work out to enable you to fulfill that desire of your heart. For example, a young woman who was a single parent wrote: "For over a year I had been working at a job which involved long hours, high stress, and very little satisfaction. Some mornings I would wake up and literally cry because I had to go to work." As a result of attending an Arnold Patent workshop, she decided to begin to do what she loved to do. She writes:

> I have created a business . . . to describe my willingness to share my talents in interior design and space planning with others.
> The Universe has totally supported me. Though the only advertisement has been word of mouth, I have many clients and enough income to support my present economic level. I know this will increase as my *Trust in Principle* [Universal Law] grows. Last week a man I know casually through my former job offered me two rooms of office space, which he will renovate any way I want, rent free for three months. After that, he's only going to charge me a nominal fee . . . These are only the most obvious and dramatic manifestations of support.[9]

MIND IS THE BUILDER OF ATTRACTION

The other important key given in the preceding reading (284-1) is that the law of attraction works for us through our thoughts because mind is the builder. The strength of our minds to build can

be understood through these simple and powerful statements in
the Cayce readings:

**"That you dwell upon . . . you become . . .
That you hate suddenly befalls you."**

(2034-1)AR

As you think about "that you dwell upon" or "that you hate," you
put energy into your aura. When you put it there, even though you
may hate something, you'll attract it to you. So don't hate anything.
Find something to like or to love. Let your mind dwell on that and
build it for you. As you do, you will put that kind of energy into your
aura, and what you like or love will come to you.[10]

Jesus understood these Universal Laws and so told us to love
our enemies. He knew that if we continue to hate them, we would
attract them to us and have to suffer the consequences!

ABILITIES ATTRACT

Edgar Cayce's work exemplified the law of attraction at work; his
gift, through which he could help people, caught the attention of
thousands in his lifetime, and tens of thousands more were drawn
to his philosophy years after his death. Whenever you have abilities
to help others or to provide a service, you will attract those who
have the need. For example, a manager of a service organization
asked:

*(Q) Are there any special ones who are not members that
would be well to see?*

(A) . . . These will be attracted when there is something to be
attracted *to*, and that is attractive in that it offers, it performs
and it serves. "By their fruits ye shall know them." (2733-2)

That would seem to be an excellent guide for putting the law to
work in attracting members, clients, or customers.

The manager of a law firm asked how to make the firm more
useful, obtain clients, and prosper financially. The reading pro-
posed a number of criteria for success that were practically unheard
of in 1937 in business. Only in the last decade have some compa-
nies begun to consider the value of these approaches which Edgar
Cayce suggested over fifty years ago:

First: Desires and purposes cannot be just for financial gain.

Second: Thought and purpose and desire must be to provide health, hope, confidence, faith, courage, and love to the clients. (Imagine a law firm loving its clients!)

Third: As these things are done, the law will attract those who may be aided; the law works.

To benefit from the power of this law, "like attracts like," and to attract customers, you need to provide the quality of service and relationships that will make it desirable, not just what "will get us by today." Every conversation with your associates, with suppliers, with clients, and with customers should be with the understanding that you are willing to meet tomorrow what you are presenting today, for by this law you inevitably meet it coming back to you. You can build your associations on the rock of Universal Law by taking this attitude, recommended to businesspeople, to your fellow employees, customers, or friends:

If you will be my friends and my associates, I will be your friend and *your* associate, and we together may, through our united effort, accomplish for each other and those we serve far more than we accomplish alone . . . (257-85)P

This advice means never taking advantage of another, financially or otherwise. It means basing all actions on high ideals and being capable of handling business in all its phases and in all its relationships. I am not suggesting idealism, but practical operations based on the solid foundation of unchangeable, totally reliable Universal Laws.

LACK DETRACTS

Another factor of attraction is our attitude toward self. Clarissa, a teacher who was having difficulty getting students for her classes, asked Edgar Cayce for help. His source advised Clarissa that her loss of self-confidence in her ability to handle the classes was being transmitted to potential class members, thus repelling rather than attracting them. She was advised to change her attitude and that all would be well. How fascinating and challenging it is to see that the law always works to present the true picture! So we must look first to ourselves to correct any lack of success that we may be experiencing.[11]

PREPARATION

At the same time, we know that as we properly prepare ourselves, the law will go to work for us—to attract those to whom we can render a service.[12]

John was interested in archaeology, but his attempts to get a job had failed. In trying to take shortcuts, he had some lessons to learn. The advice given him by Cayce minced no words:

> You speak in one manner and live another life. You proclaim in your experience that you believe this or that, and then you proceed to act as if it didn't exist! . . .
> *(Q) Why have all my efforts to make some archaeological connections failed?*
> (A) Let the *preparation* of yourself . . . [spiritually], physically, mentally, be made first. And then there may be made such connections. For what be the laws? Like attracts like! Have you not read that he who builds the best mousetrap, though he live in the midst of a forest, will have a beaten path to his door? Have you not read again, "Consecrate yourselves *this day*, wash your garments and your body and be *clean*; for on the morrow your God would speak with you"? What be the interpretations thereof? (274-10)AR

John was being told to clean up his act, to do his preparation on all three levels—physical, mental, and spiritual. There are no shortcuts.

If you're going to build the best mousetrap, it should embody the spirit of service to others—to catch mice and not to just make money or gain fame. As you serve others abundantly, you will, by the law, attract those who will serve you with abundance. The money and the fame come as a result of your preparation and your spirit.

OUR RELATIONSHIPS WITH OTHERS

What about the relationship we often see in the life of couples who greatly differ one from the other in outlook, attitudes, desires, or personalities? This seems to be contrary to the law "like attracts like" as well as to the law of repulsion. In fact, we sometimes hear the statement that opposites attract. Do they?

I believe there are no exceptions to the law. In my experience, seeming exceptions indicate further consideration is necessary. To understand these apparent contradictions, we need to look deeper than outward appearances. This extract from the readings, in discussing the seeming attraction of opposites, explains:

> For, these naturally attract opposites, and thus is growth ever made in a material expression . . . Those that are attracted to the entity are those who *need* the entity . . . (2620-2)

In other words, as we seek a mate, for example, we seek—maybe subconsciously—the person who can help us grow mentally and spiritually. In the case of opposites apparently attracting, needs exist in both people—needs to grow, to be fulfilled, to fulfill. **It is the *needs* that do the attracting—not the opposite characteristics**. The individuals are seeking greater fulfillment and greater balance. In accord with the second law of attraction, "as you seek, you attract and are attracted to that which will fulfill your search," they find someone whose opposite characteristics can bring greater balance to their lives. The Universe, in its infinite wisdom, again fulfills its purpose through the laws by allowing apparent opposites to be attracted. They are attracted not because they are opposites, but because they are complementary and thereby provide opportunities to each other for growth, for a chance for each to become familiar with the opposite, to see value in it, to learn, to grow, and to move from their individual extreme to a more balanced condition.

Perry W. Buffington, Ph.D., a writer on psychological subjects for popular magazines, summarized recent psychological research on the above subject:

> . . . an opposite-attraction relationship has special qualities which, believe it or not, promote survival. In fact, if this type of relationship is handled properly having an "opposite-type" mate can be a tonic to your health."[13]

More than fifty years ago one reading put it this way: " . . . contrasts are as an element necessary to make the perfect union." (212-1)

When we have male-female opposites, we have two cases of imbalance, each of which can be a balancing element for the other; thus, the two-way attraction. An example will help. Let's assume the woman is of a very nonstructured nature and the man very structured. Each needs to learn more about the opposite of their own characteristic. For clarity we can show it in this way:

	CHARACTER	NEED
Mr. A	structure	less structure
Mrs. A	little structure	more structure

These two people have a common interest—structure. In this regard, they are alike—having a need to better understand structure to become more balanced. It is this need that attracts, and each can teach the other what is needed to learn. The wisdom behind the working of the laws is both beautiful and incredible in that they always work for the highest good of those involved.

A simple but classic example is provided by a couple whom I have known for many years. When they were married, Jim considered an agreement to meet at a set time to be sacred. He was insistent upon being prompt. To his wife Evelyn, schedules and time were very casual arrangements. As you can imagine, this difference in values created problems and some difficult situations. Over the years, however, each has seen some wisdom in the other's attitude. Jim became more flexible; Evelyn became more prompt. Both learned much from this and from other aspects on which they differed. These differences may really make life a lot more interesting and challenging. Perhaps the greater lesson to be learned in this kind of situation is that people do see the same things differently, to accept that fact, and to love others just as they are.[14]

The Universal Laws provide us with the opportunity to express love in our relationships by attracting to us those whose presence we need to help us grow and who need us for their growth. This may naturally create friction—or a better term, "opportunities"—for each. It is through forgiving each other and looking on problems as opportunities to grow that growth really comes. To one young woman contemplating marriage and asking for guidance, a Cayce reading gave excellent advice which can apply to each of us in any relationship:

> (Q) I am practically engaged to the entity known as [. . .]. Will our union be a spiritual, mental and physical one?
>
> (A) If the choice, if the activity of each is given in such a way that you look to make of yourselves the ideal mate for the other. Not continually seeking or finding fault, either one with the other—but correcting the errors, the faults, the shortcomings in self; and you] will bring the best that is in self and that

will] make for the manifesting of the best that is in your] helpmate.

These are the manners, these are the ways that are His ways. And when other ways are used as of self-indulgence, self-purpose irrespective of the privileges, the duties, the opportunities of the other as well as of self, then there come turmoils, divisions and strife. (1722-1)

In other words, if you don't like what you see in your mate, change yourself. Make yourself the ideal mate and that will then bring out the best in your helpmate. Remember the law "like attracts like." Emmet Fox, a modern mystic and famous spiritual teacher, lecturer, and author, said it this way:

If you came to me and told me that you can't get along with people, I should tell you to get a card about the size of a postcard, and write this on it, "like attracts like," and then put it inside your closet—not where other members of your family will see it, because that would sometimes be embarrassing. When you are grumbling and finding fault they could point their finger at it, and that would be very embarrassing; so put your card inside the closet.

People come to me and say, "If you only knew the kind of family I have, if you only knew the kind of people I have to be with and work with!" I say, "The law of Being says, 'like attracts like.' "[15]

The relationships you have are important to you, whether you like them or not. In one case in the Cayce files a young lady, Sarah, was planning a trip to Europe. She asked Edgar Cayce, while in his trance state, whether she would make any valuable associations while she was there. She was told that her question was incorrect for "There is never an association that is not valuable." (212-1) He indicated there were a number of persons in Europe she would be attracted to and that these associations would bring new power, new abilities, and new conditions to be met.[16]

The effects of the law of attraction are not limited to individuals but have much greater impact. Sarah was advised to apply herself to mentally finding ways to use her new abilities to serve others. This, Cayce revealed, was necessary since, by the laws of attraction, all that is brought to us is for our development, and one of the highest purposes we can have is to use what we gain for service to others.[17]

APPLYING THE LAWS IN OUR LIVES

We have seen that the laws of attraction and repulsion can be applied in many different areas—improving relationships, creating abilities, succeeding in projects or organizations. The laws can also be used in finding health, a spiritual path, emotional healing, physical healing, or a deeper understanding of yourself and your relation to your Creator. For whatever area you choose, these are the essential steps you must utilize to make the laws effective in achieving your goals:

First: Be sensitive to your innate desire—the desire of your heart—respect it and work in accord with it.

Second: Prepare in the right spirit—desire to be of service to others through the avenues you are seeking.

Third: Prepare the mind—"dwell upon" that which you seek, upon your desire to succeed, and to be of service. You then will attract the sources you need.

Fourth: Prepare on the physical level by working with the sources and the individuals you have at hand or to whom you are attracted. Test, try, and apply that which works best for you.

Fifth: Watch what is happening in your life to "see" what is really in your consciousness. Learn those lessons and make the changes that need to be made until you have attracted into your life that which fulfills your innate desire.

There are many ways you can use these laws. If you follow the above steps, you will put into operation the forces that are conducive to your success. Things will come to you in surprising ways. Opportunities will arise of which you may never have dreamed. New thoughts will come to your mind; you will meet people who will assist you in many ways through ideas, suggestions, or actual help. The laws will open doors for you, but you have to move through them.[18] All this is possible as long as you keep your mind on the constructive and the positive and do not allow yourself to be turned aside by negative, destructive doubts and fears, whether they emanate from yourself or others.

HIGHLIGHTS OF THIS CHAPTER

The laws of attraction are:

LIKE ATTRACTS LIKE

AS YOU SEEK, YOU ATTRACT AND ARE ATTRACTED TO THAT WHICH WILL FULFILL YOUR SEARCH

The laws of repulsion are:

OPPOSITES REPEL

AS YOU SEEK, YOU REPEL AND ARE REPELLED BY THAT WHICH WILL NOT FULFILL YOUR SEARCH

Through these laws you have established your universe—the people, places, and things that exist in your life. Through these laws, you can change your life.

Chapter 5

The Power of Expectancy

In my research of the Edgar Cayce readings, I never found any specific reference to a law of expectancy; a recent computer search verified there is no such reference. But the readings emphasize frequently the importance of having an attitude of expectancy in working with the Universal Laws. They make this statement, which resembles a Universal Law: " . . . that you really expect you receive."[1] That is so because expectancy is the state of mind and spirit that gives life to our creative powers. When we have an attitude of expectancy, our mind senses it and begins to build. Without it, nothing happens. The spirit of expectancy is the key that turns on "mind the builder." The manifestation in the physical is the result. Therefore, the spirit of expectancy is an important causal factor in the operation of the laws, one that we need to learn how to use for our benefit and how to avoid using it to our detriment.

The following reading illustrates the importance of an attitude of expectancy and how it can affect your life for either good or ill:

(Q) Is there likelihood of bad health in March?
(A) If you are looking for it you can have it in February! If you want to skip March, skip it—you'll have it in June! If you want to skip June, don't have it at all this year! (3564-1)

How challenging! You really must watch what you are expecting. The degree of expectancy that you maintain is also vital:

If you expect much, you will obtain much! Expect little, you will obtain little! Expect nothing, you will obtain nothing!

(5325-1)P

Although the readings indicate that expectancy is powerful, situations don't always work out as we expect. A trip on which I expect to have a good time can end with the car breaking down, the baby getting sick, and my getting the flu. One explanation is that perhaps my expectancy was not consistent with the circumstances. If I did not get the car tuned up when I knew it needed it, if the baby needed rest and not travel, and if I was worn to a frazzle, my expectations were unrealistic. We can't violate physical laws and hope to overcome that violation with mental and spiritual forces.[2] That's not in accord with the law of balance.

BASIS FOR EXPECTANCY

Expectancy should not be confused with wishful thinking. Our expectancy should be as real for us as it is for a woman who knows she is pregnant—she is indeed expecting and with certainty.

You can be certain even when you do not have such obvious physical evidence as a pregnancy. You can base your expectancy on a solid foundation—that of the Universal Laws.

For example, consider the law of "as you sow so shall you reap." This law can be a foundation for what you can expect. You can rely on this or any of the Universal Laws because the law is unchangeable and its operation is inevitable. Therefore, **as you know your purpose and apply Universal Laws in accord with it, you will know what the results will be—and can expect that!**[3]

There are other ways of introducing certainty into our expectancy. This nugget from the Cayce readings summarizes the concept of mind and expectancy and shows how all things are made certain or possible:

For mind is the builder. This keep ever before you—the attitude of mind. If you expect to make a failure who else is going to expect you to succeed? It must be within yourself.

(3409-1)AR

EXPECTANCY OF PROBLEMS
AND DIFFICULTIES

We need to guard against cultivating an expectancy of difficulties or problems. Asked about the likelihood of an accident, Cayce's source warned: " . . . do not look for it or you will find it." (257-62)

If you are looking for an accident or you fear one, you are expecting an accident. In effect, you have an attitude or concern that it will occur. The result is that you activate a law, such as "as you sow so shall you reap," and you reap the accident.

The creative process of the Universal Laws is impartial and works in accord with your input. It is basically an energy-transforming process. In thinking about negative conditions past, present, or future, you are giving energy to such conditions. Through the creative process they will grow, expand, and manifest.

I learned such a lesson once on a trip to Virginia Beach. The hotel at which I needed to stay had previously mixed up my reservations; thus it had no room for me. On this trip, I was determined that that would not happen again. Before I left for the plane, I called the hotel to be sure the reservations were correct. They assured me all was in order. Upon my arrival, the desk clerk said he had no reservation for me! They were, just as I had expected, fouled up again! I had not only expected it, I had poured energy into that expectation by my worry and concern. What I truly expected, I received.

The following reading indicates that if a negative condition is occurring in the outside world, it will not affect you unless you expect it to:

(Q) May 1941 is given, astrologically, as the time of the beginnings of riots, tumults, and revolution in and about New York City. Is this correct and what may be looked for?

(A) This, as we have indicated, will depend upon the activities of men. As to whether this is to be, so far as the entity is concerned, will depend upon the attitude taken. If it is dwelt upon in the pessimistic manner, look for it! If it is dwelt upon in the optimistic manner, and acting in that way and manner, do not be disturbed! (1602-6)

This understanding is so important! We can be in a world of what appears to be riot, chaos, and confusion, but those things do not have to touch or disturb us. Our world can be one of peace, order, and joy no matter what may be occurring on the outside. Our world depends on how we choose to view it and, more important, how we choose to create it through our expectancy, our beliefs, and our application of the Universal Laws. What is happening in the outside world is not the determining factor unless we expect it to be.

EXPECTING THE BEST

It makes sense for us to examine thoroughly our thoughts, attitudes, and beliefs — particularly those which involve fear of something negative happening to us. We need to dismiss such attitudes. Instead, we must acknowledge that whatever happens to us will be for our highest and best good, for that is the way the Universal Laws operate. We can expect that, for nothing happens by chance.[4]

Daily Word is a popular, low-cost, nondenominational pocket-sized magazine (1,600,000 copies published monthly).[5] I highly recommend it as daily reading. It carries, for each day, an inspirational message based on truth principles and Universal Laws. The following excerpt encourages expectancy and shows many different ways you can effectively use an expectant attitude:

I EXPECT AND PREPARE FOR THE BEST

To *expect* the best keeps the door open to good at all times. It is an attitude well worth developing. I think in terms of health and I *expect* to be healthy. I know that the same Spirit that created me ever remains within me to keep me well and strong. I know that there is no lack in God's kingdom, so I *expect* and prepare for the abundance that is His good will for me. I *expect* a good outcome of all that concerns me. I believe in the good in other persons and *expect* the right and just outworking of all my affairs. When I pray, I believe in the power of prayer. I let this belief carry through in all of my thoughts and expectations. Any thought of fear or doubt is canceled as I steadfastly affirm, "I *expect* and prepare for the best." I am blessed in mind, body, and affairs as I develop the attitude of always *expecting* the best.[6]

HIGHLIGHTS OF THIS CHAPTER

An attitude of expectancy is important for "that which you really expect you receive." This applies when your expectancy is based on your application of Universal Laws.

As you know your purpose and apply Universal Laws in accord with it, you will know what the results will be—and can expect that.

Chapter 6

Laws of Cause and Effect

One of the great laws by which our lives are shaped is this simple but extremely important master law of cause and effect:

FOR EVERY EFFECT THERE IS A CAUSE

Whatever has happened to you (the effect) in your life, there was a cause for it. If you got sick or broke your leg or had an accident or gotten divorced, it was not by chance or bad luck; there was a cause. On the positive side, if you met someone who became a good friend, received unexpected money, had a wonderful day, or found the ideal job or mate, that also did not occur without reason: there was a cause behind each of these events.[1]

This law is so pervasive in our lives that the Cayce readings refer to our world as a causation world. Nothing that happens in our world or to us personally ever happens by itself or without cause. In the earth plane cause and effect is the natural law; it is the way the world works.[2]

Basically, you are the cause of all that happens to you. When you knowingly or unknowingly put a specific Universal Law into operation, the result set by that law is inevitable. The readings assure us that the effect is interlocked with and follows the cause as surely as day follows night.[3]

For example, consider the law "as you sow so shall you reap." When you sow seeds of any kind, you set the law in operation and your action of sowing the seeds is the cause. That puts the Creative

Forces to work and will inevitably bring into your life the effect—
which is the harvest from those seeds. The other two laws we have
studied are also laws of cause and effect:

The Cause	The Effect
As You Sow	You Reap
Like	Begets Like
Like	Attracts Like

In each case you are the cause: your seeds, your attitudes, or
your treatment of others sets these laws into operation.

There are many sublaws of cause and effect similar to those
given above. They are all summarized in the master law "for every
effect there is a cause." For each law *you* are the cause, as the
readings clearly state:

> This may be a hard statement for many, but you will even-
> tually come to know it is true: No fault, no hurt comes to you
> except that you have created in your consciousness, in your
> inner self, the cause. (262-83)AR

That says unequivocally that we are the cause of all we experience, totally responsible for all that happens to us. We may not be
comfortable with that fact because most of us do not really want to
take responsibility for our lives. We would rather blame our problems and failures on our parents or spouse or the government or
some other organization or condition. Our minds may bring forth a
dozen reasons why it is not possible that we are responsible for
what has happened to us. We will deal with those later.

Let's look at the positive aspect of this law. If you and I are responsible for all that happens to us, you and I have the unlimited
opportunity to make our lives exactly what we want them to be. We
can create or cause them to be what we choose. We can change them
as we wish, to make the most wonderful lives we can imagine. For
me, that possibility is so promising and so exciting that it far out-
weighs the responsibility that goes along with it. I am willing to take
the responsibility for my life if I can make it what I truly want it to be.

NO BLAME, NO GUILT

Above all, as you come to realize that you are responsible for your life, lovingly accept it as it is and accept yourself just as you are. Place no blame or guilt on yourself or others, nor harbor any guilt for the past. Such reactions are not helpful. Forgive yourself for those things which you regret. Life is not a judgment process; it is a learning process. Be thankful for all that is happening or has happened to you, for it can teach you important lessons if you accept it as an opportunity to learn and look for the good in it.

THE LAW OF CHANCE

But what about chance? Most of us grow up believing that chance, luck, and accidental events play a part, for better or worse, in our lives. But the readings say this is a law:

THERE IS NOTHING BY CHANCE.
(2946-2)

This law of chance follows from the law of cause and effect. It is a corollary of that law because it represents another way of stating "for every effect there is a cause." It is the reciprocal of that law. So in our chart showing the relationship of laws, it occupies the same position as the law of cause and effect. (See Figure 5.)

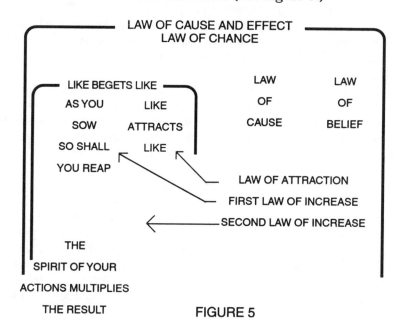

FIGURE 5

The *Kyballion*, a study of Hermetic teachings of ancient Egypt and Greece, includes in its seven basic principles of truth a profound statement regarding chance:

> Every cause has its effect; every effect has its cause; everything happens according to law; chance is but a name for a law not recognized; there are many planes of causation, but nothing escapes the law.[4]

You may still ask, "What about that accident I had?" or "What about my disastrous childhood?" We grew up believing that such unfortunate experiences surely resulted from bad luck, chance, or someone else's negligence.

If events happened by chance and without reason, we could not and would not be responsible for our lives. We would be like pins in a bowling alley, getting knocked every which way by something over which they have no control. Such a condition would be inconsistent with the nature of the Universe. The Cayce readings explain in many ways that it is a loving Universe. It respects no person more than another; it loves us all equally and gives us equal opportunity through the Universal Laws which operate impartially for all. One of the laws necessary to insure love and justice and equality for all must be that "nothing happens by chance."[5]

Under these laws of chance and of cause and effect life becomes a wonderful school in which we teach ourselves. We create situations in our lives from which we learn what we need to learn when we are ready to learn it. As we come to understand this concept and the laws that make it so, we realize that life and its problems are not mere chance. They are really the result of and show the love, the mercy of a loving Spirit who gives each of us equally the opportunity to grow mentally and spiritually, to create for ourselves the most abundant and joyful life of which we can conceive.[6]

MISPERCEPTIONS

To achieve an abundant and joyful life, we need to let go of some of our misperceptions, including our belief in "luck." The readings assure us that so-called luck, good or bad, results from the laws being carried out. There is, therefore, no such thing as good luck. The cause must be present to produce that which happens to you.

The good news is that if you have what you consider good luck, you are the cause.

The bad news is that if you have bad luck, you are the cause.

The best news is that you can create your own luck by making use of the opportunities that come to you and by applying the Universal Laws in the highest way you can. The reason there is no "luck" is that each one of us is precious in the sight of the Creative Forces. We are all treated alike and given equal opportunity to create our own circumstances—good or bad—through the Universal Laws.[7]

BIRTH AND CHANCE

You did not enter into the earth by chance. You came because you needed or wanted the experience. Through the laws of attraction you were drawn to the earth and to the place, position, race, family, and parents through which your needs could be met. The Creator does not do things haphazardly. You came by law for the purpose, as beautifully expressed in the readings, to "fill that place which no other soul may fill so well." (2533-1)[8] That is challenging! You are needed. There is a reason and a purpose for your being here. No one else can do it as well.

HAPPENINGS AND CHANCE

Once on the earth, your experiences are the result of the way you apply the Universal Laws. How you do that depends on the ideals and purposes you hold and the choices you make.

You may respond by saying, "But there are coincidences. I met my fiancé at a party—it just happened that we were both there. It certainly wasn't planned." The readings insist there was more to it:

It is true for the entity, and for most individual souls manifesting in the earth, that nothing, no meeting comes by chance. These are a design or pattern. These patterns, however, are laid out by the individual entity. For, there are laws.
(2620-2)

No friendships or associations—whether family, social, or professional—are by chance. It is all laid out by you, through your use or misuse of the Universal Laws. The Creative Forces handle the details of working out what you have directed, even though you may not even be aware that you have set them to work. You have created the pattern. There is "nothing by chance." These friendships and associations are for a purpose and have come about as another step for your development.[9]

THE UNIVERSE HANDLES THE DETAILS

A profound realization in the foregoing paragraph is that the Creative Forces handle the details. Once you have set the pattern, the Creative Forces do the work. You and your fiancé were somehow brought together—not by chance and not by luck—but by an attraction set up through your auras. Each of you set the pattern and the Creative Forces created the arrangements so that you two would meet. It is comparable to a computer that puts out signals to a network as it searches for certain information. Another computer on the network has that information. One computer may be in New York and the other in California. The electronic network provides the link between the two computers and the means through which they make the connection. This happens thousands of times a day in the computer world. It works equally well in your world. Instead of using connecting telephone lines as computers do, you and your fiancé used vibrations, which go through the atmosphere like radio waves. The Universal Laws of attraction and repulsion provide the means through which the connection is made.

The well-known motivational author and lecturer, Arnold Patent, for many years has taught the application of Universal Laws in everyday life. In the following commentary, he verifies the concept and explains another vital aspect of its use:

The Universe handles the details. This is another principle that appears to contradict common teachings.

Handling details is generally considered a conscious mind experience. It is usually an attempt to figure out the best way to function in a situation, and to plan how to achieve an objective. However, the conscious mind does not know all of the variables in any situation. Only Infinite Intelligence has this knowledge. As we relinquish this function to Infinite Intelligence, things will fall into place for us perfectly. Following our intuition, our connection with Infinite Intelligence provides us with the perfect signals or guidance without any effort on our part.

For example, each of us at some time has had the experience of going to a place because it felt right to go there. What seemed like a chance meeting with a particular person turned out to be a valuable connection. Looking back on it, we can see that there is no way we could have planned the meeting, as the existence of the other person wasn't even known to us.[10]

The Creative Forces are always available to aid us in accomplishing whatever we wish to do. The more we recognize and accept this fact, the more effectively and effortlessly we can accomplish our goals. The Universe will handle the details for us and the Universal Laws define the principles by which those details will be handled.

A KEY TO WORKING WITH THE CREATIVE FORCES

Use of your intuition—your inner guidance—is vital to your working with the Creative Forces. When you suppress it or ignore it, the difficulties begin because you are then relying solely on your conscious mind, which simply does not have the whole picture. Learning to follow your inner guidance is part of what this book is all about. That guidance is available to you here and now. Know that and start to listen to your intuition; follow it, and the road to your destination will be much smoother and far more enjoyable.[11]

You may think that you do not have such guidance because you may feel that special training or exemplary conduct is necessary to be able to receive it. Not so! The Universe impartially provides guidance for everyone, all the time. You need only to awaken to it—to the subtle feelings or thoughts or happenings that come to you as your day unfolds. Here is a simple example from my own experiences of how you can come to be aware of it:

As I am about to leave the house to go to the store, or get the mail, or go on a trip, I pause a moment and ask, "Do I have everything I need?" If I have forgotten something, I sense a feeling of resistance or lack or incompleteness or something comes to mind. If I have everything I need, it's a feeling of freedom. These feelings are subtle, but they are there. Try it—it will work for you, too, if you believe it can.

ACCIDENTS AND CHANCE

What about accidents? They certainly must be by chance. They are not planned. They come unexpectedly. Many people are sometimes killed at one time, as in an airplane crash. Those victims certainly didn't plan such an accident. Here's what one Cayce reading had to say about accidents:

> For, it is never by chance but, as with all things in this material world, there are causes, there are effects. To be sure, at times there may be what might be called accidents. But these, too, in a causation world, have their cause and effect.
>
> (2927-1)

To help you better understand this concept, I'd like to share with you an incident from Cayce's life. You will remember that I mentioned earlier that Cayce had the ability in his conscious state to see auras. In his booklet, *Auras,* he wrote that when people are about to die their auras grow dimmer and gradually disappear. He tells of one of his experiences that illustrates how the law of cause and effect operates, even in accidents, in the lives of the individuals involved and that death is not by chance. This is his story:

> One day in a large city I entered a department store to do some shopping. I was on the sixth floor and rang for the elevator. While I was waiting for it, I noticed some bright red sweaters and thought I would like to look at them. However, I had signaled for the elevator, and when it came I stepped forward to enter it. It was almost filled with people, but suddenly I was repelled. The interior of the car, although well-lighted, seemed dark to me. Something was wrong. Before I could analyze my action I said, "Go ahead," to the operator, and stepped back. I went over to look at the sweaters, and then I realized what had made me uneasy. The people in the elevator had no auras. While I was examining the sweaters, which had attracted me by their bright red hues—the color of vigor and energy—the elevator cable snapped, the car fell to the basement, and all the occupants were killed.[12]

This tragedy holds important understandings. For the elevator to fall, there had to be a cause. In this case perhaps someone had failed to properly maintain the mechanisms or had erred in the manufacture of the cable. Whatever the specific reason, the cause was there, and thus the condition was set. Those who were about to die—who, for whatever reasons, had chosen to die—arrived on schedule for their rendezvous with death. While they certainly had not acted consciously, they "caused" themselves to be there at that moment. They were ready; their auras had dimmed or disappeared. The elevator crashed, and they accomplished their objective.

Those who were not ready to die were not aboard. By some inherent sense, intuition or understanding, inner guidance, or warning—as in Cayce's case—they had been diverted elsewhere at the critical moment. It appeared to have been an accident, but, in truth, "nothing happens by chance." The laws were at work; there was cause and effect, and all was in order.

There is another example which would seem to verify the fact that there is a cause behind all happenings. Years ago I heard a report of studies which showed that commercial planes which crash have a higher cancellation rate for reservations on those flights than for noncrash flights. Apparently, those who are not ready to die are warned in some way or sense the impending disaster and change their plans!

In other events in which many people are killed or die, such as famines, war, earthquakes—these, too, have their causes. The fact that large numbers of people are involved does not change the fact that those individuals, through the choices they have made over long periods of time, have brought themselves to that place, circumstance, and involvement. Contrary to our usual assumption, they are not victims in the sense that they just happened to be there. They are there by choice, though their choices may not have been entirely conscious ones. Had they made other choices, they would not have been there. As the law states: "There is nothing by chance."

Arnold Patent, speaking of the law (he calls it principle) of cause and effect, sets forth the tremendous implications of this law and what it means to us even in the case of an "accident":

> This principle states that we cause everything that happens to us. There is no such thing as an accident. This principle mandates that we take responsibility for everything in our lives. It is a powerful principle and we gain enormous benefit, when we believe it. However, we must accept the embarrassment that comes from taking full responsibility for many things we would rather not face, including those things that appear to be the fault of others.
>
> For example, we are in an intersection collision with another vehicle whose driver went through a red light. It is easy to blame the other driver, and thus relieve ourselves of any responsibility for the collision. When we do that, however, we

are in effect saying that the law of cause and effect does not apply. We have relieved ourselves of the immediate embarrassment of being responsible for the collision. But we have relinquished all of the power that comes to us by believing in the law of cause and effect. For if we take responsibility for everything that happens to us, we now open up the opportunity to create life exactly the way we like it to be. Taking responsibility for the collision is, therefore, a small price to pay for the advantage that we gain.[13]

Even accidents have their purpose. One individual asked Cayce why he had an accident and what was its purpose. Cayce replied that it was to create an experience from which lessons might be learned.[14] In view of that realization we can add to the law of chance and make it more meaningful in our lives by expressing it as:

NOTHING HAPPENS BY CHANCE;
THERE IS A PURPOSE TO
EVERYTHING THAT HAPPENS

Here is an example of that expanded law. Some time ago I had a fender-bender auto accident, and I learned some lessons. As I thought about it afterward, I realized that I had become careless about checking traffic around me. I know that what occurs on the physical level has been created on the spiritual or mental level because, as the readings explain: spirit is the life, mind is the builder, the physical is the result. So I took time to look at what I was doing on those levels. I did this by "standing aside and watching myself go by." I found that on the mental level I had become careless about the traffic within me, that is, in my relationships to others. On the spiritual level I found that I had also become careless about the traffic around me by not seeking guidance on my decisions. I wasn't paying attention to my relationship with my inner guidance. The Universe had sent me signals before. They were warning signals— a few close calls here and there, which I had ignored. So eventually I had to create something that would get my attention—several thousand dollars' worth, as a matter of fact! I hope I have learned the lessons. I have tried to change my ways on all three levels. I know that if I don't, there will be more than a fender-bender next time. There is "nothing by chance."

Emmet Fox directly affirms the concepts we have been studying:

There is no such thing as luck. Nothing ever happens by chance. Everything, good or bad, that comes into your life is there as a result of unvarying, inescapable law. And the only operator of that law is none other than yourself. No one else has ever done you any harm of any kind, or even could do so, however much it may seem that he [or she] did. Consciously or unconsciously you have yourself at some time or other produced every condition, desirable or undesirable, that you find in either your bodily health or your circumstances today. You, and you alone, ordered those goods; and now they are being delivered. And as long as you go on thinking wrongly about yourself and about life, the same sort of difficulties will continue to harass you. For every seed must inevitably bring forth after its own kind, and thought is the seed of destiny.

Yet there is a simple way out of trouble. Learn how to think rightly instead of wrongly, and conditions at once begin to improve until, sooner or later, all ill health, poverty and inharmony must disappear. Such is the law. Life need not be a battle; it can, and should be a glorious mystical adventure; but living is a science.[15]

HOW WE ARE "AT CAUSE"

In the basic laws, "like begets like," "as you sow so shall you reap," and "like attracts like," you can see how you are the cause because the results reflect your actions. What about the more complex situations in your life—finding a job or a mate, solving a relationship problem, or accomplishing a major goal? If you are the cause in these cases (and you are), how can you be "at cause" in the highest way so as to create the best effects or results?

To answer these questions for myself, I began to search the Cayce readings, seeking to better understand how I cause things to happen. I searched for several years without success. Then one day I found a reading that gave me the answers and also told a fascinating story about how it all came to be. The discourse was given for Gladys Davis, Edgar Cayce's secretary, who recorded and transcribed many of the readings. This is her story, as she wrote it:

In late January of 1934 Edgar Cayce, Hugh Lynn Cayce, and I were visitors for the weekend at the Ladd home on Long Island. Late Sunday night Mrs. Ladd was telling me about her husband's financial difficulties; his job was insecure, and they were about to lose their home. As I got in bed, I remember wishing I could do something to help the Ladd family. It turned awfully cold that night, and I was very uncomfortable. Although the little modern cottage was steam heated, I was from the South and it seemed mighty cold to me. Early the next morning, January 29, 1934, I was awakened by this dream:

A knock on the door. I said, "Come in." Mr. Ladd stood there with a coal scuttle in his hand and wearing a lumber jacket. (I had never seen him in anything but a business suit.) He came in and made a fire in a little coal stove which stood in the room, saying, "Now the room will soon be warm so you can get up."

On the train back to New York later that morning, I told Mr. Cayce and Hugh Lynn about the dream, when relating what an uncomfortable night I had experienced. We all laughed and attributed the dream to my discomfort. Still, I remember remarking how strange it was that the room should be different from the one I was occupying—which had cute little radiators on two sides of it (too cute and too little).

In early April of 1935 while on a business trip to New York, the three of us were spending the weekend as guests of Harold J. Reilly at his Sun Air Farm in Oak Ridge, N.J. On Sunday morning, April 7, 1935, when I said "Come in" to a knock on my door, there stood Mr. Ladd in his lumber jacket, a coal bucket in his hand, and he said, "I thought you'd like to have a little fire in your stove to take the chill off while you get dressed." I immediately noticed that the little room was exactly the same as I had dreamed it over a year ago.

You see, Mr. Ladd had become manager of Sun Air Farm in January of 1935, a year after we visited him in Long Island. If he had not come to my room to make the fire, I would never have remembered the dream nor recognized the room. So many questions arose in my mind as a result of this dream coming true that I sought the answer in a reading."[16]

THE LAW OF CAUSE

During that reading, Gladys Davis asked Edgar Cayce how her dream could so accurately portray an event one year before it happened and whether the conditions were already set at the time she had the dream. The source answered with these revealing words: "The law of cause and effect is immutable [unchangeable] . . . Hence

AS THOUGHT AND PURPOSE AND AIM AND DESIRE ARE SET IN MOTION BY MINDS, THEIR EFFECT IS AS A CONDITION THAT IS."
(262-83) [Author's emphasis]

That is the law of cause. The reading had stated, in those few words, the basic elements by which we cause things to happen in our lives. It is by our **thoughts,** our **purposes,** our **aims,** and our **desires.**

Once we have set those things in our mind, by that law the effect is determined; it exists on some level; it is all set and ready to go. IT IS. In other words, the Creative Forces have recognized that our thoughts, purposes, aims, and desires are set, and the Forces then proceed to create the resulting effect. It now exists on a higher level, waiting for the right conditions and right time to manifest in the physical.

Knowing these key elements of cause, we can go back to the time that Gladys had the dream and analyze the conditions that must have existed at that time for Mr. Ladd:

Mr. Ladd's Purpose
While we cannot know exactly what his purpose may have been, possibly it was to find a way of life which would be more enjoyable for him.

Mr. Ladd's Desire
His desire may have been to be closer to nature or to get away from the city.

Mr. Ladd's Aim
His specific aim, which would fulfill his purpose and desire, could have been to manage a farm.

Mr. Ladd's Thought
Mr. Ladd probably had given much thought to his situation and made up his mind to make a change. The thought that finally counts is the one upon which we set our minds.

Through the power of his decision, Mr. Ladd had "set" the basic factors and, as a result, had put the law of cause in operation. The Creative Forces had set up the effect that would result. This was the condition Gladys picked up in her dream.

Note that we determine each of these factors within ourselves; hence, we are the cause. Another experience of mine may provide insight into how we "set in motion" our thoughts, purposes, aims, and desires.

Some years ago my wife Charlotte and I visited one of the most scenic areas of our country. We were so entranced with the beauty of the surrounding mountains that we bought a lot in the area with the **thought** that some day we might build a home for the **purpose** of retiring there. Each year we returned to that spot and our **desire** to live there increased. Even though it was many years before my retirement date, we consulted an architect as to the design of a house. When we saw the plans, there was no doubt in our minds that it was the home for us. Through the plans, our **aim** was established. Thus, all four elements had been set in motion by our minds, even though at the time we were not aware of it. Within three years we were living there. Even though it was still more than ten years to that supposed retirement—I had retired! So the law of cause is not only immutable (unchangeable, unalterable, changeless), but from my experience—once the cause is "set in motion"—the flow of events also can be powerful and precise to produce the effect—sooner than you may expect.

THE CREATIVE PROCESS

The above example shows that we are dealing with a creative process, a means by which you can literally create whatever you want to experience or have in your life. You can even use it to change your life completely. You can do this through your use of the law of cause, through knowing how to be "at cause"—knowing how you can and do create.

It is essential when using the law of cause to be aware that you are a co-worker with the Universe. You are "at cause" as you set the pattern or design of your creation with thought, purpose, aim, and desire. Like a gardener, you have a part to play in the manifestation of your creation. Once you have planted the seeds, you must water and cultivate them. In short, you must take action, doing what you know to do, using what you have. As you thus do your part, the Universe handles the details of growth and gives the increase— your creation.

Many times in the past you have used this method of creation. You probably were completely oblivious to the fact that you were using a definite process. What currently exists in your life is the evidence of how you have used this process in the past. It is another wonderful gift from the Universe, enabling you to make your life what you choose.

This creative process is impartial, so we can create havoc in our lives as well as the good and the beautiful. It may sound like a mind-control process; indeed, it is often used as such. That limited approach to its use, however, is the cause of much of the creation of chaos and confusion. It can be so much more than that when it is used in accord with the Universal Laws in the highest way. The creative process then becomes a means for holistic transformation not only of yourself but also of your universe. Keep this creative process in mind as you study the Universal Laws. They will show you how to use this process most effectively to bring you to the joys of the higher road.

When we consider this law of cause, we need to recognize that our thoughts, purposes, aims, and desires often derive from basic beliefs about ourselves and others and from programming and experiences held in our subconscious minds. We are frequently unaware of these beliefs. This explains why some of our creations turn out so differently than what we conceive in our conscious minds.

WHAT IS GOOD AND WHAT IS BAD

Before we employ this law of cause, we need need to decide what it is we really want and need, what is good for us and what is bad. Those are questions of judgment. The late Raynor Johnson, a scientist, inventor, formerly Master of Queens College in Australia, an author, lecturer, and spiritual teacher, many years ago told this apocryphal story. I have retold it numerous times because it puts the question of our judgments into a clear perspective:

A farmer in India had a very fine horse, but the horse ran away. The farmer's neighbor came to express his sympathy at the farmer's great loss. The old farmer's comment was, "Who knows what is bad and what is good?"

The next day the horse came back bringing a herd of wild horses with him. The neighbor immediately came over to express his joy at the farmer's good fortune. The old farmer again said, "Who knows what is bad and what is good?"

The next day the farmer's son, while trying to ride one of the wild horses, was thrown off and broke his leg. The neighbor came to offer his sympathy. The old farmer once again said, "Who knows what is bad and what is good?"

The next day the army came to the farm looking for recruits. They could not take the farmer's son because of his broken leg. The neighbor came over to congratulate the old farmer on the good luck that his son would still be with him. But all the old farmer would say was, **"Who knows what is bad and what is good?"**

There is a profound truth illustrated in this simple story. We really do not know in our conscious minds what is bad and what is good for ourselves, let alone for others or the world. That can be a shocking realization. It certainly is not one that would be easily accepted by most of us, for it flies in the face of our egos. None of us likes to think that we don't know what is good or bad for us. Yet so often what we think will be good for us seemingly turns out otherwise and that which we consider bad eventually proves to be a necessary step in our growth.

It is not that we do not have fine minds nor the best of education nor years of experience. None, however, is complete and none gives us the full perspective of why we are here and what life is really about. We, like the farmer in India, can only say if we are honest with ourselves, "Who knows what is bad and what is good?"

If we have any doubts about our limited ability to judge, we need only look at our world today with its ever-growing problems seemingly without solutions. We then need to realize that we—as individuals, as states, as a nation, and as a world—have created these problems. Why? One of the reasons is that the actions that have brought the problems about were undertaken with inadequate understanding of their consequences. In other words, we do not really know what is bad and what is good for us.

In reflecting upon the so-called good and bad in our lives, I challenge you to take another look and seek a higher vision. Is it not possible that, since the Universal Laws always bring to us what we have created, **what happens to us is always good, because it is always for our greater understanding, a lesson to learn, another step in our growth to a higher consciousness?**

Most persons agree that the difficult happenings in their lives have been the periods of greatest growth for them. However, life does not have to be difficult for us to learn. That is simply one way to live—the hard way. There is a better way. By learning the Universal Laws and how to apply them in the highest ways, we can transform our lives before we create the difficult situations. Through the laws we can learn how to avoid the weaknesses of our judgments and how to gain a clearer vision of what is truly for our and others' highest good and how to manifest it.

We know that the laws of cause and effect are central to how we live our lives. Our next steps, as we go through this book, are to learn more about the Universal Laws and how we can be "at cause" in the highest way. As we learn and apply, we will bring more meaning, more purpose, and more joy into our lives and the lives of others.

HIGHLIGHTS OF THIS CHAPTER

The master law of cause and effect is:

FOR EVERY EFFECT THERE IS A CAUSE

The law of chance is:

THERE IS NOTHING BY CHANCE

A corollary law is:

**NOTHING HAPPENS BY CHANCE;
THERE IS A PURPOSE TO
EVERYTHING THAT HAPPENS**

You come to the earth to fill that place which no other soul can fill so well.

If you give it a chance, the Universe handles the details of your life more effectively than you can.

There are no accidents, for there is always a cause.

The law of cause is:

**AS THOUGHT AND PURPOSE AND AIM AND DESIRE
ARE SET IN MOTION BY MINDS,
THEIR EFFECT IS AS A CONDITION THAT IS**

Chapter 7

Unique Characteristics
of the Universal Laws

Our real challenge, once we realize that we create our destiny through the Universal Laws, is to begin to make certain that our thoughts, purposes, aims, and desires plus our resulting words and acts are creating conditions we want to meet in the future. One vital link in this creative process is a more complete understanding of the Universal Laws and how they operate in our lives.

RECOGNITION OF A UNIVERSAL LAW

To distinguish a Universal Law from other ideas, teachings, beliefs, facts, or statements, first apply this criterion: Does it fit this definition of Universal Laws?

The Universal Laws are unbreakable, unchangeable principles of life that operate inevitably, in all phases of our life and existence, for all human beings everywhere, all the time.

Therefore, to determine whether or not a particular statement is a Universal Law, you could ask these questions:

1. Is it an unchangeable principle of life?
2. Does it operate inevitably?
3. Does it operate for all human beings, everywhere?
4. Does it operate all the time?

If the answer to any one of the above questions is *no*, the statement is not a Universal Law.

If the answer to all of the above is *yes*, the statement *may* be a Universal Law. But there is a further test.

If the statement makes any requirement of you by defining what you should or should not do, it is not a Universal Law. A Universal Law makes no demand on you. There are no limits or rules imposed by it. It is simply a statement of principle and of truth. For this reason it cannot be broken. You cannot break a Universal Law.

For example, consider the simple statement of this mathematical law: $2 + 2 = 4$. You can say $2 + 2 = 5$, but that does not change the fact that the truth is $2 + 2 = 4$. You cannot "break" that law of mathematics. Consider the law, "as you sow you reap." It is a statement of truth, a condition of life. You cannot break it either by doing something or by not doing something. When you take a particular action which is in the area covered by that particular law, you have set the conditions for the Creative Forces to produce the appropriate results defined by that law. The Universal Laws, therefore, are keys to the operation of life, keys to your relationship with the Universe, keys to your relationships with others, but they make no demands on you.

Therefore, the final criterion in determining whether an idea or teaching is a Universal Law is to ask this question: Does this place any limitation or requirement on me? If it does, it can be broken and is not a Universal Law.

Many statements in publications today are termed universal laws but they do not meet the above conditions. They may be fine advice or excellent teachings—or they may be hogwash, but they are not Universal Laws unless they meet the criteria defined above.

There are a number of statements that often are called universal laws but are really teachings which describe how a Universal Law may be applied in a higher way. I refer to these as lawful teachings. Consider the commandment: "Thou shalt not kill." This is not a Universal Law. It is a teaching which recognizes other Universal Laws, such as "like begets like," and teaches one aspect of living in accord with it. That commandment is, therefore, a lawful teaching. We shall distinguish between lawful teachings and the laws themselves as we progress.

UNIVERSAL TRUTHS AND UNIVERSAL LAWS

A Universal Truth is very much like a Universal Law—so much so that when I refer to a Universal Truth I, for clarity, call it a Universal Law. Both are unbreakable, unchangeable principles of life that apply in all phases of our life and existence, for all human beings everywhere, all the time. The difference between the two is that a Universal Law states an operating principle—"as you sow so shall you reap"—and a Universal Truth states only how it is; for example: "There is nothing by chance." However, the Cayce readings tell us that, in the highest sense, "Law is truth" and "Truth is law." Any difference is academic. For simplicity and clarity, I will continue to refer to Universal Truths as Universal Laws, unless there is reason to distinguish between them.

HOW DOES UNIVERSAL LAW COMPARE WITH MAN-MADE LAW?

A Universal Law is not like the laws of our government; rather, it is a basic principle of life. Instead of stating that you must do this or you must not do this—as statutory laws do—the Universal Laws explain to us how life works.

Moreover, man-made laws, such as speed limits, are changed periodically; the Universal Laws do not change and cannot be changed. The results under man-made law vary, depending on many factors, such as degrees of enforcement. Under Universal Law the results are inevitable.

The Universal Law applies everywhere; the man-made law may apply only to a particular jurisdiction or it may vary from one area to another. A Universal Law applies to everyone; a man-made law only to those in a particular area. The readings tell us that we are all equal before the Universal Laws. This is not always the case with man-made laws.

THE SCHOOL OF UNIVERSAL LAW

The key to the reason for our existence through the ages is simply that we are in school here on the earth. We are learning lessons through the Universal Laws. In this process, the readings tell us, the Universal Law becomes the schoolmaster or our school of training. We go to school every day of our lives—to the School of Universal Law! As we learn the laws and how to apply them, we can eventually graduate from this law school. That graduation is one of the major goals of our study and application of these laws.

The readings repeatedly characterize the Universal Laws as being perfect, that is, a perfect teacher. I remember a wonderful teacher, Professor Hitchcock, an older man who taught engineering math in my first year as an engineering student. He was tough. When I made a mathematical error, no matter how small or insignificant, I got a zero. I received no credit for the rest of the problem, even though I might have learned the concept and utilized it correctly. Sometimes the problems were long and involved, so we might have only one or two of them. No credit given for either one of them left my grades in shambles. Under the threat of failure I learned, as engineers must learn, that mistakes can be costly and cannot be tolerated. I learned to check and double-check and cross-check and do my work carefully, thoroughly, and accurately. Tough, yes, but exactly what I needed. At the same time, Professor Hitchcock was a loving teacher. He invited us over for evenings at his home. He tried to help us in every way possible. Even though he was tough, we loved him and respected him for it. He was a perfect teacher. So, too, are the Universal Laws tough, but only because their essence is love. They, too, are perfect teachers.

The laws are tough when you are not acting in accord with what the teacher knows is best for you—when you are being negative, destructive, evil, selfish, or when you are not paying attention to the lessons that are yours to learn. "The price must be paid! . . . You must pay the price—every whit! For, what you sow you must reap." (349-17)AR Another reading put it this way: "The law of the Lord is perfect—yea, it is as a two-edged sword, cutting as it were front and back, or dividing bone and marrow." (2275-1) In other words, the law makes a sharp distinction between right use and misuse of the law.

Although the law operates impartially to produce the results in accord with your input, there is no consolation provided—no ifs, ands, buts, or maybes—even if you are creating disastrous conditions for yourself. On the other hand, the Universal Law is like a loving teacher when you try to live in accord with your ideals. Then, according to the readings:

> . . . the law of the Lord is perfect—that if you follow therein, He may use you. And through that use may come to you the desires of your heart, in the material as well as in the mental and spiritual things. (3651-1)AR

My old math professor showed us real love by being both tough and loving. The Universal Laws are tough, but they are also loving, manifesting God's love for us and to us and bringing us our hearts' desires—when we use them in the highest ways we are capable of doing. They are indeed perfect—the perfect tough but loving teachers that we need to help us learn our lessons so that we may fulfill our purposes here in the earth and have a joyous time doing it.

LAWS OPERATE ON
PRINCIPLE—NOT QUANTITY

You may have misapplied a Universal Law many times. Perhaps you cheated others hundreds of times. If you decide to work at being honest with others and you actually do it, just that try, that effort, that change in consciousness on your part will turn the tables for you and put the law to work for you in the right way. Others will begin to be honest with you.

The Cayce readings explained to numerous individuals that certain difficulties they faced in their lives on earth were the results of acts they had committed or omitted in a previous incarnation. These were considered misapplications of the Universal Laws. Results that occur in a later lifetime from such misapplications are generally referred to as karma. (Of course, karma can also refer to positive actions from previous lives, resulting in talents and qualities that are of service to others.)

You do not have to meet the karma you have created in terms of numbers, but only in terms of principle. When you change your principle from deceit to honesty, for example, the Universe immediately is on your side because you have now chosen to work in accord with it. You are in the flow with it instead of in opposition to it. You are like a swimmer who was swimming upstream, requiring much effort. When you change direction and go with the flow, all of nature helps you, carries you along.

But you may get a test.

TESTS

Once you have successfully met a karmic condition, you need to be careful that you do not slip back to your old ways—or worse, to let your success go to your head and begin to think you are better than another. The Universe has a way of checking us out occasionally. It gives us a test. Perhaps the best way to explain is by example.

Many years ago I thought that the question of whether you were honest was like the question of whether you were pregnant—you either were or you weren't. I came to realize, however, that there seemed to be degrees of honesty. I found it easy to be honest with someone who made a mistake and gave me too much change, but when it came to a situation involving much more money, I had a greater temptation to fudge. I had the same reaction to honesty in human relations. I decided I needed to be honest under *all* circumstances. So I worked on this for a long time and began to feel I was always being honest. I had dealt very well with a number of "opportunities" that came up—as they always do when I start to work on some aspect of Universal Law. Then, an interesting situation developed.

I had a bank account in a major city bank, which I had used for a small business that I hadn't been active in for a long while. Yet I kept the account open and received monthly statements, but didn't open them because I knew there was only a small balance in the account. Then one day I opened a statement. I nearly fell off my chair. The balance in the account was over $200,000! I knew I had not put that money in the account. I quickly checked back through the unopened statements and found it had been there for more than six months. Wow! I immediately began to think of fourteen ways I could use that money.

I wish I could report that I rushed to the phone and called the bank to tell them of their error. I did not. Instead, I thought how great it was that God had found a new way to make the abundance of the Universe available to me—look at all the money I had attracted! It took several days for me to begin to pay attention to that gut feeling that told me there was another way to look at it. Finally, I did call the bank and asked them to check. They called back, apologized for the error, and assured me they would correct it immediately, little realizing they had cooperated with the Universe to give me the toughest test ever.

Since we know "nothing happens by chance," what was the reason for this situation? It could have been the result of karma that I had created; maybe in a previous lifetime I had absconded with the master's silver and, as a test, was being given the opportunity to do so again. Or I could have made enough progress in dealing with honesty to be ready for a greater opportunity. Maybe I needed strengthening in my resolve to be honest. Maybe I had grown complacent. To me, however, it felt like an actual test, and I learned a real lesson: to ever be aware that the opportunities for growth may be hidden in some strange packages![1]

Chapter 8

Using the Laws
to Create Your Destiny

As previously noted, whether one accepts any of the varied concepts of reincarnation is of no consequence in the understanding and application of the Universal Laws. There is no difference, in the eyes of the Laws, whether you created or caused a karmic condition in a past lifetime or in your present one. You will still be faced with the results of what you have done to another person or to yourself through your thoughts, words, or deeds.

In a number of Eastern religions karma entails a cycle of penalty and retribution that continues through successive lifetimes with little hope of ending.[1] The Cayce readings, however, offered specific guidelines—the Universal Laws—by which individuals could address their karma and bring about a major transformation in this lifetime.

Although in some instances the word *karma* in the Cayce readings may refer only to that condition brought from a previous lifetime, modern usage of the word includes anything that comes back to us as a result of our thoughts, words, and deeds—regardless of whether it occurred in a previous lifetime or in this one.[2] We'll use the more modern understanding of karma because the Universal Laws don't make a distinction between causes in previous lives or present lifetime.

Many tend to think of karma as being only negative. However, as stated earlier, the good you have done also comes back to you. We could term it "good" karma. Even our so-called "bad" karma comes for a worthwhile purpose: to teach us the lessons we need to learn.

So, in essence, all karma is good karma if we learn the lessons. In the terminology of the readings, taking advantage of each such learning opportunity is making stepping-stones out of the stumbling blocks before us.[3]

Life is indeed a school. To use a reincarnation analogy, think of each lifetime as a school grade in which you have chosen specific karmic lessons. The Universe brings to you the experiences from which you can learn these lessons. According to the readings, we carry with us, in our subconscious mind, the total memory of all that we have done, seen, heard, said, and experienced since our beginning as souls. So all of that information is stored there and, like bread in an electric toaster, it automatically pops up when we are ready for the experience we need. Or take the example of a computer that is programmed to bring us what we need. Daily we input where we are and what we are doing. The computer recognizes when we are ready for a lesson and sends out the signals via our thoughts, words, acts, and aura that will attract the persons or create the events needed. In other words, it creates the karma for our next opportunity to learn. This isn't done by some great power outside of us that is arranging our lives—not by some great computer in the sky. It's done by our own inherent computer, our minds.

KARMIC LAWS

What are the laws of this karma, what creates it, and what are the effects? The karmic laws are the laws of cause and effect. They are listed below, showing the basic cause in the left-hand column and the effect, or karma created, on the right.

LAWS OF CAUSE AND EFFECT
(or Karmic Laws)

CAUSE		EFFECT OR KARMA
Like	Begets	Like
Like	Attracts	Like
As You Sow		So You Reap
Thought ⎤		
Purpose ⎬		Your Creations
Aim ⎪		
Desire ⎦		

Through each one of these laws we can be "at cause" (the left column), and by that cause we create the effect (the right column). This effect can be either a new creation in your life or a karmic condition which you have unconsciously created to present you with a lesson that you need. The effect can also be in the form of a relationship, an illness or a health problem, a financial condition, or any other situation—all are opportunities for you to learn and to grow.

When you look at the list of karmic laws and see the ways in which you can be "at cause" and thereby create what happens to you, it becomes clear that you create your destiny. It is equally clear how you have created your life as it exists right now. As Arnold Patent writes in one of his books:

> Another way of describing the law of cause and effect is to say that everything that we have is what we want. Or, if we look around us and see what we have, we know that we have it because we want it. [As used in this book, *want* is synonymous with cause and create.]
>
> Again, taking responsibility for what we have now is the key to releasing the power which is inherently available to us through use of this principle.
>
> The law of cause and effect is a very precise principle. What we have, or the result we achieve, in anything and everything, is exactly what we want. In order to remind us of that precision, I suggest that we see ourselves as surrounded by 360 degrees of mirrors. Everything that we experience is a direct reflection of what we ask for.[4]

THE CYCLE OF KARMA

Let's take a moment to look at the karmic cycle: how karma from the past comes to you, how you may meet it, and its effect on your future and your destiny. The diagram (see Figure 6) illustrates this process, and its operation is explained in the four steps that follow.

STEP 1
In the past—a past life or last year, last month, or yesterday— you were "at cause"; you put the laws to work.

STEP 2

The operation of those laws creates an event in your life (an effect). That effect, the karma you created, impinges on you, here and now.

STEP 3

You react to it, based on the beliefs or typical reactions you have developed. **By the energy and nature of your reaction, you are again "at cause" and, as a result, put one or more of the laws of cause and effect into operation again.**

STEP 4

The effect created by those laws becomes your destiny and will appear again in your future—tomorrow, next month, next year, or a future lifetime.

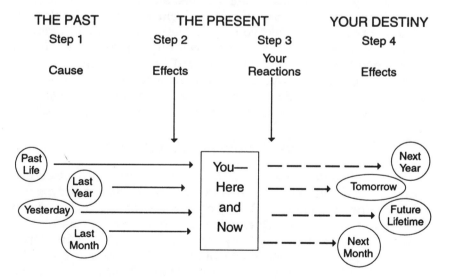

CREATING YOUR DESTINY

THE CYCLE OF KARMA

FIGURE 6

Let's consider a somewhat exaggerated example; let's assume that you are going through a traumatic period of life right now in which you just broke your leg, your house burned down, and your spouse ran off with your best friend! First, remember you set up the cause for each event in the past (Step 1). It now is manifesting in your life (Step 2). A simplified explanation might be that in the past you had broken someone's leg, burned down that individual's house, and run off with his/her spouse—now you are meeting yourself.

While this example is exaggerated, some cases of karma reported in the readings are no less dramatic or direct. Each event or experience in your life, no matter how drastic it appears to be, is your opportunity to change yourself and to create your destiny. The amazing fact is that the **actual happenings are not important; what is important is your reaction to each event.** How you react here and now is the key that determines your destiny (Step 3). If you react at the level of hate, resentment, or revenge, your reaction will create more of the same for your future. That will be your destiny. The cycle will repeat. If, however, you accept the responsibility for having created these events in your life, if you blame no one nor yourself, if you forgive each one involved and react with thoughts, words, and acts of love, peace, and forgiveness, then by the Universal Laws of cause and effect you "cause" love, peace, and forgiveness to come to you in the future. That will be your destiny. You will have ended the karmic cycle you created. By the simple process of substituting a higher reaction, you can totally change your life.[5] This kind of choice of reaction will enable you to take the high road of life instead of the low road, as far as this event is concerned.

YOUR TRANSFORMATION

It is a large order. How, in the face of such traumatic conditions, can you react with peace, love, and forgiveness? It certainly is not what is considered normal, based on the way most of us have been taught to think and act. One purpose of this book is to enable you to learn to react in a positive way. Real transformation is the step of moving—in your life and consciousness—from reacting unconsciously in ways that create negative karma to realizing the results of your reactions, enabling you then to consciously choose them to create positive results. You can do it. Others have. Such a change can be one of your most rewarding accomplishments in this life-time.[6]

BE AWARE

The key to successful change is to be aware of your reactions. Once you realize what you are doing, that you are reacting, you can begin to choose your reactions. You can choose to react with a positive attitude rather than a negative one. Your awareness of the fact that you are reacting, not choosing, is the first step in your transformation, in creating your greater destiny. You can also become aware by monitoring yourself: "by standing aside and watching yourself go by."

You may also want to be aware that any disturbing, destructive, or chaotic happening in your life is telling you there is something wrong. Such a happening should be the incentive for you to look for a better way. Even the little things that start to go wrong or that don't add up are prior warnings of something worse to come. If you pay attention to these little things, learn their lessons, and change, you can move from karma to a higher consciousness without more disastrous events happening in your life. The Universe is kind, gentle, and loving in its ways and never hits you with a two-by-four if you wake up and listen to its whisperings and its gentle suggestions.

WHEN IS IT NOT KARMA

It is easy to get so karma-oriented that we forget or do not realize that not all that happens to us is the result of karma. One notable exception is represented by cases in the Cayce readings which indicate that individuals have chosen, as part of their purpose on the earth, to take on handicaps in order to give others the opportunity to learn love, to demonstrate love, or to help others in some way. One biblical example of this purpose was the blind man who, as Jesus assured His followers, was not blinded as a result of karma but to provide an opportunity for healing that would demonstrate the love of God.[7]

I have seen a beautiful example of this in the life of a young woman whom I have known since she was a child. Grace was a quiet, shy, lovely little girl. When she was a teen-ager, she was stricken with polio and lived in an iron lung for a long period. As a result of the polio, she became a quadriplegic. But Grace has made stepping-stones out of her tremendous handicaps. Through drive and determination, she has accomplished amazing tasks. In 1988 she was one of seven U.S. women named outstanding mothers by the National Mother's Day Committee. She and her husband, Dave, have twelve adopted and three foster children. Many of the children are handicapped or come from Korea, Vietnam, or other troubled countries. In addition, Grace is the author of a number of books. The true measure of her mission in life is summed up by a neighbor and good friend who has worked with her on church committees and book publishing efforts: "I call her Amazing Grace. She is truly an inspiration for me. She is the kind of person who changes people's lives!"[8]

Grace's condition, I am sure, was not karmic but a mission to develop and show to others the beauty and power of God's love on the earth. She has fulfilled that goal. Grace is also an excellent example of the laws of destiny. She made up her mind she could do things that others said she couldn't do or shouldn't even consider. She became what she believed she could—and more. The "more" results whenever we attune to the Spirit within, for then we are utilizing spiritual powers, and the results multiply. That is in accord with the laws of increase and with some of the highest laws that are part of the process of transforming ourselves.

There are other aspects of our lives which are not karmic. Our feelings are not karmic; they are a reaction to a situation or happening—to some karma we are facing. They may result from our previous programming, "That's the way I'll always feel about that." But that attitude or feeling, while not karmic, will perpetuate or create more of the karma we are facing. We can change the way we feel about something; it is always our choice. Changing those ingrained patterns is part of what transformation is all about.[9]

We can set a policy or we can have ideas, goals, or plans for ourselves or for our business that are not karmic. They are our choice. But the manner in which we carry out such plans can create future karma—good or bad—for us to face, depending upon how we apply the Universal Laws to ourselves and in our relations with others.

OUR RESPONSIBILITY TO OTHERS FACING KARMA

Some of us, when we see others in difficulty, tend to feel they deserve it, since it is their karma. Although the other individual created it, you are involved if you are aware of it in some way. Cayce's source left no doubt as to what our responsibility is to another individual dealing with karma:

(Q) When one is working out a karma, is it right to try to help that one?

(A) . . . When there are karmic conditions in the experience of an individual, that as designates those that have the Christ-like spirit is not only in praying for them, holding meditation for them, but aiding, helping in every manner that the works of God may be manifest in their lives, and *every* meditation or prayer [for them should be]: *Your* will, O God, be done in *that* body as You see best. Would that this cup might pass from me, not my will but Yours be done!" (281-4)AR

In other words, you and I must do all we can to help others deal with karma, *not* preaching nor admonishing nor deciding for them, but helping as guided by the Spirit within us.

GROUP KARMA

Universal Laws apply to groups as well as individuals. In a brilliant and deeply insightful analysis of the Cayce readings on group karma, Linda Gerber Quest, Ph.D., in *The Politics of Hope* introduced the subject of groups and karma as follows:

For every aspect of our composite being, there is a kind of karma. Accordingly, there is physical karma, emotional karma, mental karma, psychological karma. Likewise, for every form of our social organization there is a kind of karma, too. Not only individuals have karma, but also families, races, associations of all kinds. Nations have karma. The whole of humanity has karma.

Group karma grows out of a pattern of association—association in a family, association in a nation, association in essaying a new experience, association in service, association in a special-interest organization, a religious order, or whatever . . .

Ordinarily, we might expect an association on which group karma is based to exhibit the outward signs of organization—membership, leadership, charter, bylaws, meetings, and so on. This is not a strict requirement, however. There may be real group cohesion and purpose without there being any structure or outward organization at all. A common spirit is sufficient . . .

We find, accordingly, in the Cayce readings, that the external signs of organization are not essential to the existence of a group and that the presence of all group members on the external side of life is not necessary either, provided there is the one thought and the one purpose.[10]

Group karma obviously results from the manner in which a people, as a group, applies the Universal Laws. These laws are the same for groups as for individuals. The impact and importance of the Universal Laws on groups are every bit as great as on individuals—whether the group is a family, a church, a corporation, or a nation. Whether the group succeeds or fails in its purpose for being depends not only on its competence and expertise in its field, but also—to a far greater degree than presently realized—on how the group, as a group, utilizes the Universal Laws. How it does that is determined not by any one individual but by the mass consciousness of the group.

When the group is an organized one and elects a governing Board, then the Board members are the ones responsible. How they collectively apply the Universal Laws in their decisions and actions determines the successes, the failures, the difficulties, the destiny of the group they control. Some of their responsibility is often delegated to administrative staff. Here again the staff's understanding and effective application of the Universal Laws are vital to the organization's achievement of its purpose. Problems that persist in such organizations are often the result of the consciousness that is held by those responsible. No matter how well intentioned the Board members and administrative staff may be, if they do not know and effectively apply the Universal Laws, such problems will persist.

HIGHLIGHTS OF THIS CHAPTER

In this chapter we have learned that the key to our destiny is within us. For we create our destiny by the way in which we use the karmic laws of cause and effect.

We have learned that if we wish to change our beliefs and thinking to effectively meet the karma we have created in the past, that will require a major change in consciousness. But that is only part of the story, for we each have within us far greater potential than we have any concept of when we are operating only on the cause and effect level. As a youngster, I lived in a small town and we boys always used to laugh at old farmer Hank. Farmer Hank had never wanted a car but his wife insisted they had to have one. So Hank bought one, but he would never drive it in anything but low gear! Operating unconsciously on the cause and effect level is like driving your car only in low gear. It is staying on the low road. You have far greater potential—you need to shift into higher gear, a higher consciousness (the high road), to realize your potential to achieve a greater destiny. You can make the change in consciousness by becoming aware of the transforming power of the Universal Laws. You then can create a more joyful way to live than being forever blindly subject to the laws of cause and effect.

Part 3

How You Can

Transform Your Life

with the

Higher Universal Laws

Chapter 9

The Master Law
for Your Transformation

Transformation, in a spiritual sense, means a shift or a change in consciousness from an older, limiting pattern to a higher pattern. This can be manifested in your life in many different ways: a shift from depression or despair to a positive, hopeful outlook; a change from financial lack and difficulties to material gain or effective money management; a physical healing; or the change in a difficult relationship to one of harmony and understanding.

Beyond immediate concerns, transformation can open new vistas in your life and bring you fulfillment far beyond anything you presently conceive. I am speaking now not just of creating your destiny, but going far beyond that destiny as you see it today. As previously mentioned, all Universal Laws are laws of transformation and enable us to make a change or transform our lives and our destiny because they teach us how the world and the Universe operate. Learning the laws is like learning to drive. With the greater knowledge of their operation, you are able to extend your horizons far beyond your present limits. Through knowing how the laws work, you are able to move through your universe more effectively and confidently and to achieve a higher consciousness in any area you choose. You are able to do this with far less effort and stress once you know and consciously apply the Universal Laws.

The Universal Laws of cause and effect that we have just studied are like the first few grades in school in which you learn the fundamental rules of reading, writing, and arithmetic. The laws of cause and effect give you a sound foundation on which to build. The

higher Universal Laws we'll now study will broaden your understanding of and open new doors for your further transformation.
These higher laws set forth the principles that deal with your relation to your Creator, to others, to yourself, and to your universe.
They enable you to come to more completely know yourself, to begin to understand the meaning and purpose of life and of your life,
and to understand how to live it in a way that brings the greatest
good to both yourself and others. If you are to transform yourself,
you first must know what is truly important for your life—what is it
to which you should be transforming yourself? It must not be
someone's opinion of what is best for you nor even your own idea. It
needs to be based on Universal Law, on truth.

So the question we each need to ask is the question that humankind has asked throughout the ages: What is truth?

THE MASTER LAW OF TRANSFORMATION

Truth is at the heart of the Master Law of Transformation which
was taught by Jesus:

. . . KNOW THE TRUTH
AND THE TRUTH SHALL MAKE YOU FREE.
(2809-1) (cf. John 8:32)

What is truth? Pilate asked Jesus that question nearly 2,000
years ago and Jesus remained silent. I used to wonder why He did
not answer. He certainly knew the answer and here was an opportunity to tell the world, yet He did not speak. Many years ago, at a
conference, a young ministerial student asked me the question that
Pilate had asked, yet his question was more specific. He requested
that I list what I felt were the ten basic truths of the Universe. I saw
his request as a delightful intellectual and spiritual challenge. Feeling completely capable and confident of my great wisdom in the
matter, I assured him I would have a list for him the next day.

That night, as I worked on it I had a number of realizations:

1. I was not sure whether several items I considered were or were
   not truths.
2. There were some items that I was certain were truths.
3. Some of those of which I now was certain, I had not considered truths a few years earlier.
4. Others I had once been certain were truths, I had since dis-
   carded.

It became clear to me that I could not put truth in a box—it was not a fixed absolute thing, as far as I was concerned. I realized that as I grew in understanding, my viewpoint changed and what I considered truth also changed. I couldn't give the young ministerial student a list and assure him or myself that what I had put down were the absolute truths of the universe. I suddenly realized why Jesus had kept silent. No one can tell you what your truth is. No one can put it in a box for you. If people try, they are misleading you. They can tell you what it is for them at that moment, but that does not make it your "truth." Coming to realize what is truth is a step that you must take for yourself. As you do, you must be open to new understandings of truth and be willing to grow, to change, and perhaps even to release a concept you have believed was truth, as newer, more beautiful truths and understanding come.

TRUTH IS GROWTH

I was reassured some years later to find this explanation in the Cayce readings:

> . . . truth is growth! For what is truth today may be tomorrow only partially so, to a developing soul! (1297-1)

Think of what you believed when you were a teen-ager. Compare it with your viewpoint today. How different! That does not mean you were wrong, but that you have changed. Edgar Cayce's sense of humor is evident in this story he tells to illustrate how our definition of truth changes:

> Here was an experience that came to a man. He was very much in love with his wife. He thought more of her than anything in the world, but [she died]; and when the man erected a monument in the cemetery, he had this inscribed on it: **"The light of my life has gone out."** He couldn't find anything that could reconcile him about his separation, until after a while he met a young lady he fell very much in love with and then he found that he was altogether mistaken about his first love being able to satisfy everything in his life! There was something else that had been added—he had gained the knowledge of someone else being able to fill up a portion of his life.
>
> The young lady, knowing about this inscription, said to him, "I might consent to be your wife, but I don't think I could ever

do that as long as the inscription remains as it is." So he went about to find a man who could correct this for him; and when the man who had charge of such things told him he saw how he could rectify this inscription, he went ahead with the wedding. When they came back from their honeymoon, they went out to see how it read and this is what they found: "The light of my life has gone out—but I've struck another match."

So you see there are individual experiences of truth. When we read or get an idea of some particular thought or some particular rule, we gradually build into our own selves an idea that we have gotten *the whole thing!*[1]

As the story illustrates, we never have the whole truth, even for our own lives. In fact truth, like our lives, is a continuing growth in consciousness and in understanding.

Think of truth as a brilliant jewel with many facets. You, from your point of view, see facets of that jewel that appeal to you while I, from my viewpoint, see other facets that I consider real or beautiful or true. As we move through life, our viewpoints change and so does our understanding of the beautiful jewel of truth. We, of course, need to be open to the new views. I can always put my view of the jewel in a box, close my mind, and say I know it all—sorry, I won't look at it from another point of view. In such a case, I am no longer a developing soul. I am a stagnant one. That's O.K., but I will miss so much!

One Cayce readings extract ties these thoughts together and shows us how vital truth is in our lives:

> For truth, while a growth, is indeed ever the same; and is
> the stepping-stone to material, mental and spiritual success.
>
> (1538-1)

Truth, like a jewel, is in itself ever the same—unalterable, absolute, and unchanging. While we see it as changing, the reality is that truth is not changing, but *we* are, because our perception of truth changes as we go through life.[2]

Your growth in truth is like the growth of a seed; you sow a seed in your life, then comes the first growth, the roots, later the stalk, then the flower, and finally the fruit which is ready to eat. The truth thus becomes a part of you. You do not learn truth, you earn it by applying the knowledge and understanding of the laws of truth. What are laws of truth?

TRUTH AND THE UNIVERSAL LAWS

The Universal Laws are laws of truth.[3] They are one of the most important facets of that jewel that is truth. They apply in every situation of life. When you start to apply the Universal Laws in your life, you begin to see and understand truth. You can, for example, intellectually understand and discuss the law "as you sow you reap," but the law will not become truth for you until you have experienced planting a seed, such as love or peace or hate, and then become aware of reaping the result in your life. Through that experience you come to realize that there is a divine power acting in your life, that life is not chaotic, that it operates by law.[4] That experience proves for you that "as you sow you reap" is truth, and so that law becomes a part of your "truth."

TRUTH SETS YOU FREE

Through that same step in application of the law, you can see the truth, you can know the truth, and—as the law says—the truth sets you free. You are set free from self, from the beliefs you hold within yourself that are not true, that are the veils of illusion which bind and limit you.

You have discovered the truth: that there is a higher power that is available to you, that works with you as you apply laws of truth—the Universal Laws. By that realization and by the knowing that comes from your experience of the law operating in your life, you come to realize that you are free—that you are no longer dependent on the world out there, on a job, the government, your associates, friends, or spouse.[5] It is a wonderful feeling!

With that knowing and that truth, you become free from self. You are fettered by self when you have doubts, fears, hatreds, prejudices, worry, or other negative outlooks or attitudes, for these are self-created conditions. The Master Law of Transformation assures you that as you come to know the Universal Laws—that is, apply them in your life in the highest way you know—you will be free of such negative conditions, free from the tyranny of self, from the ego self that tells you you must control your world, from the fearful self that tells you you can't control your life, from the selfish self that sets you against all others, from the fame-hungry self that demands you must succeed, from the self-demeaning self that says you are not good or not good enough—from all these selves that ride the fears you hold about life. Suddenly you find there is another way, the way of Universal Law, the way of truth, and you are free! You are free because you realize those old fears are not the truth; they are misperceptions, half truths, or outright lies. That is the law; "know the truth and the truth shall make you free"; that is the process. It may happen in a moment or take a lifetime, but it works if you are open to it.[6]

Universal laws are truth because they state how your world works. When you know how it works, you can see that you are the key to that working. The only way that makes any sense to live is to apply the law in the highest way you can. As you do, your life gets better and better. For example, today on a morning television show a young musician was interviewed about his outstanding success in establishing his own recording company. He explained he had achieved that success without any preconceived concept or goal. I thought that that couldn't have been the case. Such results only happen by law. I knew he must have, in some way, put a Universal Law to work in the right way. Just then, he explained that he felt there was a law of quality, that doing things with quality makes for success. Then he actually stated the law, "quality begets quality" [like begets like]. He said he knew somehow that there was an incredible spirit produced by that desire for quality and that that spirit attracted others of top quality [like attracts like] that made it all work out beautifully. That was his concept—his "truth"—and that is the way it worked for him, by law. He did not realize that his wise application of the laws was the cause of his success. This kind of application of the laws in our lives starts our transformation.

THE ULTIMATE TRUTH

Many of us question the reality of God, yet there exists what to me is undeniable and overwhelming practical evidence of a Power higher than ourselves.

Since 1939 many men and women have recovered from alcoholism through the efforts of the members of Alcoholics Anonymous, who themselves are recovered alcoholics. That recovery program consists of twelve important steps. The first three are:

STEP ONE: We admitted we were powerless over alcohol—that our lives had become unmanageable.

STEP TWO: Came to believe that a Power greater than ours could restore us to sanity.

STEP THREE: Made a decision to turn our will and our lives over to the care of God as we understood Him.

When these steps are sincerely taken, the alcoholic's life changes dramatically. He or she is able to regain control and start on the road to recovery. For those who try to bypass Steps Two and Three, the program does not work. That fact is attested to in the many life stories in the book, *Alcoholics Anonymous,* the "Bible" of the organization.[7] The experience of the more than 1,000,000 recovered alcoholics is dramatic evidence of the existence of a Higher Power. Their recovery is based on the realization of that Higher Power and its ability to work in their lives, when everything else they had tried had failed.

A woman writer came to Cayce for help in her work. She must have been a spiritually aware person, for she received a complete and final answer to the question, What is truth? [8] The source gave to her the jewel for which we all search, the gift of the ultimate truth, in these profound words:

> . . . you in your experience have become aware of that truth that is ALL TRUTH—that **GOD IS!!** (1152-4)AR

Most of us, if not all of us, cannot fully comprehend or understand the meaning or significance of that ultimate truth. We don't have to. The laws that we have are brilliant facets of that truth, and we can work with them and come to know them. We do need to feel and understand that those laws exist only because of and through that ultimate truth, "GOD IS."

GOD, LOVE, LAW, TRUTH

The laws, as discussed earlier in this book, are guided, guarded, watched over, and kept in accord with Divine Love. There is, as stated in the readings, a relationship among that Divine Love, the universal laws, the truth, and the source of it all, God.

The readings state the relationship very specifically:

> Truth is the unalterable, unchangeable law, ever.
> What is truth? Law!
> What is Law? Love.
> What is love? God.
> What is God? Law and love. (3574-2)

With that explanation we can make these precise statements about truth:

Truth is God
Truth is Law
Truth is Love

We also can identify these specific characteristics of God:

God is Law
God is Love
God is Truth

Lastly, from the reading we can describe the nature of universal law:

Law is God
Law is Love
Law is Truth

Since each can be described as the other, they all are one. We define them separately to help our understanding and give us points of reference. Each is a facet of that ultimate truth, GOD IS. Perhaps you can remember this more effectively from the diagram of these relationships given in Figure 7.

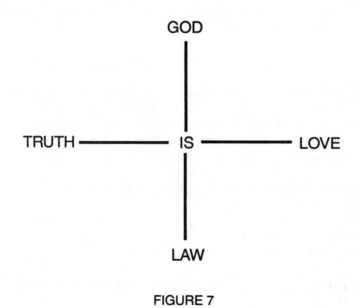

FIGURE 7

You can "read" that diagram in any direction—from top to bottom, bottom to top, side to side, or around the corners—to express these relationships of truth.

I am not attempting to define God, only to show the relationship of these aspects. Clearly the more we come to know and use in our lives law, love, and truth, the more godlike we become.

THREE STEPS TO TRANSFORMATION

At a meeting in the old Willard Hotel in Washington, D.C., in 1934, Cayce while in trance was asked what was the source of the information which came through him. His answer was:

> From the universal forces that are acceptable and accessible to those [who] in earnestness *open* their minds, their souls, to the wonderful words of truth and light. (254-83)

The first step required for transformation can be found in that statement—to earnestly open our minds to truth. If we are willing to do that, we will not have to go looking for truth. The Universe is bringing to us at all times exactly what we need to look at, exactly what lesson we need to learn, exactly the truth that we need to know:

> . . . as conditions, circumstances, opportunities present themselves day by day, so accept same, and as these work *their* way . . . so will the circumstance, the conditions, enlighten the body-mind, the physical consciousness *of* the entity, in such a way and manner . . . that the best, the conditions, the things necessary for the developments, *will* present themselves. (307-3)

In other words, we need to be open and willing to accept whatever happens to us, knowing that it is for our growth and for our greater understanding of truth. The truth is inherent within us and, as we begin to seek it, we can find it in our life's experiences. Those experiences reflect to us those truths that we are ready to see and accept.

The second step for transformation is **acceptance of the ultimate truth, GOD IS, to the extent and in the manner that you are able to do so at present.** It's like becoming an apprentice: you start at the bottom with little skill or understanding, but with a

desire to learn. You know the master you have chosen is there with
the skill and ability to teach and guide you. Such a step requires
acceptance of that master and a willingness to learn what he or she
has to teach you, even though you may not know the master very
well at the outset. As you work with the master, with the tools, and
follow his or her guidance, you will come to know him or her. The
master you need to seek and to choose for your transformation is
"GOD IS."

The third step for transformation, as Cayce's source suggests, is
**that we become discerners of truth—holding to that which is
eternal and which doesn't change in purpose or intent.** That
means, of course, that we need to hold to the Universal Laws, which
are the tools for our transformation. We need to begin to live in
accord with these laws and whatever we perceive as our truth. Begin to live these laws of truth by applying the truth you know—and
more will come.[9]

Remember: **truth is simple.** Look at the Universal Laws. They
are very simple statements of truth, yet they are the foundation
stones of life.

For many years I had doubts that Jesus was any more than a
fictional character. I began to read portions of the Bible related to
His life. I found that His answers to His adversaries' tricky questions were so simple, so wise, so direct, and so complete that I
realized He had a consciousness more profound than any individual I knew. Now I realize that He was a living person and His
answers were based on the fundamental truths of the Universal
Laws and on His attunement with the Creator.[10]

Cayce, in attunement with his source, gave this inspiring message in
urging us to seek and live the simple way of truth:

> . . . he that climbs up some other way but deludes himself
> and is lost in the maze of those material activities of others in
> the *spheres* of confusion! *Simple* the way, Truth the light!
> These are but words to many. Make them as frontlets upon
> your brow, that those who meet you—even in the way—may
> be *directed aright*! (254-83)AR

We are assured that as we do begin to live in the spirit of truth, it
will bring contentment, harmony, and peace, and we will be guided to
be better neighbors, better friends, better relatives, and better citi-
zens.[11] We will be on the higher road.

Through the three steps just discussed, as you work with the tools given you (the Universal Laws) and as you practice (life's lessons) under the guidance of the Master (GOD IS), you become a skilled craftsperson (transformed).

A well-known author, lecturer, and spiritual teacher, Eric Butterworth, is emphatic regarding the importance of the Way of Truth:

> . . . know that Truth is not something you learn or accumulate in memory, but something you unfold within yourself . . . you can release the hidden potential of your inmost self to give expression to the Truth that is the very law of your being.
>
> If you insist that Truth is limitless, and if you meet all things in the consciousness of the limitless Truth of God, then the rain may descend and the floods will come and the winds will blow—but the house will not fall, for your life is built upon rock.[12]

The Universal Laws each express some aspect of the limitless truth of God. They are the rocks upon which we can build. The results which we create through our use of the Universal Laws depend not only on our understanding of the laws, but equally on our basic belief structure—our beliefs about ourselves, our world, our relationships, and all aspects of life.

HIGHLIGHTS OF THIS CHAPTER

The Master Law of Transformation is:

KNOW THE TRUTH
AND THE TRUTH SHALL MAKE YOU FREE

The ultimate truth: **GOD IS**

God is:	**God is Love**
	God is Truth
	God is Law
Truth is:	**Truth is God**
	Truth is Law
	Truth is Love
Law is:	**Law is God**
	Law is Love
	Law is Truth

Three steps to transformation:

1. **Open your mind to truth by accepting whatever happens to you as a lesson in truth.**
2. **Accept that ultimate truth: GOD IS, as you understand it now. Seek for greater realization of that truth.**
3. **Live the laws of truth, the Universal Laws, in the highest way you can.**

Chapter 10

Why You Are Here

A fitting beginning to this chapter is to recognize and honor this admonition from the Cayce readings: " . . . we must know from where we came; how, why; and where we go—and why." (262-114)AR Human beings have sought throughout the ages to know these things. This need gives rise to these fundamental questions which you and I still ask:

1. From where did I come?
2. What am I?
3. Who am I?
4. How and why did I come here?
5. What is my purpose on the earth?

It is most important to find answers to these questions. If we do not understand our own nature and our purpose for being, our lives hold only limited meaning for us and we can find little true fulfillment. Furthermore, this knowledge is vital to our transformation, for it can help us to fully understand why we need to change our consciousness and what kind of changes are right for us.

The answers to some of these questions lie buried deep in time far beyond our conscious memory; ancient records give only tantalizing hints at what may have been. Fortunately, Cayce's incredible gifts included the ability, as he explained it, to tap a source of universal knowledge. That source gave a fascinating and sometimes astonishing chronicle of our origins and our heritage. That story also contains some of the answers to the questions posed above.

For the purposes of this book I shall touch only on those portions of our beginnings and our heritage that are essential for our study of Universal Laws.

It will be helpful in understanding and applying the laws if we take an overall look at various concepts of God as set forth in the readings.

GOD-CONCEPTS

We need to remember that the Cayce readings were given for a variety of individuals. We also need to remember that Cayce's source, when speaking to an individual, was attuned to the consciousness of that individual, and material was given in terms that could be understood by and related to him or her. For example: If his or her concept of God was anthropomorphic, as often portrayed in the Bible, the reading used such terms as "He" or "Him," speaking of God as you would of a male person. Cayce's source was interested in helping individuals, not in revising their concept of God, although the readings often spoke of how an individual's relationship to God could be improved.

To individuals open to a broader concept or asking questions as to the nature of God, the readings spoke of God as one all-pervading Spirit of love and indicated that the relationship with that Spirit can be as personal as the individual chooses to make it; that God is accessible to each of us and that we can communicate directly with that Spirit or Presence if we choose to do so.

As far as Universal Laws are concerned, it does not matter what your God-concept is. Actually we cannot define God, for whenever we define something, we limit it. God is infinite, without limit, far beyond our human comprehension.[1] We aren't prevented, however, from understanding God to a certain degree by examining some of the attributes or characteristics of God, just as we do in science when we don't understand something. To begin this process, let's consider the spiritual nature of God.

SPIRIT

During Edgar Cayce's lifetime a group of individuals began a series of readings as they sought to develop greater psychic awareness. These readings resulted eventually in the *Search for God* texts, inspiring guidebooks to spiritual development used by A.R.E. study groups. In one of the books the question, "What is Spirit?" is answered thus:

Spirit is FIRST CAUSE, the essence of Creative Power, the source of light, and the motivating influence of all life. It is God.[2]

The term First Cause means what it literally states, that the Spirit was the very first cause of the creation of our universe and of us. As noted, Spirit is the source of light. The readings explain how important this is:

What is light? That from which, through which, in which may be found all things, out of which all things come. Thus the first of everything that may be visible, in earth, in heaven, in space, is of that light—*is* that light! (2533-8)

That is an all-inclusive statement, for it says that light (of which Spirit is the source) is responsible for all, everything. This even makes sense to the conscious mind. We know from science that all mass or matter is energy, and we know light is a form of energy. It follows that since Spirit is the source of light it, too, is a form of energy. With that, what we have really said is that all is a form of energy, of Spirit, of God. We also know from science that one of the ways energy can manifest is as a force. Cayce spoke often of spiritual forces. The following indicates they are the fundamental forces of life:

Spirit forces are the animation of *all life*-giving life-producing forces in animate or inanimate forces. (900-17)

These few statements from Cayce's source tie everything we can experience to Spirit or God. Energy is the common element, one which we recognize scientifically. Physicists have found that as they work with smaller and smaller particles, as they enter the invisible world, the laws by which particles act are no longer the same as in the physical world. In my opinion, they are approaching the spiritual basis of everything, so they are encountering spiritual rather than physical laws. Cayce's source indicated that science may well find the spiritual nature of life before the religious establishment itself comes to understand it.

This interesting excerpt from *A Search for God* explains that you and I are just another aspect of that all-encompassing Spirit:

It has been given that there is One Spirit. All manifestations of life in any plane of consciousness are crystallizations of Spirit.[3]

Since you and I are certainly manifestations of life in this earth plane of consciousness, we, too, are crystallizations of Spirit. In other words, we are forms of the One Spirit.

To answer the question, Where did I come from? you and I came from that one Universal Spirit, of which we are not only a part, but also an expression.

WHAT AM I?

Let's look first at ourselves. What are you? What am I? The Cayce readings explain:

> Man finds himself a body, a mind, a soul. The body is self-evident. The mind also is at times understood. The soul or the spiritual portion is hoped for, and one may only discern same from a spiritual consciousness. (2879-1)

What is the nature and relationship of these basic elements of which we are composed? What is this mysterious spiritual nature or soul that was discerned by the spiritual consciousness that spoke through the readings? This reading gives an amazing explanation:

> In the beginning as He moved, souls—portions of Himself— came into being. (263-13)P

You and I are those souls! We are portions of God, created in the beginning! The soul which you are is your essence, your true nature, the real you. You have a physical body, but you are not your body. **You are a soul.** The readings often referred to the soul as a spiritual body or soul body. We are assured that the soul is the greatest of all creations. As such, you have some wonderful characteristics, gifts which were given you as part of your creation. You need to understand these gifts to appreciate fully what you—this soul—really are. Let's consider "you" as "you" were created in the beginning, a soul without a physical body.

THE FIRST GREAT GIFT

Spirit, in creating you as a soul, gave you four wonderful gifts. **The first gift is that you were made in the image of Spirit.** This is in accord with the basic law of the Universe "like begets like." When you look around at your fellow human beings or look in the mirror, it may be a little hard to believe that you are looking at images of Spirit. The truth is, it was your *soul* which was made in the image of your Creator, not your body or your mind.[4]

As noted, your soul is actually a portion of the Divine. The significance of this is tremendous. First of all, it means that we carry the divine portion with us always and, most important, it is within us here and now. Furthermore, it is not just at one point within us but within every cell, every atom of our bodies. Truly we do live and move and have our being in and with the Divine, as Jesus taught. In the spiritual sense we are indeed made in the image and likeness of Spirit—not only made in but are of Spirit.

The second and most amazing realization is that in this portion within us, which we might erroneously consider a "little bit" of Spirit, are all of the qualities and all of the characteristics of the Creator:

For in the beginning God said, "Let there be light." *You are one of those sparks of light* with all the ability of creation, with all [of] the knowledge of God." (5367-1)AR [Author's emphasis]

What "sparks" our souls are! They are as totally and completely like Spirit as a cup of water from the ocean is like the ocean—there is no difference between the liquid in the cup and the ocean. **Consequently we have within us the complete spiritual consciousness, all of the infinite power, total love, and the infinite wisdom to create the perfect patterns for our lives—all available to us in any way or any time we need it.**

That means that you have right within you everything you need to make your life perfect!

Be aware that "perfect" in this context means: exactly the right thing at exactly the right time and place for the greatest good for self and others.

No matter what you wish to create or to do, the perfect pattern for it can be created within you—perfect patterns for your home, your relationships, your attitudes, your talents, your health, your understanding of all things, including the Universal Laws.[5] That is why the readings make this startling statement:

**Know that the answer to every problem, to every joy, to
every sorrow, is within self.** (2581-2)

Let's take a practical example. Within you exists the wisdom to
create a perfect pattern for your health—a perfect pattern for each
part of your body. Perfect health is part of the gift to you. What you
have done with that gift depends upon how you have chosen to use
the Universal Laws of spirit, mind, and body that pertain to it.
Throughout this book we consider the basic laws through which
you can manifest in your life the perfect patterns that are available
to you.

The understanding that we are portions of the Divine leads to
another great realization:

One finds self a body, a mind, a soul; each with its own
attributes and its activity in the earth. An entity, then, is a
pattern of that which is also a spiritual fact; Father, Son, Holy
Spirit. These are one, just as an individual entity is one. *An
entity, then, is the pattern of divinity in materiality, or in the
earth.* (3357-2) [Author's emphasis]

THE SECOND GREAT GIFT

The Creator gave us, as souls, a second great gift. We were endowed with **life and consciousness.** Thus, we can be aware of
ourselves as individuals, aware of our own existence and of other
beings' existence as well as aware of the conditions of existence. In
the beginning, as souls, as spiritual beings, we were conscious of
ourselves and also of all creation. The most wonderful aspect of our
consciousness at that point was we were completely aware of Spirit,
of being spiritual companions with our Creator. We were also aware
that we were not the whole of Spirit but a part of the Creator, one
with the Creator and yet separate entities conscious of being ourselves. Therefore, we were not lost in an overwhelming relationship,
but were a real and equal part of it.[6]

Consciousness is a function of our minds. As a part of this gift,
we were endowed with mind, which also is a portion of Spirit. We
may term this the *soul mind.* It is through that mind that we are
able to be aware, to be conscious of our state. The important point
here is that life and consciousness, including all of our mental po-

tential and powers from all phases of mind, are a part of the great gifts we were given as souls in the beginning. This includes the infinite wisdom of the Creator, which is within us, available when we choose to attune to it.

THE THIRD GREAT GIFT

As a result of the creation of our souls as a portion of Spirit, we are part of that eternal consciousness that ever was, ever will be. So **we, as souls, are eternal.** This is the third great gift we were given. It is not something we must earn or deserve. You, as a soul, exist as a spiritual being before you enter and after you leave this earth. **There is no death.** What we experience as death is but a transition to another step in the fulfillment of our purpose. Spirit does not choose that any soul should perish, but has provided always a way for us to deal with whatever condition or temptation we face. The readings indicate that we are never given more than we can handle as long as we trust in Spirit. We might explain it this way—as long as one trusts in the Divine power within, there are no limits to what one can handle or deal with or achieve![7]

So the third great gift we were given as souls is eternal life.

THE FOURTH GREAT GIFT

The fourth great gift we souls were endowed with is free will. With free will, we can do whatever we choose to do with the gifts we have been given. This applies whether on this earth or in any other plane of existence. If we did not have free will, we would only be robots doing the bidding of the Creator. But Spirit wanted us as companions, true spiritual companions, with our own minds and consciousness, free to be and do what we choose, and so gave us complete and total free will.[8]

This gift is a tremendous one, for it puts you in charge of your life. Within the paradigm in which you exist, you are totally responsible for whatever happens to you. It is not up to God, your parents, your government, your spouse, or anyone else. In the words of President Harry Truman, "The buck stops here!" The buck stops with you.

The question arises as to how much free will we really have in view of the laws that apply to our lives and the fact that life is eternal. Does this not mean that we are committed to it all, whether we want to be or not? The readings indicate that we still have the choice and that we can opt out of it if we choose. This involves complete withdrawal from life, a surrendering of our souls and individuality so that we no longer exist. Thus, with free will we can even defy the Creator by negating our creation.

The concept of free will often seems to be a long way from what we observe in this world. What about the child born in poverty or who is parentally abused or is born with AIDS? Where is the free will in such a case? We need to remember that that child is a soul who, before coming into the earth, chose those parents in those circumstances, and thereby exercised its free will and accepted those possibilities. We need to remember also that while we may view such circumstances as great limitations, the soul may have chosen such a set of circumstances in order for it to grow or to help others. But often our judgments are erroneous and misleading. As St. Paul puts it: " . . . we see through a glass, darkly." (I Corinthians 13:12, KJV)

Your will is greater than any other influence in your life, greater than the patterns of astrology or numerology or colors—all of which are tendencies only. By your will, you can proceed in accord with such patterns or counteract them as you choose. The final result depends not upon them but upon what you will to be.[9]

By use of will, you can change your life as you choose—from the lowest to the highest or anything in between. The readings explain:

> What, then, is *will*? That which makes for the dividing line between the finite and the infinite, the divine and the wholly human, the carnal and the spiritual. For the *will* may be made one *with Him*, or for self alone. (262-81)

AGAIN: WHAT AM I?

Now that we understand the significance of the four great gifts, we can more completely answer the question "What am I?" We are souls, spiritual beings, blessed with four great aspects:

1. We have a portion of Spirit within us that includes all the characteristics of our Creator. Most important, it includes the wisdom with which we can create a perfect design for our lives if we choose to do so.

2. We have minds and consciousness enabling us to be aware of ourselves and others and of our existence.

3. We have eternal life.

4. We have free will to do whatever we choose.

What am I?

I am a spiritual being, a soul.

WHO AM I?

We cannot ignore the fact, nor do we wish to, that during this lifetime we have a body, but we might look at it in this way:

True, I have a body. I am in this body for a period of time. I, like the driver of a vehicle, am using this body, in charge of it for a while, as long as it serves my purposes. It is a wonderful body and serves me well, but I am not this body.

What do we really mean when we ask the question, Who am I? To answer with a recitation of our affiliations or skills or accomplishments is really avoiding the question—we are not names or skills or achievements. Who am I?

Many years ago I took my father, then in his later years, back to his hometown in eastern Canada. He had been orphaned as a child and life in the care of a relative had been difficult, so at sixteen he left and came to the United States and had not had any contact with his family since. When we arrived at his hometown and he began finding old acquaintances, I was intrigued by the conversations. Whenever an individual was mentioned, he was always identified as Harry, son of Arthur; or Bruce, son of Douglas; or Thomas, son of Donald. Heritage was clearly very important in that Scottish community. This is carried through in their names: for example, MacDonald means son of Donald, McArthur means son of Arthur. It seems to me that I am much like the Scottish people when I ask the question, Who am I? I am seeking to know my true heritage—by whom was I created? I am not asking in the sense of who produced my body; I know that. I am asking in the ultimate sense—by whom was I, this soul, created?

Several years ago one of my granddaughters was attending one of those rare schools which teaches the laws we have been discussing. Her mother has studied and practiced them for many years. I was curious as to whether they were meaningful to a child of seven years, so I asked her a number of questions. One I particularly remember asking was, "Who are you?" She replied with complete sincerity, "I am a child of God." You may be sure that that delighted me greatly, and I enthusiastically agreed with her that she was indeed a child of God. So are we all children of God, of Spirit. The readings make this statement:

> The startling thing to every soul is to awaken to the realization that it is indeed a child of God! (254-95)

There is one additional point for us to realize as children of God. Unlike the situation with our earthly parents, we are not separate from our Father-Mother-God. That Presence is within us. The vital realization is that **we are never left to go it alone!**

As I write this, I wonder if I myself have really awakened to my being a child of Spirit: I know it as an intellectual concept. I think of my father and mother, wonderful parents who tried to live in the highest way they knew, but they did not have all the background and knowledge with which I have been blessed. Yet they produced only my body. My soul came from another source long before that body was created; the real me, my soul body, was created aeons ago, when yours was created—when we all were created together—in the beginning. That was our divine birth, our true beginning, as souls, sons, and daughters of the Creator. Who am I? Who are you?

> **[I am] a child of God. (254-95)**
> **You are a child of God.**

HOW AND WHY DID I COME HERE?

The readings explain that after our creation, using our free will, we began to experiment with our own powers. As part of that experimentation, we came to this earth and became enamored with the material things of earth, becoming even a part of them. Since the vibrations of the physical level are different from those of the spiritual, as we took on bodies and became more involved with material things, we thereby changed our vibrations so that we no longer were attuned to the Spirit within us. In effect, we separated ourselves from the awareness of that Presence within us. We continue to return to the earth to search for that divine nature we lost touch with so long ago.[10]

WHAT IS MY PURPOSE ON EARTH?

You and I are here on the earth for the same reason. In fact, we share a common purpose with all humankind. True, we each have individual purposes to accomplish in this life, but first we need to learn our very basic purpose, the real reason that we all have chosen to come to the earth.

According to an old Hindu legend there was a time when all men were gods, but they so abused their divinity that Brahma, the chief god, decided to take it away from men and hide it where they would never again find it. Where to hide it became the big question.

When the lesser gods were called in council to consider this question, they said, "We will bury man's divinity deep in the earth." But Brahma said, "No, that will not do, for man will dig deep down into the earth and find it."

Then they said, "Well, we will sink his divinity into the deepest ocean." But again Brahma replied, "No, not there, for man will learn to dive into the deepest waters, will search out the ocean bed, and will find it."

Then the lesser gods said, "We will take it to the top of the highest mountain and there hide it." But again Brahma replied, "No, for man will eventually climb every high mountain on earth. He will be sure some day to find it and take it up again for himself."

Then the lesser gods gave up and concluded, "We do not know where to hide it, for it seems there is no place on earth or in the sea that man will not eventually reach."

Then Brahma said, "Here is what we will do with man's divinity. We will hide it deep down in man himself, for he will never think to look for it there." Ever since then, the legend concludes, man has been going up and down the earth, climbing, digging, diving, exploring, searching for something that is already in himself.

Two thousand years ago a man named Jesus found it and shared its secret; but in the movement that sprang up in His name, the divinity in man has been the best kept secret of the ages.[11]

Most of us have indeed lost touch with our divine nature or are only vaguely aware of our relationship with our Creator. Finding that divinity within is our soul's purpose.

Many individuals asked Edgar Cayce: What is the purpose of my life? From his trance condition, he answered in many different ways, each answer tailored to fit the consciousness of the inquiring

person. The following is a brief summary of some of these statements regarding one's basic purpose:[12]

1. **To know myself to be myself and part of the whole; not
   the whole but one with the whole.**
2. **To become one with Him.**
3. **To become one with the First Cause.**
4. **To become more and more aware of the Divine within.**
5. **To become like Him.**
6. **To become a companion with the Creator.**
7. **To so live that it will be to the glory of God and to the
   honor of self.**

There is one reading in which Cayce answers the question of our
basic purpose for all of us in a way that really rattles the rafters!

(Q) For what purpose did I incarnate this time?
**(A) . . . that you may be a light in *His* name . . . for we all
. . . are gods in the making; not *the* God, but gods in the
making! For He would have you be one with Him.**
                              (877-21) AR [Author's emphasis]

Isn't that incredible!? We are gods and goddesses in the making!
To become a god or goddess—what a purpose! That should not be
news to us, but it may well be, for it is another of those best-kept
secrets of the ages. Two thousand years ago Jesus pointed out to
His Jewish friends that, according to their own law (Old Testament),
God had said, "Ye are gods!" They didn't like that. In fact they tried
to capture Jesus and stone Him, since they felt that Jesus, a man,
was trying to make Himself a god. (John 10:33-34) So be careful to
whom you state that your purpose is to become a goddess or a god.
Check first for rocks!

HOW CAN WE BE GODS IN THE MAKING?

I must confess that when I first encountered Cayce's statement,
I was very troubled by it. We have been programmed to feel that it is
both heretical and highly egotistical to feel or imply that we are
godlike. The truth is we can be godlike without being egotistical. So
let's look at this carefully.

What does it mean that we are gods and goddesses in the making? This reading, presented earlier in this chapter, is the key:

The startling thing to every soul is to awaken to the realization that it is indeed a child of God! (254-95)

Yes, you are a child of God and, **as any human child is a man or woman in the making, so you, as a child of God, are a god or goddess in the making.** Your purpose as a soul, your reason for being here, is to become, not the God, but a goddess or a god. Cayce's source emphasizes this and explains why:

For you are indeed a god in the making because He would have you as one with Him . . . (1440-1)AR

How wonderful! Or perhaps you may think: how impossible! But not so. For it is not the purpose to become gods in flowing robes with disciples and a cross, but goddess Susan, god Bob, goddess Janet, god Charles—god or goddess YOU— as you are, where you are, doing what you do as a parent, a teacher, a dentist, an executive, a gardener, or a secretary; **in whatever you are doing to be godlike to the world!**

You can do that because it is inherent within you as this reading, quoted earlier, affirms:

One finds self a body, a mind, a soul; each with its own attributes and its activity in the earth. An entity, then, is a pattern of that which is also a spiritual fact; Father, Son, Holy Spirit. These are one, just as an individual entity is one. *An entity, then, is the pattern of divinity in materiality, or in the earth.* (3357-2) [Author's emphasis]

What does it cost to accept this basic purpose of being a goddess or a god and to begin living it? You give up nothing except pain and sorrow, struggle and fear. You move your limits from not knowing, not being aware, to the potential for knowing and complete awareness—to peace and joy, abundance and fulfilling relationships and happiness.

To become the goddess or god you are meant to be is the ultimate in transformation. It is the high road of life. There is absolutely no reason that you cannot do this—if you choose to—for the Universal Laws show us how it can be done.

Why do we have this incredible purpose? Since we were created by Spirit, that great fundamental law of the universe "like begets like" means that we are indeed like Spirit. Since another basic law is "like attracts like," we are continually attracted to and seeking to find the Spirit. In and by everything we do, we are seeking that love, that light, that companionship we once knew in the beginning. This search is at the heart of all we do, whether we are nursing a baby, playing golf, or robbing a bank, each is just our unique way of searching for that Spirit at that moment. That is what we are always about—whether or not we recognize it. We are seeking Spirit.

The basic reason for our creation was Spirit's desire for companionship and expression. It's, therefore, in accord with the spiritual nature within us to desire companionship and expression; "like begets like." The ultimate fulfillment of that desire would be to return to that original oneness with the Creator which we lost so many aeons ago. On some level we realize that desire is the basis for our soul-purpose on the earth—to return to that state of oneness with our Creator. One of the readings defines soul as:

That which the Maker gave to every entity or individual in the beginning, and which is seeking the home or place of the Maker. (3744-2)[13]

That reminds us that we could also state our basic purpose as: to be one with Spirit or to be one with God. We need to be aware and acknowledge that our basic purpose—"to become a goddess or a god"—can also be stated in many other ways: the search for the Holy Grail, for God realization, for Cosmic Consciousness, for Oneness, for samadhi, or—in the more common terminology of the readings—the search for the Kingdom of God or for the Christ Consciousness. The search may take many forms, but it's the same goal no matter how you name it.

Through use of our free will, we separated ourselves from our Creator by putting other things first in our lives. We now find ourselves earthbound souls encased in physical bodies. Why do we have to go through this if our souls are perfect as created in the beginning? Because we lost the awareness of our own divine nature. It still exists, but we have very poor reception and communication with it—similar to a poorly tuned radio.

Without the infinite wisdom of the Divine within to lead us, we rely solely on intellect for guidance. Since intellect does not have the overall picture, we create difficulties and situations that are not completely fulfilling or satisfying. Our earthly experience is designed to bring us to the realization that we have a higher purpose than merely living life. To find the high road—the path to complete fulfill-ment—we need to re-establish the connection with the Divine wisdom within to guide us. We can begin that process by con-sciously making it our purpose to become the god or goddess we were meant to be.

As we begin to live in accord with this purpose, we attune our vibrations, our consciousness to greater awareness of the Divine within. As we get more in tune, our "reception" and communication with the Divine improves. As we follow its guidance, we find that our lives become more fulfilling, more satisfying, more meaningful, more worthwhile. Thus, we begin to fulfill our basic purpose which is: to become the goddesses and gods we were meant to be.

In summary, the reasons for such a soul's purpose are:

1. We are attracted to our Creator by the operation of the Uni-versal Laws.
2. As souls, we desire the companionship of our Creator.
3. We lost our understanding and awareness of the divinity within. Yet, it is our only reliable guide through life. As we begin to live our higher basic purpose (to become a god or goddess), we achieve greater attunement with that Divine within, and its guidance will enable us to live in the highest way and to fulfill our overall purpose in the earth.

THE UNIVERSAL LAWS: KEYS TO FULFILLING YOUR PURPOSE

The basic purpose of the Universal Laws, I believe, is to re-estab-lish our awareness of the Spirit within. We learn our lessons in the earth plane through what happens to us as a result of what we think, say, do, or have done to our fellow humans or to ourselves. These lessons are brought back to us through the operation of the Universal Laws and gradually bring us to the realization that there must be a better way. So we begin our search, which leads eventu-ally to the awareness of the Spirit within.

As you study the Universal Laws, you are taking a major step in the direction of understanding and fulfilling your basic purpose and living a life of joy and total well-being while you are learning. This is true because "God is Law" and, as you learn these laws and live them in accord with your guidance from within, you will be-come more godlike, which is the essence of our purpose and is the transformation we all seek.

USING THE UNIVERSAL LAWS
IN THE HIGHEST WAY

The pattern of divinity within us is not just an abstract idea. It includes characteristics we can manifest every hour, every day. These are vital keys to fulfilling your basic purpose. They are known as fruits of the Spirit or seeds of the Spirit:

Seeds/Fruits of the Spirit
(As Given in the Edgar Cayce Readings)

Love	Truth	Peace
Gentleness	Hope	Obedience
Kindness	Persistence	Humbleness
Self-Control	The Loving Word	Harmony
Brotherly Love	Faith	Understanding
Patience	Goodness	Grace
Fellowship	Joy	Honor
Mercy	Meekness	Contentment
Selflessness	Justice	Consistency in Acts and Speech

These are repeatedly referred to in the readings as ideal aspects of God. The important point is that we have been given these; they are within us. As previously explained, we can develop and express them if we choose. As we use and make these fruits of the Spirit a part of our lives, we begin to fulfill our basic purpose. They become steps to higher consciousness, to transformation, to that perfect life![14]

Chapter 11

Laws of Self

Full understanding of the higher Universal Laws begins with the laws of self. Understanding of all truth is found in self. Understanding your relationship with Spirit is found in self. As you begin to apply the laws of self, you start your progression up the ladder of the higher laws to ultimately becoming the goddess or god you are meant to be—to Oneness—to the Christ Consciousness.

In previous chapters we established a base of understanding the nature of the Universal Laws, experienced some basic laws, and learned of our relationship to God, Law, Love, and Truth. We now have a solid base on which to build and progress with the all-important laws of self. This base and our progression to this point is illustrated in Figure 8.

KNOW THYSELF

Throughout the ages spiritual teachers have advised: Know thyself! Cayce's source often expressed this ancient wisdom by suggesting that it is important to "first find self."[1]

Unfortunately it is easy to turn away from the task of finding self because we do not realize its importance nor fully understand what it means. As you come to know the laws of self, you will understand that finding self is the most important thing you have to do—it is (or should be) top priority.[2]

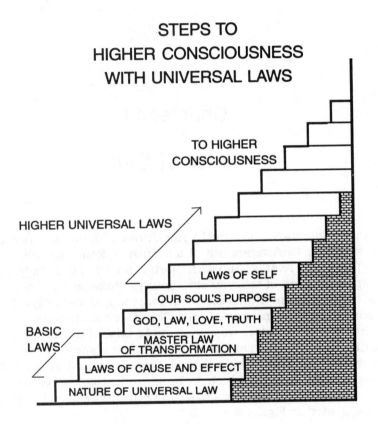

STEPS TO
HIGHER CONSCIOUSNESS
WITH UNIVERSAL LAWS

TO HIGHER
CONSCIOUSNESS

HIGHER UNIVERSAL LAWS

LAWS OF SELF

OUR SOUL'S PURPOSE

GOD, LAW, LOVE, TRUTH

BASIC
LAWS

MASTER LAW
OF TRANSFORMATION

LAWS OF CAUSE AND EFFECT

NATURE OF UNIVERSAL LAW

FIGURE 8

YOU

The first step in finding yourself is to realize you are the most important person in your world. What you see out there and what you think, feel, experience, and know is your own world. In fact, it is *your* universe. No other person sees it the way you do. By use of the Universal Laws, you have created it, developed it, "peopled" it, and by those laws you can change it in accord with your wants and needs. That is why the Universal Laws are the keys to your life and your universe.

The readings have a fascinating concept which expresses your importance:

Are you doing your job or trusting someone else to do it for you? It can't be done! Each soul is just as each atom, as each corpuscle [blood cell]. For, remember, you are as corpuscles in the body of God. Each with a duty, a function to perform if the world would be better for your having lived in it, and this is your purpose in the earth. (3481-2)AR

One of the greatest mistakes you can make in trying to know yourself is to compare yourself with others. We are all beloved children of Spirit. We all have unlimited potential. Where you are—as compared with anyone else—is not important. You and everyone else have been attending the school of law through each lifetime. We all have been learning our lessons. No one, not even you, knows what grade you are in or how you compare with others. The Spirit within does not judge you, but knows rather the infinite potential that exists within you. To know yourself is to know and use these infinite potentials.

PERSONALITY AND INDIVIDUALITY

We have learned this truth of self: Spirit is within us. That spiritual part of us, the living God within, is like an inner light which we have wrapped in veils of illusion, so that we are only dimly aware of it. To know self, we must unwrap those veils in which we have hidden our soul, the God within us.[3]

The Cayce readings have a practical approach to understanding this condition. They use the term *personality* to describe how others see us. Personality is the act put on by our ego self to show what we want others to see; we think we need to hide our doubts, fears, guilt, and other negatives. Unfortunately personality is part of the veil of illusion which masks our soul qualities.

The term *individuality*, different from personality, is defined as "that which shines out from within, separating one from another." (345-2) Your individuality is your real self—the God part, your soul, "the lamp within"—as it has developed over the aeons of time into the spiritual being you now are. It is that being you seek when you search for self. You do not have to create it, it is there; you only need to find it, to "first find self," and allow it to manifest. This is a process of releasing the guilt, the fear, the negative and misleading concepts of self and allowing your God-self lamp to shine in the world. The laws of self are key to unwrapping those veils of illusion and finding your true individuality.

LAW OF INDIVIDUALITY

There are several laws of self. They are expressed in terms of our relationship to others. They deal directly with the self-concept we hold and its relation to others, for that is where we each must start if we are to understand self.[4]

Service to others is one of the basic requirements for spiritual growth. Effective service is the expression of our individuality, our God-self to others; demonstrating our love, kindness, peace, joy, compassion, and other fruits of the Spirit. The law of individuality gives us a measure of how effective our service to others will be. It is:

AS YOU HONOR, RESPECT, AND LOVE YOUR OWN UNIQUE INDIVIDUALITY, SO YOU HONOR, RESPECT, AND LOVE THE INDIVIDUALITY OF OTHERS.[5]

This is, also, a basic law of truly successful relationships. Only to the degree you know and love yourself (your individuality) can you truly know and love others.

LAW OF EQUALITY

This law of self is based on the understanding that all of us come from the same source and were created equal, each being a child of God and each having God within us. The law is:

YOUR TRUE NEEDS, WANTS, DESIRES, HOPES, DREAMS, WISHES, AND THEIR FULFILLMENT ARE AS IMPORTANT AS THOSE OF ANY OTHER SOUL IN EXISTENCE.

This law emphasizes that you should consider yourself not higher, not lower, but equal to others and treat yourself (your God within) in that way. One Cayce reading explains why this is so:

. . . the care of each soul, each individual, is just as necessary—[as that of any other] because each is just as precious as the other in the sight of the Creative Force or God. (4047-2)

To apply this law of equality in the highest way—in accord with your basic purpose—you need to know what makes you joyful, what makes you comfortable deep within, what feels right to you, and what you love to do. These are your true needs, wants, and desires that stem from your deep-feeling level, the intuitive level of the Spirit within. They are the needs, wants, and goals of the real you. In determining these and honoring them, you are recognizing your divine essence. By that act alone, you are beginning to fulfill this law.

The importance of the equality among us, which is the message of this law, is expressed by the readings in another statement:

. . . that which would be ideal for self must also be that which would be ideal for others. (2185-1)

Therefore, on the same basis of equality, in considering what we should do for others, it is, of course, true that that which is ideal for others must also be ideal for self.

LAW OF PRIORITY

This reading gives the basic consideration on which this law of self is established:

In the material conditions in life, consider first that as is necessary that the mental and the spiritual may have a place of manifesting; for the body physical is truly the temple of the soul, the dwelling place of the mind, of the mental body, through this material plane, and needs same for physical manifestation. Care *first* and *foremost* for these . . . (5615-1)

Note the reading does not say take care of your mind and body when something goes wrong. It says to do it first and foremost!

If you wish to help others, this law requires that your first priority be to care for self spiritually, mentally, and physically. The law is:

YOU MUST FIRST "SAVE" SELF IF YOU WOULD "SAVE" ANOTHER

"Save" = Serve = Help = Care For = Love = Know

Our purpose on earth is in essence to "save self." If you neglect self for "saving" another, you are defeating your purpose.

Cayce and modern-day psychics point out that violation of this law is at the heart of many of the world's problems. We hypocritically try to straighten out others and the rest of the world without first "saving" self. The psychics indicate that by such actions we create the earthquakes, tornadoes, and other physical aberrations that occur.

THE SIGNIFICANCE OF THESE LAWS OF SELF

The key to these three laws is recognition, acceptance, and honoring of the divinity within self. Regardless of who or what you are, what you have done or not done, they make it clear that:
1. There is as much of Spirit in you as in anyone else.
2. Your needs and wants are as important as those of anyone else—because of that divinity within you.
3. You should give care of yourself first priority as compared with anyone or anything else you are involved with—because of that divinity within.

APPLYING THE LAWS OF SELF

In applying the preceding laws of self, you give of yourself in any activity only to that point at which you do not feel depleted—physically, mentally, or emotionally. You do not move in opposition to what feels right for you, even if this conflicts with another. Even when you have the best of intentions, when you go beyond the point that depletion of self begins, you are no longer in accord with these laws of self and no longer honoring the Presence within. You have placed another person or another situation or condition higher than that Presence. It is, therefore, not only right, but important, to love and nurture yourself as much as you love and nurture anyone else.

Living these simple laws of self can bring a new view of life. It can be a challenge to you. If you have viewed the needs, wants, and goals of another as more important than your own, you have been saying that the Spirit within you is less important than that in some other soul. Since it is the same Spirit in all of us, that statement is not fair to you, to the Spirit within you, or to the other person.[6]

If, on the other hand, you have considered your needs, wants, and goals more important than those of another, you have said that the Spirit within you is greater, more important, or better than that in the other. That cannot be if it is the same Spirit and we are all created equal.

The following Cayce readings excerpt gives us some insights as to the laws of self:

> While one must think highly of self do not be overdemocratic; neither too self-sufficient. There is the medium ground on which all may meet. For God is not a respecter of persons as individuals sometimes are. (3474-1)

" . . . do not be overdemocratic" means: don't feel you must have approval of the majority. Don't be "too self-sufficient" means be aware that others, too, have much to offer you. The phrase, "God is not a respecter of persons" means that God cares no more and has no more respect for the president than for the janitor, no more for the millionaire than the person who is broke or in debt, no more for the person with a brilliant mind than for the slow learner, no more for you than for any other. God is love and cares for each one of us, just as we are, completely, totally, and unconditionally. It is that value system of equality of all on which the laws of self are based.

WE ALL ARE INDEPENDENT UNITS OF GOD

We were all created as independent units of God. As such, we are independent of all others in the sense that our primary relationship is with the Spirit within. In that sense, we have no responsibility to others. Our only responsibility is to that Presence within. As we live attuned to that, we will be directed or guided by it into knowing what is required by another.

We have many concepts of our responsibilities to others that are often based on beliefs derived from mass-mind consciousness or misperceptions of our relationship to Spirit. These are seldom based on laws. Universal Law ascribes no responsibility to us for others. Our only responsibility is to the Spirit within.

Here is a reading from Cayce that leaves no question as to where our responsibility lies:

Fulfill your purpose in your relationship to your Maker, not to any individual, not to any group, not to any organization, not to any activity outside of self other than to your Creator! (1391-1)AR

You are, of course, free to undertake any responsibilities with and for others. You can do this in many forms—marriage or other relationships, parenting, community service, in a professional capacity, or as a friend. Such an effort may be beneficial to others as well as to you, providing you recognize the laws of self and don't allow your concern for responsibilities that involve others to have greater weight than your concern for your own temple. The ideal in working with others was expressed by Cayce in this way:

. . . all are to work in unison for the good of all. (3976-23)

I have, in essence, said that you and I are responsible for our own well-being and not that of anyone else. You came into the earth alone and will leave the same way. You are here by the grace of God and by your choice. You have others with whom you experience life, but within that existence you are not responsible for them. You are alone except for that Presence within, which is closer than anyone else can ever be, and to that alone are you responsible.

YOU ARE YOUR BROTHER'S OR SISTER'S KEEPER

In seeming contradiction to the laws of self, the Cayce readings often remind us that we are our brother's keeper. That certainly is a responsibility, although it has often been misunderstood and misinterpreted. The actual responsibility is not to your neighbor; it is to yourself—the God-self within. If I am my brother's or sister's keeper, what must I keep? I must keep my integrity with my Creator. As I do, I fulfill the law in the highest way. By fulfilling the law, I manifest my integrity. I thereby become an example to my neighbor and that is the highest service I can perform for him or her. That is the finest way to be my neighbor's keeper. Whenever we fulfill any of the Universal Laws in the highest way we can—we are maintaining our integrity, we are being an example, we are being the love, the light, the goddess or god we are meant to be.

So you are your brother's or sister's keeper, but you are not responsible for or to him or her. You are responsible only for being all that you can be—using the gifts and talents you have been given to enable you to fulfill your life's purpose. As you do that in the highest way you can, you are helping your neighbor by your example.

You are not your brother's or sister's keeper in the sense that you are required to house, clothe, feed, reform him or her or to take over his or her responsibilities. When you do that, you are taking from that individual, demeaning his or her integrity, and treating that person as a lesser being than yourself. It is arrogant to believe that you can do something for another that the person is not capable of doing for himself or herself. That is saying that the Spirit within that individual is less complete, less perfect, and less capable than the Spirit within you.

Do we do nothing about those who are in need, suffering, ill, starving, or who seem relatively powerless over their lives? The readings had much to say about such service.

GIVING OF SELF IN SERVICE TO OTHERS

The Cayce readings sometimes seem overwhelming in their insistence on serving others. Quoting Jesus, they tell us: " . . . he that is the greatest among you is the servant of all!" (1264-1) They also proclaim that the greatest service to God is service to others and indicate that in service alone may any soul find advancement or development. Service is essential to our growth. It is a Universal Law that as we aid others, more help comes to us, providing that our purpose is right; "like begets like." We need to find the answer to the question of how we can be of help to others without sacrificing self, without "taking over" or "playing God" or imposing on them our ideas of what they ought to do or be.[7]

I have learned that when I can *best* be of help to others is when they ASK for help. Then I am free to respond to their request, that and nothing more, and only if my guidance permits it! It is so easy to go off on a do-good ego trip.

There are times when I may have an urge to be of help or have a feeling or an idea how I can aid another. Only when I check with my inner guidance and receive approval and instructions for doing it, can I successfully help another. Thus, I am recognizing that my only hope of success in my endeavor is to turn within for guidance so that I will fulfill the laws of self in the highest way. If I rely on my emotions or the mental level alone, I frequently end up in difficulty and cause more problems than I solve. To distinguish between being helpful and serving your own ego, ask yourself these questions about the help you propose to give; first, with regard for the divinity in the other person:

1. Would my help give the individual greater independence?
2. Would my help aid the individual to know his/her own capability, talents, or power?
3. Would my action or advice in any way promote dependency or be only a temporary means of easing that individual's difficulties?

Second, with regard to the divinity within you, ask:

4. Will my help serve truth or apply a Universal Law in the highest way I can?
5. How will this change affect my care of my own body temple? Will it be a joyous change?

If the answers to those questions feel right to you, then ask inner guidance as to whether or not you should do this.

As you seek to be of service, be aware of your spiritual ideal:

Rather set an ideal in the *spiritual* sense, and know that he that would be greatest among men will be the servant of all. The servant *cannot* be selfish, either in nature, in person, in fact, but prefers the other in preference to self. (912-1)

This sounds paradoxical in light of the preceding laws of self. How can we prefer others in preference to self and yet give our true wants, needs, and goals equal weight with theirs? Let's consider an example:

Assume that you have a business or profession. You know the business, know what you can do, and how you can conduct it to be of greatest service to others. As you do so, you are indeed a servant, serving all in the highest way. You are then conducting your business for others in preference to self. As long as that is the ideal and purpose that you apply in your business, your devotion to it is not selfishness but "become[s] rather *blessedness* in the eyes of those the body mentally, physically, would serve." (912-1)

You can conduct your business for others and, at the same time, fulfill your true wants, needs, and goals. They aren't in opposition if they are not selfish in nature. The law asks only that you give equal weight to both—to others and to self. You conduct your business for others in preference to conducting it for self, but you do not ignore self nor take advantage of self for others. An example of that would be in making your business that which you love to do.

The same principle can apply in your work, your home, and your other activities. As you live in accord with the laws of self and value others as you value self, you become selfless. In that state, your true needs, wants, and goals are just as important as those of others. Neglect of self or of your true needs, wants, and goals will eventually cause self-deterioration. That, in turn, will result in neglect of others. So a requirement for being of service to others is that you must honor, respect, and take care of yourself and consider yourself and your needs on an equal basis with others'.[8]

MANAGING YOUR LIFE

The final proof of how well you apply the laws of self is reflected in how you manage your life. The following questions about your time and decisions will highlight where you place yourself in relation to others. Consider a typical day in your life and indicate the number of times in that day that you do the following:

1. How often during the day do I allow periods of time primarily for myself, other than that time specifically relegated to the physical? _____

2. How often during the day do I allow time for mental and emotional serenity? _____

3. How often during the day do I allow periods of time for the Spirit? _____

4. In summary of the above, how often during the day do I allow time just for myself without intrusion from others?
_____

5. How often are my decisions based upon the wants, desires, or needs of others? _____

6. How often in this process (question #5) do my needs, wants, and goals become less important than those of others?
_____

7. How often do I allow for others that which seems not the better for myself? _____

Allowing for self is not selfish. None of these laws is to imply that you should not help others. Instead, when you do help, it is because it is in accord with your ideal and purpose and the laws of self. If it is in such accord, you do not violate your own body temple and your responsibility to the Presence within you.

BECOMING SELFLESS

The key to the higher ground is to have a spiritual ideal and live in accord with it. The readings explain this as becoming selfless:

Then, self must become selfless, and not in any form or manner desire those things that would be advantageous over others in that others would have to suffer that self might have the advantage—for that is selfishness, and not selflessness.

And selflessness is that to which each entity, each soul, must attain through the varied experiences in the material plane. (2185-1)

Selfishness, a characteristic of the personality, can manifest as neglect of others. To be selfless is of the individuality. We need to work to have less and less of the ego, the personality, and to have more and more of our God-self, our individuality. This requires a shift to trust the spiritual power within and the development of guidance from within. As you make that shift, you find increasing peace, harmony, happiness, and joy in anything you are guided to do, all without sacrificing self.[9]

The matter of becoming selfless is frequently misunderstood. Selflessness does not mean you are not important. You should not pity, condemn, or belittle yourself—these are actually forms of selfishness and are not selfless.[10]

We can transform our consciousness and raise it to a level of being selfless by recognizing and living in accord with the laws of self and by basing our thoughts, words, and deeds on our spiritually derived purposes, ideals, and guidance.

We can summarize the above as an instruction for each of us to change our attitude and purpose from one of service to others because we think we should serve, to service to others as

an extension of the Spirit of love within us. Then we are not doing it for self or for others, but recognizing our true source and responsibility.

LAW FOR MANIFESTATION
OF YOUR HIGHER SELF

This law is the basis for the readings that urge us to put "first things first":[11]

AS YOU PUT THE GOD WITHIN FIRST IN YOUR LIFE, SO YOU MANIFEST THE GOD YOU ARE.

These are the steps to put God first:

1. Accept that you have that God Presence within.
2. Acknowledge that you are a spiritual being by living that concept. If you don't acknowledge the Presence within, you are dishonoring it. For example, when you mistreat your body in any way—such as allowing yourself to get too tired—you are not caring for the body temple, you are in your own consciousness disregarding the Presence within. You are not putting God first.
3. We put God first by attunement through:
   a) prayer, meditation, faith—the basics;
   b) seeking, asking, knocking—the laws of guidance; and
   c) holding an awareness of the God Presence.
4. We remember to apply and to live as we are guided; that is, to do the will of Spirit within. "Not my will but Thine." In this way we respect, honor, and glorify the God-self within us. This Presence is not telling us we are bad and wrong or judging or condemning us. It just loves us. So as we accept this understanding, we then are able to start loving ourselves, too.
5. We do our best to put God first continually, hour by hour, moment by moment, in our daily lives.[12]

The vital point in applying this law is to put God first always. This is a real challenge because our world doesn't help. It produces dozens of exciting diversions for us every hour. We cannot go off to a cave or mountain; we have to accept these diversions as a part of our world, and go right on putting God first and dealing with them— whatever they are—from that higher point of view.

I use a "gimmick" to help me in remembering to put God first. I have a watch with a timer that I set to go off every fifteen minutes—

to remind myself to put God first in whatever I am doing. It really helps. Otherwise, I can easily forget and go for hours or days without giving God a thought.

As we begin to put God first, we begin to think as God, to love as God, and to live as the goddess or god we are. We come to see that God is with us at all times as our conscience, so we gain confidence in the Presence and have its constant guidance.

LAW OF MASTERY OF SELF

This law of self is a law of restoration through which we can restore the power we have given away to others or to our lower nature, fears, doubts, and confusion. It's in the nature of a promise; but since it is a law, it is a guarantee that:

AS YOU BECOME MASTER OF YOUR LOWER SELF, SO ALL THINGS, CONDITIONS, AND ELEMENTS BECOME SUBJECT UNTO YOU.[13]

Begin to master your lower self. Recognize its existence in the form of your fears, anxiety, guilt, shame, selfishness, and other negative aspects of your ego and personality. Whenever you become aware of such thoughts, feelings, or emotions, accept each lovingly as your creation. Then release it by explaining to yourself that you do not need it any more because you know a higher thought. For example, if a friend should make a remark to which you react negatively, release your negative feeling by thanking the feeling lovingly and explaining that you now understand it is showing you a point at which you need to grow. Be grateful for that.

As you become selfless, you master self. As you attune yourself to the voice within and follow its leading, you master self. As you recognize and live in accord with the laws of self and other Universal Laws, you master self. As you come to know self, you master self. As you put God first, you master self. As you become master of self, you become the goddess or god you are meant to be, with all things, conditions, and elements subject unto you. There are no limits.

JESUS THE EXAMPLE

Jesus took time despite the demands of crowds and the needs of many to rest and pray and meditate—to care for His body temple in the physical, mental, emotional, and spiritual aspects. In this way He was recognizing and honoring the Presence within. He was an excellent example for us in terms of the application of the laws of self.

As the readings explain, " . . . self, death, hell and the grave even, become subservient unto Him *through* the conquering of self in that made flesh . . . " (364-7) So He is our example. Remember that He said we could do it, too.

HIGHLIGHTS OF THIS CHAPTER

1. Law of Service:

AS YOU HONOR, RESPECT, AND LOVE YOUR OWN UNIQUE INDIVIDUALITY, SO YOU HONOR, RESPECT, AND LOVE THE INDIVIDUALITY OF OTHERS.

2. Law of Equality:

YOUR TRUE NEEDS, WANTS, DESIRES, HOPES, DREAMS, WISHES, AND THEIR FULFILLMENT ARE AS IMPORTANT AS THOSE OF ANY OTHER SOUL IN EXISTENCE.

3. Law of Priority:

YOU MUST FIRST "SAVE" SELF IF YOU WOULD "SAVE" ANOTHER.

"Save" = Serve = Help = Care For = Love = Know

4. Law for Manifestation of Your Higher Self:

AS YOU PUT THE GOD WITHIN FIRST IN YOUR LIFE, SO YOU MANIFEST THE GOD YOU ARE.

5. Law of Mastery of Self:

AS YOU BECOME MASTER OF YOUR LOWER SELF, SO ALL THINGS, CONDITIONS, AND ELEMENTS BECOME SUBJECT UNTO YOU.

Chapter 12

Consciously Creating Results with the Master Law of Manifestation

One of the most important laws of transformation is the one involving the relationship among the basic elements of our being—spirit, mind, and body. With this law we often create the physical results we see in our lives. It is the Master Law of Manifestation:

**SPIRIT IS THE LIFE,
MIND IS THE BUILDER,
PHYSICAL IS THE RESULT.**[1]

SPIRIT IS THE LIFE

As already discussed, our soul nature or Spirit is the beginning of all things in our world. For Spirit is both the beginning and the end of all self-development. You and I, as souls, were Spirit in the beginning, are Spirit plus a body now, and at the end will still be Spirit.[2]

Spirit is the basis for all the higher Universal Laws of transformation and attunement. A spiritual consciousness operates at a different frequency or vibration than a mental consciousness. The purpose of learning and applying these Higher Laws is to help us to become aware again of our inherent spiritual consciousness.

Spirit is the life force which permeates every cell of our body and mind. The proof of this lies in the simplest of actions. Move your fingers, move your toes, move your head, or think about something. What is the force involved, required, present, that makes the parts of the body move or enables you to think? It is the life force, the Spirit within you. If you had just died, there would be no movement or thought. All your muscles and blood and brain cells would be there, but the life force produced by Spirit is gone. Spirit is the very life force within you.

Spirit, the life force within, is also the creative force of your life. How you use this creative life force determines what you will be and what your experiences will be.

. . . the activity is first in spirit, then in mind, and *then* it may become a *material* manifestation. One is the projection as it were of the other into materialization, as we see about us in the earth. (1597-1)

In essence that reading defines a step-by-step process in which each step is a projection of the preceding one, and the ultimate result is the manifestation in the physical. It can be diagrammed as follows:[3]

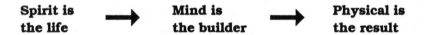

Spirit is ➝ **Mind is** ➝ **Physical is**
the life   **the builder**   **the result**

Everything is first derived from the Spirit, the creative life force within us. The readings express this by stating that Spirit is the First Cause. This is a simple concept but a profound truth, which explains the key to the application of this law in our lives.

We cannot emphasize enough that this law of manifestation is the statement of the natural flow of the life force, of the energy with which we live and move and have our being. It states the fundamental process of life. Let me explain:

The dream symbol for pure Spirit is often that of clear water or a stream. I have lived in the mountains for many years and I have always loved the beauty of the clear mountain streams. I have always enjoyed the sparkle and the singing sounds of the water as it tumbles purposefully on its way from above, bringing life to all below. It has always seemed appropriate to think of the Spirit within that gives me life as a pure mountain stream flowing from above without limit, ever energizing, ever renewing, and ever inspiring in accord with my every need. If you have not experienced the joy of mountain streams, perhaps the concept of a sparkling white fountain with its pure water of Spirit welling up within you would also be meaningful.

The kind of Spirit to which this law of manifestation refers is available to each of us. It is pure, it is perfect, it is unchangeable, it is a living Spirit, and it is the highest form of spirit we can attain. It is not out there somewhere; it is within you right now. No one has more and others less—we each have all we need.

Just as we must drink the water of a mountain stream to quench our thirst, we need to open ourselves if we are to use the life-giving energy of Spirit. We can make use of the Spirit by attuning our mind to it. When we do that, it will build and manifest the perfect pattern in the physical.

INFINITE POWER OF SPIRIT

A young man asked Cayce how he might develop self-mastery. The answer given to him applies to all of us:

> Study that from the spiritual angle, if there would be that power, that might to succeed. For, as has been given, all first finds concept in the spiritual. The mental is the builder. This is true in planning the life, the relationships, and every phase of man's existence or experience. (2322-2)

At another time, speaking of the spiritual within us, Cayce noted "the spiritual from which emanates the essence of all power, might and strength!" and urged us to "Rely upon that more." (2390-1) Another individual was cautioned to "forget not the *sources* of *all* power as may be manifested in the earth." (1743-2)

It is the nature of power to be manifested in many ways. How you may utilize it depends on your unique characteristics. This is explained in a passage from another psychic source of high consciousness channeled by Grady Claire Porter, co-author of one of my favorite books, *Conversations with JC:*

> Recognizing that you are *consciously,* and that is the key word, that you are consciously in harmony with the Universal Laws, gives you all the power of those laws. Power means infinite ability to express ability, capability, flexibility, sensibility, lovability, and on and on.[4]

Each one of us has full access to that power. It is an infinite power without limit available for you and for all. Spirit is the infinite power of the universe. **Spirit is the life.**

UNLIMITED ABUNDANCE OF SPIRIT

If we are to use this power, we need to recognize it as the source of all power, as our life force, our source of energy. Just as we approach a mountain stream knowing it is the source of the unlimited, cooling, thirst-quenching water we seek, we approach the Spirit within knowing that it is the source of life, of all power, all might, all strength of all we seek, that it holds nothing from us, that it gives to us all that we ever need or ever want.

That is the key. Spirit within is the infinite source of all. If you don't use that key, you fall into the trap of thinking from the mental or physical point of view that the supply is limited, that I don't have enough, that someone else has more than I have, or that I am not worthy or qualified or don't know how to get it. Rubbish! If that is the spirit in which you view it, that is the spirit in which you are applying the law of manifestation, and that is exactly what will result in the physical for you, by law! It does not have to be that way; by the same law, you can change it. If you attune your mind to a higher level, to a spirit of abundance, to the Spirit within that is life, not lack, the conditions you find in your life will change because you are then applying the law in a higher way.

The following readings excerpt affirms the abundance available to us and explains that the source of our supply is not in the outer world. It also gives us the keys by which we can tap that abundance:

(Q) Have I a right to demand abundance, or should I be content with my small income?

(A) Be *content* with what you have, but never be *satisfied* with what you have. Abundance is the lot of him who is in accord with those truths of the Creative Energy . . .(2842-2)AR

The "truths of the Creative Energy" are the Universal Laws applied in accord with the Spirit within you. That will create abundance in your life.

Another excerpt explains further:

For, as He has given, be not anxious how you shall be clothed nor how you shall be fed. For, the Father knows that you have need of these things. When you apply the spiritual life in your relationships to others, there will be the supply. For, does He not clothe all nature? Are not the silver and gold His? Then act in that manner! (3538-1)AR

You can apply the spiritual life in your relationships to others by applying the law "spirit is the life, mind is the builder, physical is the result." You do this by keeping your mind attuned to the Spirit within on all things regarding your relationships with others. You "act in that manner" by putting your trust in the Spirit within.

Abundance is the natural state of the universe. There are no limits. The apparent limits are caused only by our own limited mental concepts and activities. I remember articles published in respected technical journals more than forty years ago predicting a severe oil shortage because the world's known reserves at that time equalled a ten years' supply. The authors had a spirit of lack. Fortunately, others in the industry had a spirit of abundance as proven by extensive discoveries made since then and that continue to this day.

Abundance will manifest in your life if you choose to have it and apply the laws accordingly. The infinite Spirit energy available is not limited to any one form. You can manifest its abundance in a multitude of ways—as peace, love, joy, as a brilliant mind, as a loving healing touch, as beautiful art and music, as material things, home, job, money, or cars. There is no limit. Spirit is the infinite abundance of the universe. Spirit is the life.

It is through the law "spirit is the life, mind is the builder, physical is the result" that we are able to manifest abundance in our lives.

In summary, "spirit is the life" because:
1. It is the beginning of all things.
2. It is the first element, the first step in manifestation of anything in the universe.
3. All is first conceived in Spirit. It is conceived perfectly. The pattern or concept given is perfect. Spirit is our source of wisdom.
4. It is infinite in supply for each one of us.
5. It is the essence of all power, might, and strength.
6. It is available to us all equally.
7. It is the life force (energy) within us.

What will you do with this Spirit, this unlimited life force within you? The answer lies in how you use the next step in this law, "mind is the builder."

MIND IS THE BUILDER

Our minds are the connecting and communicating link between us and Spirit, so they are a natural part of the flow of Spirit into and through our lives. Our minds are the builders between things spiritual from which all emanates and that which is material. The purpose of our minds is to bring manifestations into our experience. The mental is always the builder; this is true whether we are planning our lives, establishing relationships, or for any and all phases of our existence and our experiences. In other words, our minds are the controlling and building force in all that we create in our physical beings and in our worlds. They give us the abilities to grasp and rebuild aspects of the physical—whether of the body or of conditions around us or of our experiences. We can also use our minds to change aspects of the mental and spiritual in our lives; so our minds are truly the architect, the planner, and the caretaker as well as the builder of our lives.[5]

Where does spirit come into this? Cayce was once asked how spirit compared with mind; here was his answer:

Spirit is the First Cause. Mind is an effect, or an active force that partakes of spiritual as well as material import. Mind is an essence or a flow between Spirit and that which is made manifest materially. (262-123)

Since everything is conceived in Spirit, it is conceived in perfection. The concept is presented to your mind as a perfect pattern with all the energy of spirit that your mind, as the builder, needs in order to form, shape, and create the ultimate result. So with a perfect concept and with infinite energy available, your mind creates the perfect result—the perfect job, the perfect relationship, perfect peace and contentment! Since few of us have that, what is it that goes wrong?

As previously noted, all manifestations of life are crystallizations of Spirit. The law of manifestation is the process by which that occurs. There is only one Spirit. Humans, through exercising free will, often choose to misdirect and divert the power of Spirit to selfish purposes, thereby building negative and destructive forms of spirit, such as selfishness, hate, envy, and so on.[6]

Readings given for individuals who had difficulties in their lives repeatedly point out that the solution to their problems lies not in trying to change or manipulate the outer events or conditions, but turning to the Spirit within. They needed to shift from trust in the intellect and outer forces to trust in the inner Spirit. That change needed to be made because Spirit is the beginning and the only source of good for all concerned.[7]

Let's take a parallel creative life situation as an example of what often happens. Consider the building of a house. Energy (spirit) is brought to the building site in such forms as spirit of cement, spirit of bricks, spirit of wood, spirit of hammer, spirit of labor, and spirit of design. Assume that these forms of energy are all perfect. The builder, Mr. Mind, starts to work with them to shape the house. What Mr. Mind does, according to his consciousness, with this perfect material and perfect design to form it, shape it, and build it determines whether it turns out to be a perfect house or a leaky shack. The physical is the result of *both* the spiritual input and the building done by the mind.

If Mr. Mind's consciousness is spiritually developed and attuned to the perfect pattern, the house will be in accord with the perfect energy and pattern given to the builder. It will be perfect. If the builder is attuned to factors other than the highest, such as the spirit of build-it-fast-and-cheap, that will prevail, and there will be a major deviation from the perfect result originally conceived by Spirit.

The point of this example is: The result comes from what your mind is attuned to *while* it builds. What is your consciousness? Is it a "perfect house consciousness" or a "leaky shack consciousness"? Spirit will give you correct concepts, pure energy, and a perfect pattern to start with and to use. But what you, your mind, does with it is up to you—up to how you use that other great gift you were given—your will. Your will is the master of your mind if you choose to make it so.[8]

With your will, you choose the pattern to which you set your mind: the "perfect house" pattern of Spirit or the "leaky shack" pattern of the world. **Mr. Mind, the builder, follows through precisely as YOU have directed, and the physical is the result of the choices YOU have made. Your consciousness manifests! By this law your consciousness manifests whatever you are attuned to.** What are our minds often attuned to? To the spirit of the world, as the chart (Figure 9) shows.

As the diagram illustrates, we allow our minds to dwell on spirit, but it is the spirit of the world outside of us, the mass consciousness, by which we are surrounded. If you do this too often, you can easily develop a "leaky shack" consciousness of hate, envy, fear, doubt, greed, lack, judgment, criticism, and condemnation.

From such negative consciousness, your mind then builds in your physical life illness, poverty, accidents, misery, unfulfilled relationships, and chaos—by this law.

But it doesn't have to be this way. These negatives are not the truth about you. The truth is that you are a child of God and, as such, you are love, peace, joy, light, and beauty, and all the seeds of the Spirit within. Your need is to release the "leaky shack" misconceptions and transform your consciousness. You can do this without more learning, but by simply remembering that you are a child of God. You can release the negatives you have absorbed from the world and let the goddess or god you are shine forth.

You can do that by attuning to the God Spirit within you. (See Figure 10.)

When you attune to the Higher Spirit, as shown, the picture changes and the real you comes forth with a "perfect house" consciousness of wisdom, love, peace, joy, and harmony. Your mind builds in accord with that to give you abundance, health, fulfilling relationships, and other aspects of a more wonderful life. It is all in accord with the Master Law of Manifestation.

Let's examine in more detail the physical results that this law produces in our lives.

THE PHYSICAL IS THE RESULT

This simple phrase—"the physical is the result"—has in reality tremendous scope, for it covers all the material aspects of our lives. The results that manifest can be either crimes or miracles:

> The spiritual the creator, the mental the builder, the material—that of the result of a life, a thought, a deed; for thoughts are deeds and may be miracles or crimes in their execution and the end thereof. (5680-1)

The crimes or the miracles are manifested in many ways and in many areas of our lives. Our physical body is the result of our application of this law. Our material success is determined through this law, as explained in this statement:

> It is the universal consciousness, the desire for harmonious expressions for the good of all, that is the heritage in man, if there is the acceptance of the way and manner such may be

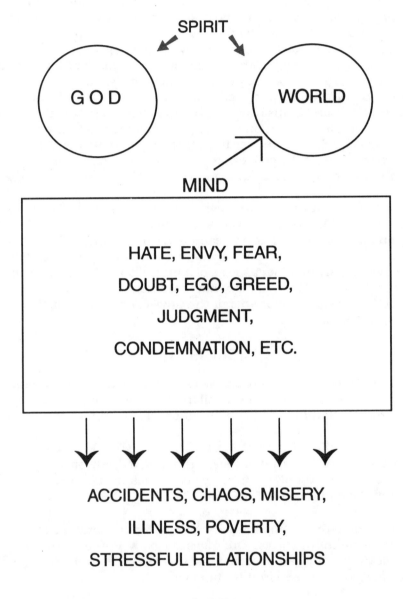

FIGURE 9

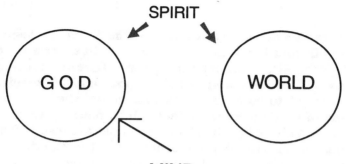

SPIRIT

G O D

WORLD

MIND

LOVE, ABUNDANCE,

WISDOM, TRUTH, FAITH,

JOY, PEACE,

PERFECT PATTERNS

HEALTH, HAPPINESS,

FULFILLING RELATIONSHIPS,

SUCCESS, JOY, PEACE

FIGURE 10

applied, first in the spiritual purpose and then in the mental application, and the material success will be pleasing to any.
(3350-1)

The reading above says to us that the Universe desires the good of all; that is our heritage. We are told we can have that good by accepting and applying this law—first by choosing with our free will to have a spiritual purpose and by keeping the mind focused to build from that. As we do, the result will be the kind of material success that will be pleasing to us.

Whether we have health or sickness or disease results from this interconnectedness of body, mind, and spirit. The following excerpt, from a reading for a person having physical problems, emphasizes this interconnectedness:

An at-variance to the divine law! Hence it may truly be said that to be at-variance may bring sickness, dis-ease, disruption, distress in a physical body . . . The awareness, the interconsciousness of the *body*, the mind, the spirit . . . O that all would gain *just* that! and not feel, "Yes, I understand—but my desires and my body and my weaknesses and this or that—and I didn't do it." Who else did? (262-83)

In other words, you are responsible for all that occurs in your body. It depends on you because the physical is the result of how you apply the Universal Laws.

Likewise, all healing, whether of our spiritual life, mental life, or physical life is governed by the law of manifestation:

. . . all healing, all correcting of the spiritual and of the mental life must come from the Divine within, and the results in the physical being will be in keeping with that which is developed in the spiritual self. (3064-1)

LIVING IN THE FLOW

To be living in the flow is to be so in accord with the principles and purposes of the Universe that you begin to experience in your life the highest good for yourself and others. When you are living in the flow, wondrous things happen.

Being in attunement with Spirit and in accord on all three levels is the secret of being in the flow with life and the Uni-

verse. If we are not in accord, we create conflict and negate the desired effect. To have our spirit, mind, and body cooperate fully sounds like a big order, but the laws make it simple for us. Let's consider an example.[9]

You and I want peace in our lives. It is not enough to manifest peace on the material plane by refraining from violence. To truly have peace we must first develop a spirit of peace within us; that is, we must feel that peace is important to us and seek to be peaceful in spirit. We can do that, as we have discussed, through attunement and seeking a spirit of peace. The wondrous results of this simple step are beautifully explained in this reading:

> For, according to the true law of spirit, like begets like. Thus as harmony and beauty and grace reign within the consciousness of an entity [a person], it gives that to others—and others wonder what moved them to feel different, when no one spoke, no one even appeared to be anxious. This is the manner in which the spirit of truth operates among the children of men.
>
> (3098-2)

As others feel that peace we hold in consciousness, the law of "like begets like" operates to bring it back to us. This all occurs on the spiritual level (see Figure 11).

FIGURE 11

Note that the flow of the Spirit occurs on this level from us to others and returns on the same level. The flow is created by the law "like begets like."

By choosing and holding the spirit of peace on the spiritual level, we start another flow. By the law "spirit is the life, mind is the builder, physical is the result" our mind picks up and builds on whatever spirit we hold.[10] So, on the mental level we begin to think peaceful thoughts, which flow as shown (Figure 12).

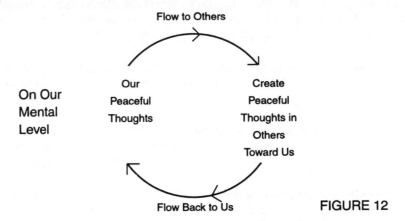

Flow to Others

On Our
Mental
Level

Our
Peaceful
Thoughts

Create
Peaceful
Thoughts in
Others
Toward Us

Flow Back to Us   FIGURE 12

Our peaceful thoughts on this level flow to others and are returned to us.

With a peaceful spirit and peaceful thoughts, our activities and words become peaceful. So the flow then moves outward to others on the physical level and institutes the return flow which occurs through the action of the law "like begets like" (see Figure 13).

Flow to Others

On Our
Physi-
cal
Level

Our
Peaceful
Words
and Acts

Create Peaceful
Words and Acts
of Others
Toward Us

Flow Back to Us   FIGURE 13

While we can think of and picture these as separate levels, they are really one. Each level affects the others. Only when we manifest peace on all three levels will we truly have peace in our lives. If we try to hold it only on one or two levels, we are out of balance and the flow is incomplete. A great deal of effort and stress is required to even attempt to maintain a peaceful state on one level if we are not peaceful on the other levels.

Figure 14 shows how it all works together when we are living in the flow.

We can see from this diagram (Figure 14) how it all ties together in a supporting flow pattern from our spirit to our physical activities, from the inner to the outer, and then back again on all levels. We can see that our spirit is the key and starting point of it all. We can see also why we need to live the law on all three levels, because to do otherwise would disrupt the flow and cause conflicts within us. We can achieve any other result we may choose—such as harmony, patience, gentleness, or kindness—by starting with that spirit and going with this flow. Thus, with the Universal Laws you and I can change not only our lives, but also the world around us in wonderful ways.

WHAT WILL YOU BUILD?

A young woman, twenty-four years old, asked Cayce in his trance state, "How can I improve myself during 1928, physically, mentally, spiritually, and socially?" His reply is as valid and as challenging today as it was then:

> Physically, mentally, spiritually and socially, by application [of Universal Laws]. Remembering that as has just been given. The mental, the spiritual, are unseen forces; the activities are the result of mental application; physical conditions—whether pertaining to social, to money, to station in life, to likes and dislikes—are the application of those mental images builded within the body, seated, guided, directed, by the spiritual application of that of the spirit within bearing witness within self to the spirit of the universe, or to God, and the forces as are seen are *results! What will you build within yourself!*
>
> (349-4)AR

This is the question we all must face, no matter who or where we are. What will you build within yourself? Will you take the high

LIVING IN THE FLOW

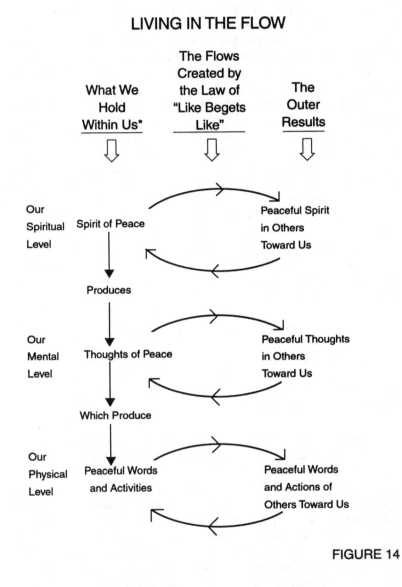

What We Hold Within Us*	The Flows Created by the Law of "Like Begets Like"	The Outer Results

⇩   ⇩   ⇩

Our Spiritual Level   Spirit of Peace   Peaceful Spirit in Others Toward Us

Produces

Our Mental Level   Thoughts of Peace   Peaceful Thoughts in Others Toward Us

Which Produce

Our Physical Level   Peaceful Words and Activities   Peaceful Words and Actions of Others Toward Us

FIGURE 14

*The flow created by the law: "spirit is the life, mind is the builder, physical is the result."

road or the low road? The choice is always yours. The Master Law of Manifestation—

**SPIRIT IS THE LIFE,
MIND IS THE BUILDER,
PHYSICAL IS THE RESULT**

—defines the process by which you build, but you must choose your purpose and the consciousness from which you act: these are the keys to the result. With these keys and this law you can consciously create the desired results in your life.

Chapter 13

Making the Right Choices for Your Life

LAW OF CHOICE

We learned that the key to building what we really want in our lives is to keep our minds attuned to Spirit within. We will consider a further aspect of building our lives by looking at another law, which is a sublaw of "spirit is the life, mind is the builder, physical is the result." It is the law of choice, which leaves no doubt as to the importance of the decisions we make. It is stated thus:

LIFE IS THE EXPERIENCE OF YOUR CHOICES

By the choices you make throughout your day, you create your life. This is both similar to and different from the karmic laws by which we create our destiny. It is similar because all laws are creative as we use them; through all laws we create our destiny. However, it is different because we now view the laws from a higher perspective and we understand that our inner wisdom shows us the perfect pattern to guide us, enabling the choice to be between the perfect pattern or a lesser one.[1] Behind each choice presented to us is this basic question: Will I do it the way I have chosen in the past or will I choose a higher way, that of the Spirit within me? This is the crucial decision to make if we are going to transform our lives. This is the choice that we can make today and each day for each event and each experience. The question will come in many ways and many guises, but the choice is always the same.[2]

This law of choice is telling us that if we wish to change our

lives, we must change our choices. In one sense, we have no choice for we always choose from the level of consciousness that we hold at the time of our choice. If our level has not changed since the last time we made that choice, there will be no change in the result. If we wish to choose a higher way, we must prepare ourselves by working to raise our consciousness from the present lesser patterns to the perfect patterns in accord with our inner guidance. That is our *real* choice—to choose to change our consciousness. To change our consciousness is the purpose for our choosing the path of Universal Law. The Universal Laws, as we know, are laws of consciousness; as such, they are the keys to changing consciousness. The master key to changing consciousness is:

THE MASTER LAW OF ATTUNEMENT

How do we attune to the Spirit within? How do we transform our consciousness? The master law of attunement shows us the direction we need to follow to find answers to all our questions and all our needs. It is:

. . . "IF YOU WILL BE MY PEOPLE, *I WILL BE YOUR GOD!*"

(257-85)[3]AR

In that simple statement lies the solution to your problems, to my problems, and to the problems of the world. Note first that the solution is up to us. If we choose to turn to the Creator of all, to attune ourselves to the source of life, then that Creator will be our source of all—all power, all knowledge, all wisdom, all good, and all abundance—because that is its nature.

The Cayce readings insist that the divine forces are the only safe and sane power to depend upon and that the law of attunement is the key to our relationship with the Divine. We ignore the law at our own peril:

Man has ever . . . when in distress, either mental, spiritual *or* physical, sought to know his association, his connection, with the divine forces that brought the worlds into being. As these are sought, so does the promise hold true—or that given man from the beginning, "Will you be my children, I will be your God!" "You turn your face from me, my face is turned

from you," and those things you have builded in your own
endeavor to make manifest your own powers bring those certain destructions in the lives of individuals in the present . . .
Do not ignore those divine powers that are so tabu by the
worldly-wise, that are looked upon as old men's tales and
women's fables; yet in the strength of such forces do *worlds*
come into being! (367-11)AR

The law of attunement strongly implies that if we choose to depend on ourselves—our wills and our ideas—to try to manipulate
or control others or the world or we put our faith in what is going on
around us, that is all we have. If we put our faith and trust in the
Creative Force, we, as a co-worker with that Force, will be taken
care of—problems and all—no matter what the conditions around
us may be. It is that simple. As you put Spirit first, you will be cared
for. If you do not put Spirit first, you are on your own. That's O.K.,
but it's the hard way, the low road.

It is a question of whether we are willing to rely on that divine
power within us rather than trying to gain, develop, acquire, or use
our own power or influence others on our behalf who seem to have
the power out there. There is a vast difference between these two
understandings of where the power is.

THE GREAT CHOICE

The master law of attunement challenges us to make the ultimate decision of our lives—the life-changing choice of the high road
or the low road! In all its beauty and simplicity the law asks us,
"Will you be my people?" Will you be what you really are—the sons
and daughters of God? Are you willing to accept yourselves as such
and seek to be the goddesses and gods it is your birthright to be? If
your answer is YES, you have made the great choice!

If you choose not to decide now, that's all right. You will continue, as millions of others of us have done for years, to vacillate
between the high and the low road—and your life will, too. The
opportunity to choose will come again, and again, and again.

If you do choose to accept this relationship, then Spirit is bound
to that relationship by this law and becomes your source and supply for as long as you decide to maintain and live in accord with
that consciousness.

Whether or not the master law of attunement will become active
in your life is up to you. The choice is yours.

THE LAW OF SUPPLY

If you make the great choice for the high road, the only requirement is that you attune yourself to the Spirit of God instead of to
the illusory spirit of the world. Along with that requirement goes a
better guarantee than you can get anywhere else: a guarantee of an
infinite supply of all that you need. It is the law of supply:

**SEEK . . . FIRST THE SPIRIT WITHIN AND ALL THINGS
SHALL BE ADDED YOU HAVE NEED OF!**
(262-89)[4]AR

The master law of attunement "if you will be my people, I will be
your God" raises this question: What does "I will be your God"
mean? The law of supply answers that question. "I will be your God"
means Spirit will provide everything you need—whether the need is
spiritual, mental, or physical.

If you need a house, a car, a mate, a dog, a new job, money, or—
more important—a life with joy, peace, love, happiness, and
fulfillment, then "Seek . . . first the Spirit within and all things shall
be added you have *need of!*" (262-89)AR This is practical advice.
Note the requirement is that we seek *first*, that we make this search
the first priority in our lives. This is not just an arbitrary requirement. It is a recognition that the law of manifestation—"spirit is the
life, mind is the builder, physical is the result"—gives fulfillment
only when we attune ourselves to the Spirit within us because it is
the source of all we need. As we previously learned, seeking first
the Spirit within is the way to put that law to work.

HOW DO WE "SEEK FIRST THE SPIRIT"?

You seek the Spirit just as you seek a station on your radio or
television set—you tune in to its frequency (vibration). We receive
what we are attuned to; "like begets like." Life—God—in its essence
is vibration, and we are, too. In the body, sight, hearing, taste, and
speech are simply different vibrations to which we consciously attune and so become aware of them. We can also learn to attune
to the vibrations which are the essence of the God force within
us.[5]

As we attune to Spirit, we are establishing a relationship with
Spirit. What kind of relationship this will be depends entirely upon
you:

Know that the Creative Energy called God may be as personal as an individual will allow same to be; for the Spirit is in the image of the Creative Forces and seeks manifestation.

(391-4)

METHODS OF ATTUNEMENT

One reading excerpt gives us the key to attunement: "Necessary for the perfect union [attunement] that each be in accord." (5756-4) A very basic requirement for attunement by any method is some faith that there is a Higher Power to attune to, to be in accord with.

There are many ways in which we can seek to become more in accord with, more perfectly attuned to, Spirit. The Cayce readings stress at least seven methods:

1. and 2. Meditation and Prayer

Meditation and prayer are vital elements of raising consciousness. Nothing else is as essential as these for attuning to the Spirit within.

3. Study of Dreams

The use of dreams for guidance can be a very helpful tool for greater accord with Spirit.

4. Service to Others

The readings stress the importance of service to others as a means of attunement.

5. Define Your Life's Purpose

When you take this step, you set the direction for your life in accord with the purpose of the Higher Self within.

6. Establish Your Ideals

In taking this step, you establish the guidelines by which you will live and by which you can coordinate your will, your inner Spirit, your mind, and your body.

7. Laws of Guidance

These laws, presented in the next chapter, enable you to obtain guidance for any aspect of life. The guidance will be that best suited to your own nature and to where you are in your spiritual growth. It will be that which brings greater attunement.

These methods of attunement can be used most effectively when:

1. The importance of the master law of attunement is recognized and accepted, and the choice is made to live it.

2. They are utilized in accord with the Universal Laws that apply.

3. The purpose behind their use is in accord with the purpose of the Universe: love for all, including ourselves.

HIGHLIGHTS OF THIS CHAPTER

The law of choice is:

LIFE IS THE EXPERIENCE OF YOUR CHOICES.

The master law of attunement is:

IF YOU WILL BE MY PEOPLE, I WILL BE YOUR GOD.

The law of supply is:

SEEK FIRST THE SPIRIT WITHIN
AND ALL THINGS SHALL BE ADDED
YOU HAVE NEED OF.

Chapter 14

All the Answers

Life so often seems to require an unending stream of answers but provides few reliable sources from which to receive them. This appears to be true, regardless of the importance of the questions that we face. If anything, the more important the question, the harder it is to find the right answer. Fortunately there are Universal Laws that tell us how to get the very best answers to any and all our questions.

LAWS OF GUIDANCE

There are three laws that define how to get the guidance you need in order to deal with any situation in your life. These three laws are not just suggestions or techniques, but Universal Laws. You can, therefore, by law achieve guidance as you apply them.

These three laws were stated in the readings hundreds of times to those who came to Cayce for help. The laws are not new; as far as we know, they were recorded nearly 2,000 years ago and attributed to Jesus as part of His great truth-teaching in the Sermon on the Mount.

FIRST LAW OF GUIDANCE

The first of these laws is commonly stated as: "Seek and you will find." But wait a minute! The Universal Laws always work without fail. Yet how many times have you sought and not found? What's wrong then? The problem is that the law as given above is not complete. "Seek and you will find" should be stated in full as:

SEEK FIRST THE SPIRIT WITHIN AND YOU WILL FIND

This law defines the first step for obtaining guidance on any question, problem, or need. It really says: Seek first the Spirit within and you will find the source of all the answers that you need.

SEEKING

You need to become a very special kind of seeker, one who knows, feels, senses, believes, or accepts—to some degree—that there is a Higher Power on which you can rely, in which you can trust. As long as you feel that you by yourself can do the job better, you are putting yourself first. You are not complying with "seek first the Spirit within," so the law does not apply to you and does not operate. You have not put it to work.

To put the law to work, you don't even need to know specifically what you are seeking. You only need to know you have a need and seek an answer. By seeking, you set out on a quest, a voyage of discovery. By this law, you know Spirit will help you find what you really need.

Knowing this law, I am now able to recognize a critical time in my life when I unconsciously put it to work. It was long before I knew anything about Universal Law. The last of our three children had gone away to school. My wife and I had devoted ourselves to our children and their activities, and we suddenly realized much of that was at an end. I began to wonder what life was really all about, what was its real meaning and purpose from here on. As an executive, I was used to searching for answers. The obvious sources, such as religion, philosophy, and psychology, however, didn't have any answers that appealed to me or offered me any sense of fulfillment. After long and fruitless searching, I had to admit that I didn't know where else to look. Then a strange thing happened. I was visiting for the first time a town of ancient cultural heritage—Santa Fe, New Mexico. As I walked down the street past an old Spanish inn with its sunbaked adobe walls, I saw books displayed in the window. One of them—*Search for the Truth*—caught my eye.[1] I knew instantly that that was what I was searching for—the Truth—and that I had to read that book. I did. The book also told the story of Edgar Cayce, which eventually led me to the truth of Universal Laws and to a fulfillment far greater than I had ever dreamed possible.

Note that nothing happened in my search until I gave up the possibility of getting the answer myself. As long as I felt that I could find it myself, the law did not operate. Only as I gave up—surrendered, accepted that I needed help, even though I didn't have any idea of what kind or where to get it; by that act of getting myself out of the way—did I put the law to work, and Spirit provided the answer.

If we are to find, our search needs to be on the spiritual level in order to seek the pattern for what we wish to manifest. Our mind can then build from this perfect pattern, the perfect result in the spiritual, mental, or physical. Such a result will be right for us and for others. It will have come from that higher source within us which knows all there is to know.

The readings offer many suggestions to aid you as a seeker.

IDEAL REQUIREMENTS FOR A SEEKER[2]

1. Seek first the Spirit within with the desire for spiritual guidance.

2. Seek in earnest, willingly, sincerely, with a higher purpose than for self-gratification, but rather to be creative and constructive in the physical, mental, and spiritual for self and for others.

3. Seek at all times to do His will by seeking to do the highest that you know and to better understand His will for you.

4. Do not seek to take advantage over others in body, mind, or material things.

5. Put into practice what you already know. Use what you have available to you today. Act only in accord with your purpose and ideals.

6. Trust in Spirit and the Universal Laws rather than in self. Expect to find what you seek.

7. Seek in a balanced manner, consistently, persistently, and with openness to receiving answers from many different sources.

Because we are unique individuals, what is right for one of us is not necessarily right for another. However, by seeking the Spirit within and keeping our mind attuned to it, we can find what is right for ourselves. Here's an example from the readings of the choice we have:

Mary was a young girl of seventeen. The reading explained that she had one of two paths to follow: a path with constructive influences (the high road) or one that responded to her indulgences (the low road). Mary was told that if she chose to seek to know herself (Spirit within), she could find the way, become content, and have much joy, peace, and happiness in her life even though the way might be hard. If, however, she chose to feed self-indulgence and self-interests without tempering them by seeking spiritual guidance, she would find hardships, turmoils, and strife—even though she might find an abundance of earthly goods.[3]

The individuals who came to Cayce for help were seeking a variety of things. Regardless, however, of what they were seeking, the wisdom expressed through the readings inevitably pointed in the same direction, urging them to seek the spiritual. The following are typical of such advice:[4]

1. Seek to know God and your relationship to Him.
2. Seek to know His love, His law, His will, His guidance.
3. Seek the universal Spirit as a source for helping self and others.

The readings assured their recipients that as they sought the spiritual, the law "seek first the Spirit within and you shall find" would bring the desired effects. I was fascinated by the incredible variety of wonderful results mentioned in the readings that would come from such seeking:

As you seek the Spirit:[5]

1. You will know what you may do to fulfill your purpose.
2. You will purify the body and the mind, and the growth of the soul will be assured.
3. Spirit will give you the answer to every question.
4. Spirit will provide a way of escape from every temptation, every error, every fault.
5. Such seeking will bring knowledge of the relationships that should exist between self and your Creator.

SECOND LAW OF GUIDANCE

Now let's consider the second law of guidance which, stated in full, is:

ASK THE SPIRIT, WITH FAITH,
AND YOU WILL RECEIVE

For years I had the impression that faith was the act of believing in something I didn't really understand. That's not faith at all. Faith is one of the fruits of the Spirit. You have it and I have it; it is as inherent in us as our eyes and our ears. As previously noted, faith is the ability to perceive that anything is possible through the infinite power and wisdom of Spirit working through the Universal Laws. Remember, the inherent nature of that Spirit includes all the power you need plus the perfect pattern and the guidance to achieve it. So, indeed, nothing is impossible. By your free will, you can choose to have two percent faith or 100 percent faith in the infinite possibilities of the Spirit within. As always, it is up to you.

WHY SHOULD YOU ASK?

Whenever we have difficulties, needs, or problems, it's very easy to get caught up in the drama of the situation. We have been taught to solve a problem by working with the problem. This is wrong. The readings point out that the answer to every problem is to discover the truth about it. The only viewpoint from which we can see the truth and learn its lesson is to reach a consciousness that's higher than the one from which we created the problem. Since we create problems by using our mental/emotional faculties, we need to go higher—to seek the spiritual level where the truth is known.[6] That is one reason why we need to turn to Spirit within and ask for guidance.

If you get a wretched deal or bad advice from another, you know better than to approach that person for advice the next time. Yet we do exactly that with the difficulties in our lives. We create problems by relying on our minds for answers, then we expect that same mind to figure out the right answer. "How dumb can we be!" Or you may go to an expert. Unless that expert is attuned to his or her spiritual source, the answer will be based on mind and experience only. Likewise for friends; unless they turn to the Spirit within or help you to do so, their answers may not be what you need. The best advice they could ever give you or you could give them when the situation is reversed is: Ask the Spirit within you for help.[7]

We often feel that "God knows what I need; let Him show me"— but that is not the way it works. One reading says:

Know that the divine powers that be . . . work with *you* in the earth only upon your *own* invitation. (2437-1)AR

For that reason it is essential to ask the Higher Power for help, if you want it. The Spirit within you is an infinite Spirit that wants you to have complete and total abundance, joy, and peace. Furthermore, Spirit knows what you need, but leaves it up to you to invite it to be a part of your life by asking. This signifies that you are ready for and willing to make use of whatever you request. By asking Spirit, you put the law to work in the right way. By using your mind to decide what to ask, you are doing your part as a co-creator.[8]

If you wish to develop a personal relationship with the Divine within, you need to ask for it:

How personal is your God? Just as personal as you will let Him be! How close is the Christ as was manifested in the physical body, Jesus? Just as near, just as dear as you will let Him be! (1158-9)AR

WHEN TO ASK

You should ask whenever you have a question, whenever you need an answer, whenever you are not sure what to do next. Even when I am sure, I have found that I really need to ask; otherwise, that is when I am most likely to make a mistake. When should we ask? *Always!*

KNOCKING

Let's now consider the last of the three laws of guidance:

KNOCK, WITH FAITH IN SPIRIT, AND THE DOOR WILL BE OPENED

This law defines the third step you must take to achieve complete guidance. It is often presented in the readings in conjunction with the preceding one, as "Seek and you shall find. Knock and it shall be opened unto you." (4121-3)AR It's as if your search is your journey to find what you're seeking, but when you arrive, the door is not open. An additional effort is required to fulfill your search. It is up to you to knock.

You knock by accepting and using that which you find or receive. This law recognizes your free will and your role as a co-creator. You may seek and you will find. You may ask and you will receive. However, you still have the right to make the final free-will decision about whether you will accept and use that which you find or receive. There is no requirement to do either. If you choose not to knock or if you choose to act in accord with your own will, that's all right. Nothing, however, will come of your seeking and asking. This law makes it clear that if you do knock (accept and act on what you have been given), then the door is "opened unto you." This means that as you apply in your life what you have found or received, the door of your consciousness will be opened to greater understanding and to a higher consciousness.

There is another message in this law that came in a dream I once had. In the dream, as I climbed to the top of a mountain, I was scaling a vertical rock wall high above the valley floor. Then I came to a huge ledge which loomed over me. There was no way around it, over it, or through it, nor could I back down. I was trapped, clinging to the face of the rock with no way to move. I had reached the limit of my powers and knowledge and understanding. I felt it was the end for me. Then something told me to trust and let go. I did so, but instead of falling I felt myself being lifted up. Suddenly I found myself on top of the mountain! It was a beautiful and exhilarating moment, one of complete attunement, but it was achieved only by letting go and trusting in the Higher Power. That, I believe, is the message of this law.

Whenever you are faced with a situation in which you don't know what to do or the condition seems hopeless or all doors seem to be closed to you, knock—by putting your trust totally in the highest power, turning it all over to Spirit. A door will be opened and you will be guided as to what to do. To knock is to turn to the presence of the Divine within you and accept it as a vital living part of your life and your experience. You are the only one who can open the door of your heart to the Presence. It is up to you to knock.

USING THE LAWS OF GUIDANCE

Using the laws of guidance can be as simple as thought, a desire, an awareness, or a surrender turned inward, and an openness to receive. There are no other prerequisites.

There is much we can do, however, to enhance the process and to make it an integral part of our lives. Let's look at the overall picture of these three laws of guidance and how they relate to the process of attunement.

We can consider attunement to the Higher Source in this way: It is like a three-legged stool. (See Figure 15.)

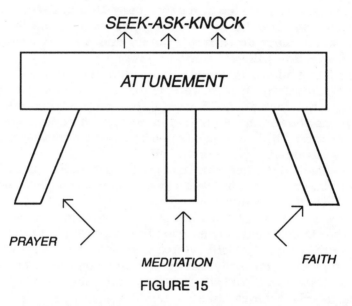

FIGURE 15

The legs, the foundations of attunement, are prayer, meditation, and faith. These are not absolute prerequisites for attunement because we all have by our inherent godlike nature a degree of attunement. But, as you establish this base, you clear away obstacles such as fear and doubt, become more effectively attuned, and can ask, seek, and knock to get the guidance you need for every aspect of your life.

When we "ask," God speaks to us. The *Search for God* book explains:

There is in all of us that still Voice that teaches sacrifice [of the ego], love, and service, that warns of every catastrophe and protects from all danger. When it is listened to and followed, no mistakes are made, no wars are fought, no homes are broken up; for then we seek the good of our neighbors and the will of the Creator.[9]

In other words, when we listen to that voice, we get perfect guidance. The readings give many different ways in which we can communicate with Spirit. I would like to share one that I enthusiastically recommend as a daily practice.

Each day before you begin your daily meditation, write your questions out in a notebook. At the end of a meditation period and while you are still in attunement, ask your question either silently or aloud. Listen intently; really listen; listen expectantly. As any thought, idea, feelings, or words come into your mind, write them down immediately and keep on writing as they come. You will get your answers![10]

This is not automatic writing. By meditation, you have attuned to the Spirit within. By being receptive through listening, you have opened the door to guidance which comes through your superconscious mind, your Higher Self. As it comes, you consciously record it. I write in my notebook with my eyes closed so that my attunement is not disturbed.

The basic requirement for this to work for you is to believe that this guidance is available, and expect to receive it. Disbelief and doubt turn off the connection.

Like any other skill, this takes practice. By doing it every day, it will begin to flow smoothly for you. The most wonderful results of this are that a great weight is lifted from you. Joy comes with the realization that you really can get guidance on any concern you have and that there is a loving, caring Source always with you and willing to aid whenever you seek it.

USING THE LAWS OF GUIDANCE
FOR GREATER ATTUNEMENT

We previously asked the question, How can we attune ourselves to Spirit? As noted, there are many methods of attunement. What works best for me may not work well for you. You can use the three laws of guidance to learn the methods and ways that are best for you in achieving greater attunement.

WALKING AND TALKING
WITH HIM—FOR GUIDANCE

The readings assure us that God will walk and talk with us here and now, if we choose to establish that relationship. This is one of the privileges we have as we accept and apply the master law of attunement: "If you will be my people I will be your God." The readings explain:

How beautiful the face of those whom the Lord, the Christ, smiles upon! He would walk and talk with you, my children, if you will but put away from your mind those things and conditions that you *feel* are in the way. For, they are as naught compared to the great love that He has bestowed upon His brethren, you and I." (254-76)AR

It took me a long time to believe that I could talk with the Spirit within, that it would work for me, that I was good enough. Fortunately you do not have to be "good enough." You simply have to try it expectantly. Remember that you are His child. The readings said this to one mother:

Enter into your inner chamber with your Lord; meet Him there; seek and you shall know. For He would speak with you as you would with your child. As you as a mother loves that which is born of you, of your own body, of your own blood, then know . . . that as you . . . would be patient, your heavenly Father would be more patient with you? *Trust* in Him; *speak* often with Him. (922-1)AR

Men and women throughout the ages have spoken with that Presence:

. . . all the various stages of developments that have come to man through the ages have been those periods when He walked and talked with man. (364-8)

(Q) Will I contact my Master in this lifetime?
(A) . . . He will walk and talk with you; if you seek to do His bidding. (2405-1)AR

Choose to so conduct your life that He may walk and talk with you as face to face, as He walks in the way. Let *Him* be your guide in your going ins, in your coming out, in your meditations—be not afraid. (537-1)AR

USING THE LAWS OF GUIDANCE
IN MAKING IMPORTANT DECISIONS

Many individuals came to Cayce with questions which his source said should be answered within themselves. The Creative Forces would not take away anyone's right of free will to choose, particularly in making life's major decisions—such as, which job to accept or whom to marry. However, the questioners were often given a process which enabled them to make their own decisions and to check that decision with the Spirit within to make sure their choice was right for them. This is a seven-step process:[11]

STEPS OF THE
DECISION-MAKING PROCESS

1. Analyze carefully the situation about which you wish to make a decision. Consider all its aspects such as: circumstances, changes involved, individuals involved, your basic purpose, your ideals, the alternatives.

2. Pose the decision you need to make as a question that may be answered by a "yes" or a "no." Write the question out.

3. Mentally make a logical, rational decision, "yes" or "no." Be willing to act in accord with this decision.

4. Seek attunement to your Higher Self by prayer, meditation, or any method that works best for you. Remember, at this stage, do not meditate upon the question or decision—go within simply for the attunement.

5. When you are attuned, ask: HAVE I MADE THE RIGHT DECISION? Listen, sense, know, or feel the answer from within.

6. If the answer is "yes," your conscious self and divine self are in accord; you have made the right decision. If they disagree, the answer will be "no." In that case DO NOT just assume your mental decision was wrong. A "no" answer indicates there is a problem to be resolved before you can proceed. Start again at Step 1 and go through the entire process. Perhaps you had not considered all the alternatives or considered all aspects of the situation. Double-check to make sure you do not have a hidden purpose. Perhaps you did not ask the right question. Complete all the steps again.

7.   Do not proceed with your decision until you get a "yes" answer in Step 5. When you do, do not fail to act on your decision.

I find this seven-step method important for making major decisions because it makes me think through all aspects and look at the basic questions involved before I make a decision. This is important, for we are co-creators and need to first know and do our part by using our minds and will—then check it out with Spirit.

No matter what form of guidance you use, be aware that your strongly held opinions and prejudices can distort the results if you are not fully attuned. Know that guidance from Spirit will never condemn nor judge you or others or suggest that you take advantage of someone or require that you harm yourself or another in any way. Any such advice is not from your Higher Self.

One more important point: Perfect guidance does not mean a perfect situation will result as seen with your human consciousness. Rather, it means that the perfect situation for your spiritual growth and understanding will manifest. Often this may appear a more difficult way and might be particularly hard on the ego at times. But our guidance leads us to and through the experiences of life that will teach us the lessons we need to learn for greater spiritual growth. Through time we will see the infinite wisdom and the good in those lessons. Through time these lessons will help us to become the goddesses and gods we are meant to be.

THE TRANSITION

A gentle warning is appropriate as you enter the transition period from depending on your old ways to coordinating with the Spirit within. This transition may happen overnight or it can take years or lifetimes. It is up to you.

Through the thousands of past choices you have made, you have established your life as it exists today. In addition, you have yet to experience the results of many of your past choices. Once you open yourself to a higher consciousness, you will have the opportunity to deal with many of the experiences you have created. Life suddenly may seem to be filled with more and greater difficulties. Remember, though, you are not alone; you have new strength and guidance.

The following example illustrates what can be done by coming to know and consciously apply the Universal Laws in your life:

Louis and Ann were a wonderful young couple whom we knew many years ago. They had promising careers, two lovely children, and their future looked bright. We moved away and lost touch with them until about four years ago, when we met Ann again. Her husband had become an alcoholic, her daughter seemed hopelessly lost in the drug scene, and her job, though a responsible one, was frustrating and unfulfilling. Ann felt she was a miserable failure. She lived far away from us but kept in occasional touch by phone, and we always shared with her the concepts of Universal Laws. She worked with the steps for attunement and gained new courage and guidance. As a result, she began to apply the Universal Laws in a higher way. She eventually went through a divorce and began to make a new life for herself in another part of the country.

Ann has found fresh meaning and purpose and has truly transformed her life. There have been ripple effects: her ex-husband has stopped drinking and her daughter has begun treatment for her addictions. In the last year the family has met together several times. Contrary to past experiences, they were able to enjoy each other and share some good times together. Most important, Ann has proven for herself that life can become joyous and fulfilling, regardless of the circumstances, if you choose to take the higher road.

SUPPORT GROUPS

You can help yourself in this process of transformation by joining a support or study group that works with Universal Laws.

Such groups provide an opportunity for in-depth discussion and for learning about others' experiences in working with the principles. The group becomes a laboratory for trying to live the laws. The sharing of ideas and experiences helps expand the understanding of every group member and often inspires members to greater accomplishments. At the same time, the group helps to moderate or correct excuses, errors, and misunderstandings of which members may not be aware.

These groups are easily available—sometimes in surprising places. When I first looked years ago, I learned there was one in the small town where I lived. Following are addresses of two organizations that have such groups. They will assist you in contacting a group in your area. If there are none nearby, they will advise you on how to start your own support group for working with Universal Laws.

A.R.E. STUDY GROUPS

Study Group Department
Association for Research and Enlightenment, Inc.
P.O. Box 595
Virginia Beach, VA 23451-0595

An A.R.E. Study Group usually consists of from two to ten persons meeting weekly with these purposes:

1. To assist each individual to meditate and pray in an effective and helpful manner;

2. To show by practical application how each one may know his/her relationship to God and to others and how to manifest love to all;

3. To furnish a safe way for soul growth;

4. To help each member to live a balanced life;

5. To inform each member about the broad areas of information that may be found in the Edgar Cayce readings; and

6. To support each other in living a more useful and fulfilling life.

Group leadership rests with a loving God not with a human master, guru, or teacher. The only requirement for group membership is a desire to cooperate in group study.[12]

I know from experience that becoming a member of such a group can be one of the greatest experiences for you and your growth. A member of one such group wrote A.R.E.: "Becoming involved in this work is the most important and most wonderful thing that ever happened to me and I did *not* lead a secluded life before. But somehow one's values change; things which were of prime importance are replaced by things of eternal importance. You find yourself working with such beautiful people and looking for ways to show them you love them."[13]

ARNOLD PATENT SUPPORT GROUPS

Information on Arnold Patent support groups may be obtained by writing to the following:

Celebration Publishing Co.
Rt. 3, Box 365AA
Sylva, NC 28779

or by calling: 1-800-476-4785

Arnold Patent support groups are small groups that meet frequently to support their members in achieving a more fulfilling life
by living in accord with Universal principles (Laws). Groups alternate leaders at subsequent meetings. They emphasize individual
and group purpose, provide opportunities for study, discussion,
and applying principles, and offer support for members in doing
so.[14]

SOME HIGHLIGHTS OF THIS CHAPTER

The three laws of guidance are:

**SEEK FIRST THE SPIRIT WITHIN
AND YOU WILL FIND**

**ASK THE SPIRIT, WITH FAITH,
AND YOU WILL RECEIVE**

**KNOCK, WITH FAITH IN SPIRIT,
AND THE DOOR WILL BE OPENED**

Chapter 15

Finding Your Life's Purpose

Your life has a purpose which is based on the principles set forth by the Universal Laws. When you know your life's purpose you can more effectively and consistently apply the Universal Laws to achieve that purpose.

Finding the purpose for your life can be far more significant for your transformation than it may at first appear. It is easy to dismiss as a mere exercise or technique. However, this exercise needs to be seriously considered, for it gives a practical means of coordinating your life with the Spirit within.

THE MISSION OF YOUR LIFE

We previously defined the common purpose we all share—our basic purpose—which is to manifest the god or goddess you really are. However, you also came into this life for a purpose that is unique to you. The readings refer to that purpose as your mission:

> For, each soul enters with a mission . . . we all have a mission to perform. . . . (3003-1)

Your life's purpose or reason for being here on earth consists of your basic purpose plus the mission you have come here to accomplish. Each contributes to the other. Together they define your life's purpose. You should be able to express it with a simple, clear statement that answers both of these questions: Why am I here? and

What am I going to do with my life?

Your mission is related to your unique talents, qualities, and characteristics. The readings always encouraged individuals to find, develop, and use their particular talents. They recognized that these were unique gifts that that individual had brought to fulfill the mission for which that person had come into the earth. Your unique gifts are represented by the things you love to do. As previously discussed, your life should be an expression of doing what you love to do. Those things should be a part of your life's purpose.

Defining your purpose is a consciousness-raising experience because it helps you to open your awareness to your potentials. It can get you on the track that is right for you and save years of lost time in looking and searching for you-know-not-what.

When you are ready to take this important step of finding your life's purpose, do the workshop that follows:[1]

WORKSHOP FOR FINDING YOUR LIFE'S PURPOSE

Your life's purpose or reason for being here in the earth consists of your basic purpose plus the mission you came here to accomplish, as we stated earlier. Each contributes to the other; together they define your life's purpose. In Part I of this workshop you will define your soul's purpose, in Parts II and III your mission. You will then combine these to define your life's purpose.

PART I: DETERMINING YOUR OWN BASIC PURPOSE

The Cayce readings emphasize that we all have the same ultimate purpose: to become a god. This can be expressed in many ways. A number of individuals asked Cayce what their life's purpose was, and he defined it for each in a different way, suited to his or her consciousness and understanding. Likewise, you need to define your purpose in a way that is meaningful to you.

To determine your basic purpose, proceed as follows:

1. Read through the following list of typical ones given in the readings; check any that feel right.

2. Prepare yourself with meditation; use these possible affirmations: "I am guided in all ways" or "I am perfectly guided."

3. When you have attuned yourself, ask **"What is my life's basic purpose?"** If you are given one—use it. If not, select from the

following list or create one of your own as guided.

4. Write it on the blank lines below this list, expressing it in your own words:

EXAMPLES OF YOUR LIFE'S BASIC PURPOSE:

Live the Christ Consciousness

Become godlike

Make the world a better place

Become a god or goddess

Be an ambassador here for Him

Live the fruits of the Spirit

Be a channel of blessings to others

Be a servant to all

Manifest the love of the Creative Forces/God

Purify self

Strengthen and develop my soul for greater service

Expand my view of the Christ

Be a living example of oneness with God

Learn patience

Manifest (truth) (principle) (universal laws) (God)

Be a helpful force to others

Learn my lessons for greater soul expression

Be a light to others

Be and do all in accord with God's will

Know the spirit within that I may be of greater help to others

Be one with the purpose of the Creative Forces/God

Become aware of my relationship to the Creative Forces/God/Spirit

Work in cooperation with others for the good of all

Become more aware of the Divine within

Be one with and an expression of the Creative Forces/ God

Live and move and have my being in the Creative Forces/ God/Spirit

Magnify the Creative Forces/ God rather than the self

Prepare myself to be a companion with the Creator

Be a living example of the fact that God is

It is my basic purpose to: _____

_____

_____

PART II: DETERMINING YOUR MISSION IN LIFE

To determine your mission, proceed as follows:

1. Read through the following list; check any words that feel right to you or add your own.

2. Prepare yourself with meditation; use these possible affirmations: "I am guided in all ways" or "I am perfectly guided."

3. When you have attuned yourself, ask **"Which of my natural qualities or spirit do I most love to use in my life?"** Write your answers on the blanks provided below.

Select from the suggested nouns below *or* use your own:

Alertness	**Attentiveness**	**Awareness**
Beauty	**Beliefs**	**Centeredness**
Commitment	**Communion**	**Compassion**
Consistency	**Confidence**	**Courage**
Creativity	**Curiosity**	**Direction**

Enthusiasm	**Endurance**	**Expressiveness**
Faith	**Friendliness**	**Generosity**
Geniality	**Graciousness**	**Guidance**
Health	**Honesty**	**Humor**
Image	**Independence**	**Insight**
Intention	**Intimacy**	**Intuition**
Joy	**Laughter**	**Leadership**
Love	**Nurturance**	**Open-Mindedness**
Peacefulness	**Patience**	**Security**
Self-Awareness	**Self-Esteem**	**Sensitivity**
Serenity	**Stability**	**Supportiveness**
Tolerance	**Trust**	**Vision**
Understanding	**Wisdom**	**Unconditional Love**

Vitality

(Others) _____

_____

_____

Write your selections here:

1. _____ 2. _____

PART III: DETERMINING TALENTS AND ABILITIES

To determine your talents and abilities proceed as follows:

1. Read through the following list; check any words that feel right to you or add your own.

2. Prepare yourself with meditation; use these possible affirmations: "I am guided in all ways" or "I am perfectly guided."

3. When you have attuned yourself, ask **"What talents, abilities, or other means of expression do I most love to use in my life?"** Write your answers on the blanks provided below.

Select from examples below *or* use your own:

Accounting	**Artistry**	**Acting**
Building	**Cooking**	**Caring**
Centering	**Composing**	**Coordinating**
Counseling	**Dancing**	**Communicating**
Designing	**Encouraging**	**Engineering**
Fishing	**Healing**	**Inspiring**
Leading	**Learning**	**Listening**
Managing	**Massaging**	**Meditating**
Nursing	**Organizing**	**Painting**
Parenting	**Performing**	**Planning**
Plumbing	**Sculpting**	**Serving**
Sharing	**Singing**	**Studying**
Sporting Activities	**Supporting**	**Teaching**
Training	**Writing**	**Homemaking**
Selling	**Creating**	**Gardening**
		(Others) _____
		_____
		_____

Write your selections here:

1._____ 2._____

NOW PUT THE THREE PARTS TOGETHER:

It is my life's purpose to:

Part I:_____

Part II (and to use my):_____

Part III (in/to):_____

Rearrange, revise, or add words to make it a clear, smooth, and satisfying statement for you. Write it here:

_____

_____

_____

Review your purpose daily to make it an ever-present part of your consciousness. As you grow and change, be aware that it will change. Modify your purpose as you feel it is necessary.

Use your purpose in your planning and decision making. It will make a vital difference!

FINDING YOUR HIDDEN TALENTS

As previously noted, your unique talents are represented by what you love to do; they should be a part of your purpose. However, we often are not aware of the talents we have. Arnold Patent gives an exercise which can help us find our hidden talents:

The way we locate the particular talent that is perfect for us at any specific time in our lives is to look at what we love to do. For what we love to do naturally is what we have a natural talent to do. The two are really one and the same.

We all know what it is we love to do. However, we often keep this information from our conscious minds. Doing the following exercise will put you in touch with what you love to do right now. When you are in touch with what you love to do, you will have discovered your talent . . .

Make a list of the things you love to do. Limit the list to those activities that create an excitement in you at the mere thought of them. The shorter the list, the easier it is to reach the desired result . . .

It is best to do this daily. Keep a separate book for this exercise. Do not judge the ideas that come to mind as you do this exercise. Write down every idea that flows through your mind, no matter how silly or meaningless it may seem. The purpose of the exercise is to stimulate your creative mind.

After doing the exercise for a period of time, you will have developed a habit pattern that will continually produce creative ways to express what you love to do. The number of ways you can express yourself by doing what you love has no limit. Using your creativity to produce these ideas is one way to experience the abundance of the Universe . . . [2]

When you discover a hidden talent, you may wish to incorporate it into your life's purpose by doing the workshop again.

Chapter 16

Setting Your Ideals
in Accord with Spirit

One of the most important steps in beginning to transform your life is to establish your ideals, then work diligently to achieve them. Your ideals set standards for you, and they are excellent guides for choices which can transform your life. The Cayce readings pointed out frequently that, if we wish to make our lives successful in the highest sense, we must establish our ideals and live according to them.

The dictionary defines an ideal as "a conception of something in its perfection; a standard of perfection or excellence" *(Random House College Dictionary)*. That sounds great. What are your ideals? If you are like I was when I was first confronted with that question, you don't know. I quickly came up with some high-sounding phrases to cover up my ignorance and confusion. But I knew I didn't know what they were and I'm sure the person who asked me the question was also aware that I didn't know. My phrases bore little relation to me and my life.

Actually we all have ideals. Our problem is that they may be misdirected—like those held by a bank robber, or by the tycoon whose only ideal is to make a lot of money, or by Joe whose ideal is to have a car bigger than Jim's, or by Mary whose ideal is to marry a rich man. These are ideals of a sort. They're O.K. for those individuals and they may indeed achieve such ideals. Those kinds of ideals, however, will not bring happiness because they are founded on a limited base. We need to set ideals on a higher level because the readings caution us that:

. . . those activities of man or woman in the earth may not excel . . . the individual's ideal. (3407-1)

When you hold limited ideals—such as in the examples described above—you actually restrict yourself, because you use ideals in important ways of which you are not even aware. For example:

1. Your ideals are the standards by which you make your choices. They are like a road map which you use to guide you to your destination.
2. Your ideals set the attitudes by which you live.
3. Your ideals determine the path and the direction in which you are moving in consciousness.
4. Your ideals determine what and whom you attract to you as you put them into effect.
5. Your ideals provide the balancing tie among body, mind, and soul. Through them you coordinate the Spirit within, the mind, and your physical aspects.

Clearly anything that affects you and your life in such vital ways should be well thought out and should be something you have developed and chosen from the highest consciousness you can achieve.

As you know, Cayce gave readings for thousands of people with difficulties and problems of every imaginable kind. As part of the solution, he often recommended that these individuals set ideals for themselves—not just general ideals, but spiritual ideals, mental ideals, and physical ideals—so all the basic aspects of life would be in accord. We have at least a three-dimensional consciousness and must fully recognize and work with all three elements—spirit, mind, and physical—if we are going to deal with ourselves in a holistic manner.[1]

Setting your ideals to the highest levels of which you can conceive and choosing to live by them can bring you these benefits:

1. Enable you to change your consciousness by establishing guideposts for living in accord with your Higher Self and so change your life for the better.
2. Set a definite direction for your pathway of life and provide a guide for making the best possible decisions for your life.
3. Help in resolving the difficult areas of life.
4. Bring you joy and contentment.

5. Become the guides for you in your use of the Universal Laws and in your creative efforts so that what you create is truly what you want to have in your life and is of benefit to all.
6. Bring greater balance into your life and enable you to live a more holistic life.
7. Enable you to be a positive influence on others in your life.

Knowing your ideals and using them are essential for effective application of the Universal Laws and vital for use of the Higher Laws.[2] Setting your ideals gives foundation and direction and a quality of motivation to achieving your transformation.

Following is a workshop through which you can establish your ideals. I urge you to work with this now.

IDEALS WORKSHOP[3]

Complete each step before moving on to the next.
Materials needed:
1.   Circular Ideals Chart (see Figure 16)
2.   Pencil or pen

STEP #1: SELECTION OF YOUR AREA OF FOCUS

A. Select from the following list an area of your life that you would like to make more joyous or choose one of your own:

spouse	**health**	**family**
self	**spiritual growth**	**time**
children	**a relative**	**school**
job	**recreation**	**church**
finances	**social life**	**education**
		(Others) _____
		_____
		_____

B. When you have selected the area, write it on the Circular Ideals Chart, Figure 16, on the line marked #1 in Quadrant A.

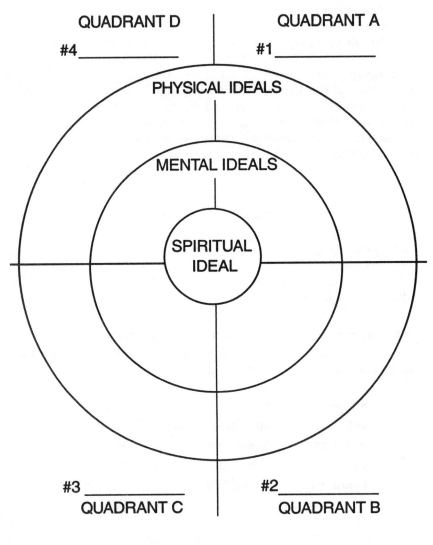

QUADRANT D   QUADRANT A

#4 _____   #1 _____

PHYSICAL IDEALS

MENTAL IDEALS

SPIRITUAL
IDEAL

#3 _____   #2 _____
QUADRANT C   QUADRANT B

FIGURE 16

C. Your ideals for this area of your life will be entered on this upper right-hand quadrant of the chart.

STEP #2: SELECTION OF YOUR SPIRITUAL IDEAL

A. Study the following "fruits" or "seeds" of the Spirit, any one of which would make an excellent spiritual ideal:

love	mercy	meekness
truth	gentleness	peace
hope	kindness	obedience
persistence	self-control	humbleness
patience	brotherly love	harmony
faith	fellowship	understanding
goodness	consistency in acts and speech	selflessness
contentment	forgiveness	joy

B. To make your selection, use either option 1 or 2 below—whichever feels right to you:

Option 1. After a period of meditation, turn inward and search in your mind for the most joyous, fulfilling spiritual experience you have ever known. This might have been a conversation with someone, a dream, a vision, something you have read that was meaningful to you, or another form of experience. Review it in your mind, trying to experience its essence, and describe it in one word or short phrase (possibly one of the above). This will be your spiritual ideal. Write it on the Circular Ideals Chart in the center circle labeled SPIRITUAL IDEAL.

Option 2. To select your spiritual ideal, attune yourself in whatever way works best for you and use your preferred method of obtaining guidance. Ask what your ideal should be, or select from the list above. When you have found or selected it, write it on the Circular Ideals Chart in the center circle labeled SPIRITUAL IDEAL.

STEP #3: SELECTION OF MENTAL IDEALS

A. The mental ideal you are about to select is for application in that area of your life that you wish to make more joyous. This is the area you selected in Step 1 and marked on line #1.

B. The mental ideal is a "be"-attitude, the attitude you will hold in this area of your life. It needs to be in accord with your spiritual ideal. It is as if the spiritual ideal actually flows into the mental attitudes or emotions and together they produce the mental ideal.

C. Therefore, ask yourself: "What 'be-attitude,' what attitude of 'be'-ing, should I hold and use that is in accord with my spiritual ideal and will make this area of my life more joyous?"

SOME POSSIBLE SUGGESTIONS

BE-loving	BE-self-controlled	BE-hopeful
BE-gentle	BE-brotherly love	BE-persistent
BE-kind	BE-understanding	BE-patient
BE-merciful	BE-appreciative	BE-faithful
BE-truthful	BE-harmonious	BE-selfless
BE-content	BE-constructive	BE-thoughtful
BE-positive	BE-generous (giving)	BE-tolerant
BE-good	BE-helpful	BE-cooperative
BE-joyous	BE-encouraging	BE-forgiving
BE-meek	BE-happy	BE-disciplined
BE-peaceful	BE-moderate	BE-honest
BE-humble	BE-sincere	BE-a servant
BE-confident	BE-compassionate	BE-just
BE-trustful	BE-temperate	BE-graceful
BE-one		(Others) _____

_____

_____

D. You may wish to select more than one of the above or ones of your own choosing. Enter your choices on the ideals chart in the section of the circle in Quadrant A marked MENTAL IDEALS.

STEP #4: SELECTION OF PHYSICAL IDEALS

A. Your physical ideals are what you will be "do"-ing to bring into expression/manifestation on the physical plane the spiritual and mental ideals you have set for this area of your life.

B. The physical ideals can be expressed through the ways in which you use various aspects of your physical body or your possessions. For example, ask yourself, "How can I use my ears to manifest my mental ideal of being cooperative?" Your answer might be: "Listen to Jane." That would then be one of your physical ideals. You may wish to select several for each area of your life.

ears	sharing know-how	legs	sex
eyes	sharing possessions	feet	words
nose	sharing facilities	hands	song
mouth	furniture	house	time
car	recipes	face	arms
money	clothes	tools	effort
voice	energy	food	(Others) _____
			_____
			_____

C. As you make your selections, write them in the section of the circle marked PHYSICAL IDEALS in Quadrant A.

D. Your chart should now look similar to Figure 17. This shows an ideals chart with Quadrant A completed.

STEP #5: COMPLETION OF IDEALS CHART

Return to Step 1 and select **another** area of your life you wish to make more joyous. Enter this on line #2 in Quadrant B.

Skip Step #2—The spiritual ideal you have selected applies to **all** areas of your life.

Do Step 3 and Step 4 for this same area of your life.

Repeat this procedure for as many areas of your life for which you wish to set ideals.

To be effective you need to review your ideals daily, to make them a part of your consciousness. Work with each, trying to achieve it. As you achieve each ideal, you will need to change or modify it. Your ideals should grow with you.

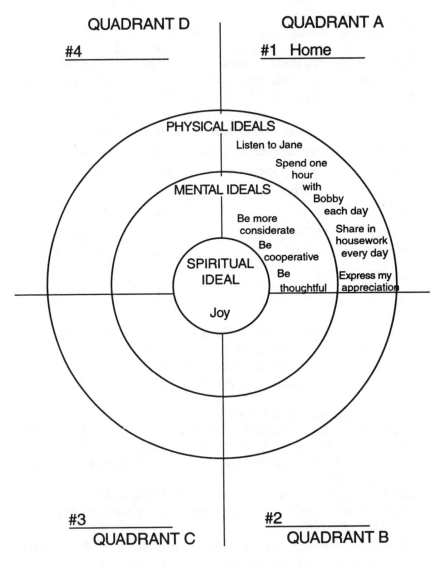

QUADRANT D   QUADRANT A

#4 _____   #1   Home_____

PHYSICAL IDEALS
Listen to Jane
Spend one
hour
with
MENTAL IDEALS   Bobby
                       each day
Be more
considerate   Share in
Be   housework
cooperative   every day
SPIRITUAL
Be   Express my
IDEAL
thoughtful   appreciation
Joy

#3 _____   #2 _____
QUADRANT C   QUADRANT B

FIGURE 17

PROGRESS ON THE PATH OF UNIVERSAL LAW

It is time to look back and see our progression in taking the steps to higher consciousness. Figure 18 shows we've made much progress—but we've further yet to go!

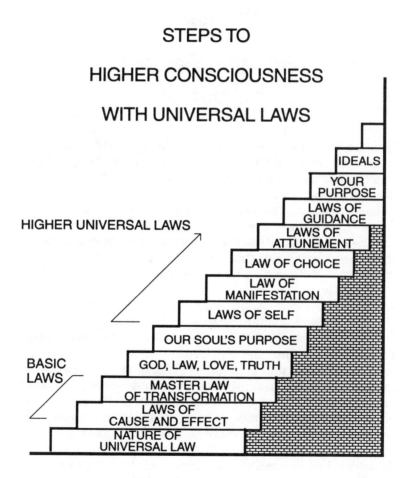

STEPS TO

HIGHER CONSCIOUSNESS

WITH UNIVERSAL LAWS

IDEALS

YOUR PURPOSE

LAWS OF GUIDANCE

HIGHER UNIVERSAL LAWS

LAWS OF ATTUNEMENT

LAW OF CHOICE

LAW OF MANIFESTATION

LAWS OF SELF

OUR SOUL'S PURPOSE

GOD, LAW, LOVE, TRUTH

BASIC LAWS

MASTER LAW OF TRANSFORMATION

LAWS OF CAUSE AND EFFECT

NATURE OF UNIVERSAL LAW

FIGURE 18

Chapter 17

Bringing Balance
to Your Life

Balance is a state of equilibrium—of health on the physical level, fulfillment on the mental level, and joyousness on the spiritual level. Balance is handling all aspects of life in a way that results in the greatest good for you and for others.

Imbalance in our lives is akin to an unbalanced wheel on a car, a vibration that signals a destructive condition. In our lives imbalance can create difficulties that disturb us, that grow in magnitude, that limit our activities, that frustrate us in achieving our goals, that use up our energy, and eventually destroy our ability to function effectively.

What we truly seek—to be the gods and goddesses we can be—is a dynamic balance, a condition in which we are attuned and aware, flexible and capable. Then we can travel the road of life, taking all of it, including its bumps, tough climbs, and sharp curves with understanding, poise, and composure, handling each aspect of it in ways that are joyous and fulfilling to us and inspiring to others. A dynamic balance is one that flexes, moves, shifts, and adjusts to meet new challenges, allows us to learn from them, to change and grow, and through it all to move to a condition of equilibrium regardless of what happens.

Consider that we are trying to balance in three dimensions. Only one of the dimensions, the physical, is visible. We cannot even see the mental and spiritual. Each dimension needs to be balanced in itself and also balanced with the other dimensions.

REASONS FOR BALANCE

Without dynamic balance, we don't have the essential ingredient for transformation, and we cannot achieve the purpose for which we came in the present experience.[1] When we become ill, which is the result of an imbalance, the illness can completely disrupt our work, our family life, our recreation, or any other activity or interest we may have. When we create such conditions, it is a cry from our hearts for greater balance in our lives. If we recognize this underlying need, then find and correct the area of imbalance, we will have made another step in our transformation. Better still is to work for balance in each area of our lives so that we do not have to learn our lessons the hard way.

THE LAW OF BALANCE

The law of balance is founded on the fundamental nature of the universe: love. It provides that all interactions within the universe are *equal* exchanges. It insures that balance will always be maintained in the universe for the law is:[2]

ALL EXCHANGES BALANCE

Obviously not all exchanges are balanced. This law means that *eventually* they are balanced. That is the nature of the Universe. If we don't make a balanced exchange, the Universe will balance it — at our expense!

We can enjoy a balanced life by knowing and living in accord with this law — by making equal or positive exchanges. One of the basic causes of human troubles is disregard of this law.

Any exchange that you make is balanced when what you give is equal to or greater than what you receive. If you give less than you receive, there is an imbalance which remains; by this law you will eventually have to face that imbalance and deal with it. A simple example — on the physical level — would be: If you sell something and feel that what you sell is worth what you receive, the exchange is balanced as far as your involvement is concerned.

If you are the buyer, and you feel that what you pay is worth what you receive, then your interchange is balanced.

The criterion for balance does not involve the other person's view or opinion. It is personal. You only need to meet the standards of the Spirit within you, which is a loving Spirit. No matter how the interchange may be made, you will know subconsciously, if not consciously, whether you met the criterion of giving in equal measure to what you receive. When you do give equal to what you receive, the exchange then is a balanced one and there is no effect on you or the universe. When you give greater than what you receive, there is a positive balance (not an imbalance) in your favor because you are in accord with the purpose of the Universe.

Another example: As noted earlier, when you are out of balance in the treatment of yourself, illness can result. You are not making an equal exchange in some area of your life. You may be overworking, and the illness may be the way which you have unconsciously created to balance this discrepancy by requiring rest.

You are so constituted that when you make an exchange that isn't neutral or positively balanced, you create within yourself the difference (the imbalance) that is needed to equalize the transaction. *You* keep score within yourself, either for you or against you. If you act in accord with love—the fundamental principle of the Universe—and give more than you receive, the score is positive. If you give less than you receive, the result is a negative and takes the form of a tension. The troubles that you or I or the world are suffering from today are the result of an accumulation of such tensions. If these tensions are not resolved, the increasing imbalance can eventually destroy the underlying structure, whether it's the life of an individual, a family, a corporation, or a country.[3] The results of such tensions may manifest personally in many ways—as illness, confusion, overweight, fatigue, anger, frustration, as problems reflecting the cause of the tension. On the national level, they may manifest as strikes, riots, wars, and other such disasters.

We also know the positive and the negative scores which we create through the law of balance as karma. This law gives us an understanding of how we create our karma and a reason, based on Universal Law, of why karma exists. Our so-called "bad" karma is the result of the negative imbalances we have created in our exchanges.

There are four broad areas of interchange in our lives:

1. Interchanges with our environment
2. Interchanges with others (individuals and groups)
3. Interchanges with self (physical, mental, spiritual)
4. Interchanges with the Creative Forces.

ENVIRONMENTAL INTERCHANGE

The world's realization of the importance of the environment has brought constructive changes in protection by individuals and government. We ignored the law of balance with the earth's environment for so long that the resultant accumulation of imbalances produced life-threatening conditions. We have been forced to recognize our mistakes and to begin to take action to restore balance. I hope it is not too little and too late.

INTERCHANGES WITH OTHERS

Universal Laws are inherently laws of balance, insuring equalization in the universe by making every exchange equal. For example: "For every effect there is a cause," "like begets like," and "as you sow you reap" are statements of balance as well as laws governing interchanges.

Know that if we want to create good effects, we need to use the laws in the highest way we can—by applying the fruits of the Spirit in our lives. As we act with love, peace, joy, and kindness, we balance our exchanges with others or make positive ones, and so are in accord with the law of balance.

INTERCHANGES WITH SELF

The responsibility for keeping your life balanced is totally yours. Balance or imbalance depends on the interchanges you make within yourself on the physical, mental, and spiritual levels. Balancing is not just a one-time effort, but a continuous process. Life is constantly changing, and we need to continually rebalance. Much of this we do inherently and naturally.

THE PHYSICAL LEVEL

If we're not in good health, we're out of balance in some way. We can start a program of balance by changing how we treat our bodies. This is not just a physical process. We need to love ourselves enough to take excellent care of our bodies. This involves the spiritual—loving ourselves and seeking guidance within. It also requires the mental—finding the best ways of healing through doctors, medicine, prayer, exercise, or whatever else is needed. Each physical activity we perform is an exchange to which the law of balance applies.

Exercise can be wonderful if done in a balanced way—not too easy and not too strenuous, but just right for our condition.

Eating requires balance in both content and quantity. There is good reason for the readings' insistence that we deal first with our physical problems. When we are in ill health or in poor physical condition, we are less effective mentally and spiritually, for the body is not in balance. We are not taking care of the temple of the Presence within.[4]

THE MENTAL LEVEL

We make interchanges on the mental level by thoughts and beliefs about ourselves, conditions, things, others, and our relationships. We need to analyze self and do all we can to straighten out the mental before we try to balance it with the physical and the spiritual. For example: If, on the mental level, we worry about a certain problem, condition, or person, such an approach will usually bring us more to worry about, for "like begets like." Many readings cautioned against worry:

> (Q) What may be done to overcome the worry?
> (A) Quit worrying! (294-134)
> (Q) How may the body better leave off the mental worries . . . ?
> (A) Fill the mind with something else! (294-91)
> Worry does not change anything. (295-5)

So eliminating unnecessary and debilitating worry will help us balance the mental.

INTERCHANGES WITH THE CREATIVE FORCES

In previous chapters we emphasized the need for conscious exchange with the Creative Forces. In deciding how to apply the law of balance, we are often not the best judges of ourselves. Again Cayce's source tells us that help is readily available from our inner self, which gives us an informal way of obtaining that guidance:

> As in studies of all natures, as in studies of how to play, how to rest, how to read, how to make for better social attainments and the like. Think on these things, then *leave* them to your inner self and work at them as they present themselves in their proper order. (257-173)AR

Tapping the wisdom of the inner self is a simple process:

1. **Study and think about the question, problem, or condition that concerns you.**

2. **Leave it to your inner self for a period of time.**

3. **Be open to guidance which comes; it may be thoughts, ideas, concepts, spiritual occurrences, hunches, gut feelings, things that don't readily translate into the mental or into orderly, logical phenomena. But they are valid, important, exciting evidence of the workings of the Divine within you. Work with and use the guidance you receive.**

This help is available to every one of us. Some people use it all the time; others only as a last resort. The more you use it, the better it will work for you. Especially important to maintaining balance and stability in your life is to check with your higher self before taking action on any important issue. Stop, think, and check out your decision. This will save you from taking actions that create crises, problems, and imbalance.[5]

The readings give us seven tools to achieve greater balance in any aspect of life:

TOOL #1: ANALYZE SELF

One example of this tool—analyze self—is the case of a young mother who devoted herself totally to the needs of her children, husband, and others without consideration for herself. She developed a serious health problem. The best of medical help gave no relief. She told me that in desperation she sat down and began to analyze her life. She had a very practical approach. She first listed everything she did in a day and throughout a month, from the moment she awoke until she went to sleep. She began to study the list and ask herself: Why am I doing this? How do I feel about it? Does it give me a lift, or a pain, a headache, a peaceful feeling, or a knot in the belly? Here is one example of her analysis:

"When I go to see so-and-so, is it to impress them, or someone else, or because I have to, or is it a joy to return joy given?

"When I dress, do I have a good feeling, am I content or am I unhappy with my clothes, with myself, or do I want to change myself? Why? When I look at myself in a mirror can I honestly say 'You are great' or 'You are a rubber-stamp' (that is: just doing the same thing over and over that others expect of you)."

She was doing a wonderful job of learning to know herself. When she found a point of tension such as pain, unhappiness, fear, or anger, she realized it signaled an imbalance. She began to work to restore balance in that interchange. Such work required changing what she was doing, why she was doing it, her attitude about it, or whatever created the pain, unhappiness, fear, or anger. As she did this and began to achieve a balance in her life, the illness disappeared.

TOOL #2: TIME AND BALANCE

One of Cayce's most enthusiastic clients was a sales executive who had more than 200 readings. He repeatedly asked questions about management of his mental and physical condition and was repeatedly advised to get his life into better balance by budgeting his time. Why? Because **a time budget insures that no important aspect of our lives is neglected.** His readings suggested that he budget his time for these activities, essential for all of us:[6]

1. **Work and associated aspects**

2. **Play—mental and physical recreation**

3. **Development of mental and physical abilities**

4. **Eating**

5. **Rest, relaxation, recuperation, and sleep**

6. **Social activities**

7. **Spiritual activities and meditation, study and time for self**

Those items were to include, where appropriate:

A. Activities which have special appeal, such as hobbies

B. Activities to keep body and mind ever alert and in accord with purposes, needs, wants, and desires of self

C. Activities to improve the material surroundings

D. Activities to appreciate the values of all aspects of life

E. Activities to be of service to others

F. Activities which are necessary, such as buying groceries

These lists give you essential activities to include in your time budget. I suggest using a chart (see Figures 19A and 19B) to schedule your activities to assure that you don't neglect any essential aspects of living, as just listed. That does not mean they should be given equal time; rather, they should receive equal consideration.

Don't impose your schedule on others in your household or expect others to adjust their schedules to fit yours.

TOOL #3: BALANCING THE SPIRITUAL, MENTAL, AND PHYSICAL

The importance of budgeting your time cannot be overemphasized. If you do it with understanding, you can achieve one of the most important aspects of balance. The readings explain:

[Keep] an equal balance in the physical, mental and spiritual aspects of the body-functioning . . . For, every phase of the physical, mental and spiritual life is dependent upon the other. They are one, as the Father-God is one. (2533-3)

We can live an unbalanced life for long periods of time, but results inevitably will materialize. This is true no matter how well intentioned you may be or how beneficial you think your activities are.

A young minister I know chose a small church so that he could really work with the people. He loved the teaching, the classes, the counseling, the spiritual challenge, and giving the Sunday sermon; he devoted himself totally to these endeavors and was highly successful. About three years later, on a day that a counseling appointment was cancelled, he realized that he felt a great sense of relief, that the Sunday sermon had become a chore, and that he didn't want to talk to anyone. He was burned out. He had not maintained a balance among the spiritual, mental, and physical. He had to tell his church Board that he needed a rest—a time to get himself in balance.[7]

It is equally easy to become a mental giant, but a spiritual and physical pygmy, or a physical giant and a mental and spiritual pygmy.

Balancing the spiritual, mental, and physical does not mean they must have equal time, rather each must be given *equal emphasis*.

BUDGETING MY TIME

TIME	SUNDAY	MONDAY	TUESDAY	WEDNESDAY	THURSDAY	FRIDAY	SATURDAY
6 a.m.							
7							
8							
9							
10							
11							
12 noon							
1 p.m.							
2							

FIGURE 19A

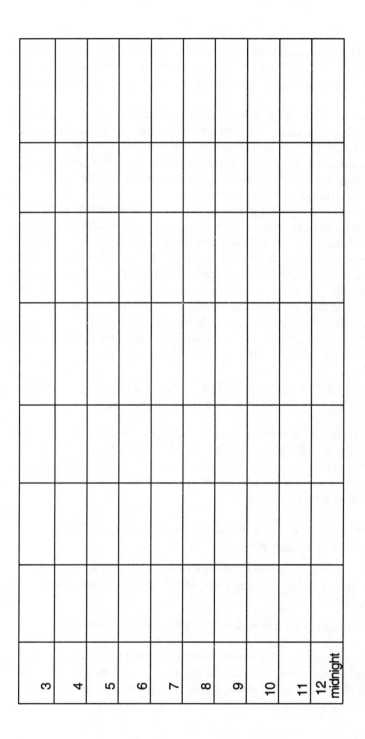

FIGURE 19B

This means that you don't neglect one for another. To keep physically fit may only require half an hour a day of good aerobic exercise. The point is to be sure that the exercises are done effectively and consistently.

For spiritual balance, maintain a prayer and meditation time. Even half an hour a day can contribute greatly to your spiritual "fitness" if it is effectively and consistently utilized.

For mental balance, if your work is not mentally challenging, find something outside of it that is—a good book, a course, or learning about something that appeals to you.

Your daily work may be primarily physical, or mental, or spiritual, depending on your vocation. In most cases, it is some mixture of the three. Analyze your work and your participation in it to estimate how much of each aspect is involved. Make a list of actions you can take to create greater balance. For example, regardless of the work you do, you can shift the emphasis of your day to the spiritual by changing your attitudes about work and about others. Simply apply the fruits of the Spirit or silently use affirmations or short prayers as you go about your day. Treat others lovingly, and you will transform any job into a spiritual experience.

TOOL #4: KEEP YOUR ACTIVITIES IN ACCORD WITH YOUR PURPOSE AND MISSION

Dynamic balance is only achieved through effective use of: (1) your life's purpose, (2) your ideals, and (3) spiritual guidance in your life. You can check how well you are doing in achieving dynamic balance by reviewing your weekly activities and asking these questions about each activity:

1. **Is this activity in accord with or contributing to achievement of my purpose?**

2. **In this activity are my thoughts and attitudes, words and acts in accord with my spiritual, mental, and physical ideals?**

3. **Is this activity in accord with my spiritual guidance?**

If you can answer "yes" to those three questions, you have made a team of your spirit, mind, and body; they are coordinated and cooperative. If you cannot answer "yes," you have changes to make for a better balance.

TOOL #5: FLEXIBILITY

Don't set up rigid rules and regulations for yourself. They make life a drudge rather than a pleasure.[8]

When we budget our time, we are making a plan. Plans should never be cast in concrete, but should be like a road map. They show the best way to go, but if the happenings of the moment make an alternate course advisable, take it. It's essential to allow in each day's schedule some unbudgeted time for unexpected interruptions, changes, or whatever becomes necessary or has special appeal at the moment. This keeps your schedule from becoming too rigid or too extreme and makes it more practical and enjoyable.

A friend gave me a technique which recognizes the need for a schedule, yet allows me to keep in tune with my inner guidance:

Begin with whatever plan you've already made for the day. As soon as you hit a glitch, an obstacle, a problem, an irritation, or whatever derails your plan, be aware that you've just tripped over one of the threads in the weavings of Spirit. Allow your awareness (body, mind, and spirit) to rest lightly on this glitch and see what comes to you. If something does, take it up at once and go where it leads. *Never argue with yourself about it.* When you come to a stopping point, pick up your original plan and go on until another anomalous thing manifests itself. Then follow it. And so on. In this way, you can live the adventures of Spirit, and you will become more and more unified, and be able to live longer and longer outside The Illusion [the limitations of the structured world]. This exercise builds faith, partly because the world revealed is much stranger than fiction and is not governed by the logic of a human's conscious mind. To accept and continue at all requires a leap of faith.[9]

TOOL #6: MODERATION; AVOID EXCESS

To become a top-notch business person or a social lion or a great spiritual teacher is not enough. There must be a well-rounded balance with moderation in all we do and in all our relationships.[10]

The well-rounded aspect of balance includes having the ability to play as well as work, to relax as well as to drive yourself, and to be appreciative of the finer aspects of life as well as of material success.

The readings urge "Moderation in all things, excess in none" (294-7) and point out that "Some people use the theory that if it is good for a little, more would be better. Usually, more is worse—in most anything. The best is to keep well balanced . . . " (1861-16)P

"[*Be normal*], not extreme in any manner! and there will be shown you day by day that which will be the necessary for your *own* development." (5752-2)P [See also reading 1885-2.]

We need to analyze self frequently to keep from becoming lop-sided; most of us don't stay balanced but become overzealous about one phase of life without proper consideration for its other aspects.[11]

To achieve success in anything at the expense of your body, your mind, your home, your marriage, or your relation with Spirit will prevent you from achieving a true contentment, an inherent spiritual need and desire of every person.[12]

It isn't that those things which satisfy the mind or the physical body are tabu; rather, each of them are to be used in moderation so they become beneficial rather than detrimental to you and in your dealings with others.[13]

TOOL #7: STABILITY

Do not allow discouraging and disorderly events in others' lives disturb your equilibrium. Their problems are not yours unless you choose to make them so.

Balance creates stability. If you react to a friend's difficulties by being angry or sad, you are allowing outside forces to affect your stability. That's not helpful to you or to your friend.[14]

When someone criticizes you, instead of feeling angry you can try to keep your sense of balance. If that person's negative energy is beginning to unbalance you, send them love.[15] As you do, you restore your balance because you have tapped the higher power within you. Remember, if people are angry with you, that's their problem, not yours. Don't make it yours by becoming emotionally involved. Look at it from a balanced and stable state. You then can more readily find the true message the Universe is sending to you. Nothing happens by chance, so there is something there for you, generally different than the angry words indicate. Recognize that the person is doing you a favor and be thankful for the outburst.

BALANCE AND WHOLENESS

Riane Eisler, author of *The Chalice and the Blade*, shows through research of archaeological and historical records that our world once was a world of peace. Put another way, it was a world of greater balance than we know today.[16] She concludes that the peaceful condition resulted from more balanced relationships between the sexes—a partnership, so to speak. Our present male-dominated world is clearly out of balance. As a result, we have tremendous challenges and problems. Under the Universal Laws, there is no gender distinction. The more nearly we can approach this nondistinction, the more balanced our world will become. We also achieve greater equality and wholeness as individuals when we work to balance our feminine and masculine natures within self.

We are body, mind, and spirit; these are one. The way we can become whole, balanced persons is to live in a holistic manner by fully recognizing, honoring, and coordinating all three aspects of our being in all that we do.[17] We are then living from inner to outer and, therefore, reflecting our inherent wholeness of which balance is a vital element.

Chapter 18

Law of Belief

The law of belief is a fascinating one because it shows us that our beliefs actually manifest in our lives, even though we may not know what they are or where they originate! It is another law of manifestation. The law of belief is:

AS YOU BELIEVE, SO IT BECOMES FOR YOU

Jesus taught the law of belief in this way: " . . . as thou hast believed, so be it done unto thee." (Matthew 8:13, KJV)

The phrase "as you believe" as used in this Universal Law refers not only to religious concepts, but to all that you think or feel is true about yourself, any aspect of life, or your understanding of how anything operates. One dictionary defines belief as "mental acceptance or conviction in the truth or actuality of something."[1]

OUR BELIEFS

Our beliefs are the base from which we apply the Universal Laws, which are the major determinants in creating every aspect of our lives. Our beliefs are also the filters through which we screen all that comes to us as well as all that we think, say, and do. Beliefs are the basics of our consciousness. If we are going to transform our consciousness, we need to change our beliefs.

The operation of the law of belief can be understood in terms of the law of attraction, "like attracts like." Since our beliefs, in a great sense, are what we are like, we attract that which is in accord with our beliefs and it becomes a part of our lives. "As you believe, so it becomes for you."

Our beliefs also create through the law of cause: "As thought, purpose, aim, and desire are set in motion by our minds, their effect is as a condition that is." Since our thoughts and purposes and aims and desires come from our beliefs and are shaped by them, we see how our belief structure is a major causative factor in our lives and why the law is "as you believe, so it becomes for you." It doesn't matter what kind of belief you hold. It may be completely erroneous, but the law works for you, and your life is as if that belief were factual. Here's a simple example from the past: In the time of Columbus, the prevailing belief was that the world was flat, so it was thought that if you went beyond known limits, you would go over the edge. Consequently, no one ventured farther. To them, it was as if the world really was flat. Columbus, however, believed the world was round, so he was able to live and act in accord with that belief.

WHAT DO YOU BELIEVE?

Most of us are not consciously aware of all that we believe. In addition to our conscious learning, our beliefs consist of much unconscious "programming" as well as carryover material from previous experiences and other sources. We are unaware of the extent of either. As a result, we create our lives from beliefs which we don't even know exist within us. That situation doesn't have to continue. **Every happening in your life comes as a result of some belief you hold. Each happening is, therefore, an opportunity to examine and change that belief, if you want to**. Any difficulty is a red flag raised by the Universe to let you know you have a belief that is not in accord with the Universe's flow and love. These flags may appear as financial problems, difficulties in a relationship, or any unhappy aspect of your life. Be thankful for them and seek the lesson each holds for you. That lesson will show you where your belief needs to be changed to create for yourself greater happiness.

For example, a woman might look at her life and become aware that she repeatedly attracts men who turn out to be "no good," according to her standards. Life is telling her she holds the belief that men are no good. By the law "as you believe, so it becomes for you," "no-good" men are manifested in her life. Her first step to correct this condition is to accept—without any self-condemnation or self-judgment—that she has that belief. The second step is to ask herself whether she really wants to continue believing it. If not, she can release that belief. The release of an undesirable belief can, in most cases, be done very easily—if you believe it can. Release it and substitute a more positive belief. Of course, if you think that releasing the belief is difficult for you to do, it will be—in accord with the operation of this law.

Whatever new belief you substitute for the old one should be in accord with your purpose and ideals. We are continually bombarded with others' ideas of what we should believe. Only *your* inner guidance knows what is best for *you*. Consider the ideas from other sources, but check them with your inner guidance.

In some cases in which the belief you hold is the result of deep emotional involvement or trauma, professional counseling may be necessary to release it. One such source, the Option Institute and Fellowship, originated with Barry and Suzi Kaufman, who brought their own son from the "incurable" illness of autism to a highly verbal, extroverted, happy young man, with a near-genius I.Q. Their work now includes adults and adolescents, as well as children. Basic to the process they use is in-depth work on beliefs, showing how happiness and love are possible as a sustained experience, not just in the future, but today. The Option Institute has tapes, books, and programs that provide a process by which you can discover and change your beliefs.[2]

BELIEF, CONSCIOUSNESS, AND ACHIEVEMENT

Since our belief structure is such a basic part of our consciousness, the law of belief is key to transformation of our consciousness. Recognizing this, Eric Butterworth, author, lecturer, and spiritual teacher, gives a basic concept for transformation as a simple formula:

$$C + B = A$$

In other words: **That which you can conceive (C), plus that which you can believe (B), is that which you can achieve (A).**[3]

We conceive through the creative process of the law of cause by establishing our thoughts, purposes, aims, and desires. To do this from the highest consciousness requires attunement first to Spirit. Mind is the builder and will build what you conceive through the Universal Laws and Creative Forces, if you believe that it is possible and that it can and will be done. This is the certainty, the expectancy you must provide. To the degree these ingredients are present and not negated by interfering doubts or fears or misapplication of other laws, you will achieve that which you conceived and believed.

You do not need to know how you will achieve your goal. This can be a step-by-step process in which you hold the ultimate goal in mind and each day conceive and achieve the next step until you finally reach your goal.

Like all laws, the law of belief is impartial. You may conceive a great idea. If you believe you can make it fly, you will. If you also hold a belief that you cannot succeed or you fear success, you will bring the idea to a point of success and then make decisions that will cause you to fail. I have seen this happen in business. Searching out and releasing fear-based beliefs can completely change the results.

We usually think of achievement in terms of material success. The laws are not so limited. They work equally well to provide peace, joy, patience, love, and other conditions. Such goals of your transformation are in accord with the purpose of the Universe and can bring greater contentment than material goals alone. **Only through seeking these god-like aspects, as well as our material goals, can we achieve contentment and fulfillment**.

There is a warning about seeking material goals only. You can, by the powers of mind and physical effort alone, achieve great wealth and great fame. The price you pay, however, may be enormous—in broken health, in ruined relationships, and in lack of fulfillment. It is not necessary to pay such a price. You can achieve such goals if your seeking is based on guidance by attunement to Spirit. As you do that, believing that your material and other needs will be met, they will be, by law. It is the question of what path of belief you choose to follow: the high road, guided by the Spirit within you, or the low road, guided only by your mind and mass-mind consciousness.

HIGHLIGHTS OF THIS CHAPTER

The law of belief is:

AS YOU BELIEVE, SO IT BECOMES FOR YOU

Your life reflects your beliefs. To change your life, change your beliefs.

That which you can conceive, plus that which you can believe, is that which you can achieve.

Chapter 19

Nothing Is Impossible

THE LAW OF FAITH

The readings referred occasionally to the law of faith, but I could not find a specific statement about this law. Jesus taught the law as:

"WHATEVER YOU ASK IN PRAYER,
YOU WILL RECEIVE, IF YOU HAVE FAITH."
(Matthew 21:22, RSV)

Most of us can recall times when we asked in prayer but didn't receive what we asked for. It is clear from the law that asking without any faith in the power of Spirit doesn't put the law in operation. When you do pray and ask with faith in Spirit, you bring the Creative Forces into play and the results are assured—*if* you have not previously set other laws into operation that counter your request. For example, you might have created through karmic laws a condition in your life which is there to teach you a lesson. This could be a financial, health, relationship, or other problem. You may ask with faith for that condition to be resolved. It will be, but only when you have learned the lesson that that condition is bringing to you. It may take years or lifetimes for you to make this step. So it seems that your asking is in vain. Also, the resolution of the problem may not occur in the way you want it resolved. The Universe always operates for the highest and best good for all concerned. Sometimes we are unable to recognize this fact when it occurs, so it may seem that our prayer is not being answered.

Another example is the situation in which we ask with faith for healing for self or another, and death is the result. Death can often be a healing, of the highest and best for all concerned. It is not imposed by God but comes through the laws which that person set in operation. With our limited view and understanding, we often do not see it that way and erroneously think that our asking is in vain or that we do not have enough faith.

The Universe is aware that we, as souls, do not die but are eternal; that the passing of the body is another step forward in our development. Therefore, death in the universal sense is a positive change, rather than the very negative view most of us take of it.

Because the law of faith is a Universal Law, we can be assured it will always work. We must also recognize that we or others for whom we pray often have other agendas and may have put other laws into operation that will affect the results.

PRAYER

The law of faith is a Universal Law which is spiritual in nature. To comprehend and apply it effectively, you need to understand the basics of its two spiritual elements: prayer and faith. What is prayer? It is not a technique nor is it just a way of making requests of Spirit. Rather,

> Prayer is the concerted effort of the physical consciousness to become attuned to the consciousness of the Creator, either collectively or individually! (281-13)

Prayer is a process of attuning yourself to reach a higher point of view—of wholeness, of understanding, of oneness with Spirit. As previously discussed, there are many ways of making that attunement.

Charles Fillmore, co-founder of Silent Unity, an organization which has maintained continuous prayer twenty-four hours a day for over a hundred years, challenges our prayer practice with these seven necessary [ideal] conditions for truly effective prayer:[1]

1. God should be recognized as Father-Mother.
2. Oneness with God should be acknowledged.
3. Prayer must be made within, in "the secret place" (Psalm 91).
4. The door must be closed on all thoughts and interests of the outer world.
5. The one who prays must believe that he or she has received.

6. The kingdom of God [Christ Consciousness] must be desired above all things and sought first.

7. The mind must let go of every unforgiving thought.

FAITH

I previously noted that faith is an important foundation for attunement. It is one of the fruits of the Spirit. You have it and I have it; it is as inherent in us as our eyes and nose. **Faith is simply the ability to perceive that through the infinite power and wisdom of the Spirit within, working through the Universal Laws, nothing is impossible**. Remember, the inherent nature of that Spirit includes all the power you need, plus the perfect pattern and the guidance to achieve it; so, indeed, anything is possible. You, by your free will, can choose to have two percent faith or 100 percent faith in the infinite possibilities of the Spirit within. We block faith with doubts and fears. What can we do about them?

> For, live each day as if you were to meet Him the next; in that expectancy, in that glory, and let not those things that would hinder have a place in your consciousness. Thus do *His* children, His brethren, manifest that faith that removes mountains. (262-46)AR

We can move step by step from "those things that would hinder" to faith. We can release the doubts and fears by giving them no energy and no thought, turning instead to Spirit within for guidance. As our mind builds from that base, we can first hope. Then, as those hopes are realized, we gain confidence in our guidance. As our confidence grows, we begin to trust. Then our trust grows. As we, through experience, see that we can truly trust the Spirit within, we finally realize that **as we use our mind directed by Spirit in applying the Universal Laws, nothing is impossible and everything is possible—we have arrived at faith.**

Those are transforming steps. Taking them, we move to a higher consciousness and to greater understanding of the higher laws.

We particularly need to bolster our faith when we are faced with situations which seem impossible to our limited vision. The following statement has helped me often at those times:

I HAVE FAITH
I have faith in God as my instant,
constant, and abundant supply.
I have faith in God to open ways where
to human sense there is no way.
I have faith in God to guide, protect,
and direct me in His service.
I have faith in God to help me raise my
human understanding to His higher understanding.
I have faith in myself as a son/daughter
of God eager to do His bidding.[2]

Faith lifts us beyond our limited beliefs, doubts, and fears to the higher dimensions of consciousness. With faith we realize that the infinite power and intelligence of the Spirit within are available to us and will guide us in every aspect of our life in our application of the Universal Laws.

Jesus gave us a graphic description of the power and the use of the law of faith:

Have faith in God. I tell you this: if anyone says to this mountain [your problem or difficulty], "Be lifted from your place and hurled into the sea" [be eliminated or dissolved]," and has no inward doubts, but believes that what he says is happening, it will be done for him. I tell you, then, whatever you ask for in prayer, believe that you have received it and it will be yours. (Mark 11:22-24, NEB)

APPLYING THE LAW OF FAITH TO HEALING

If we need healing and do all we know to do with faith and expectancy of achieving what we desire, it may come to pass. Why "may"? Our use of the law of faith *can* heal us. But if we are misapplying other Universal Laws, the healing may be only temporary. In such cases we can seek medical help and/or our own inner guidance to remove the blocks to healing.[3]

WHEN WE NEED GREATER FAITH

Sometimes we have more doubt and fear than faith. To a young man in his late thirties, Cayce in trance had recommended certain treatments. In this brief but wise statement, he summarized the requirements for his healing:

> Do these. Be consistent, be persistent, be prayerful. Expect
> something to happen. Know what you believe spiritually. Know
> the source of your healing. For all healing must come from the
> attuning of self to the divine creative forces as may manifest in
> self. (3779-1)AR

The above requirements are excellent substitutes for our doubts
and fears and for development of our faith. Infinite Spirit knows
our needs, but it is up to us, using our free will, to decide what we
want, to do our part, and to ask in prayer because: "*Know* that
prayer must be the basis of the hope and the expectancy." (1424-1)

We previously learned about the power of expectancy. It is a step-
ping-stone to developing our faith. In a fascinating book *Jesus and
Mastership,* dictated through James Coyle Morgan, a Unity minister, this explanation is given by Jesus of how those who have not
developed their faith can be healed:

> . . . they seek an outward or visible object through which to
> receive their good. I help them raise their expectation high
> enough so they expect to be healed and then they are. There is
> no disease or malformation of the body that God power can-
> not heal when **faith** and **expectation** are strong enough.[4]

Through prayer we can attune ourselves to the Creative Forces.
Having attuned and asked, we have a solid basis for expecting results. But we need to live our faith—with no doubts or fears, but
believing that we have received and acting in that manner.[5]

OTHER STEPS TO TRANSFORMATION

Each Universal Law gives you a key to transform some aspect of
your consciousness. As you apply these laws for transformation of
self, the important point is to always be certain of the foundation
from which you are operating. As you use the solid foundation of
the best within you—the Spirit within as your guide—then each
application of the law becomes a step to higher consciousness.

As you begin to walk the path by seeking the guidance within
and developing and using your ideals and purposes in applying the
Universal Laws, you gain more hope, more confidence, more trust,
and more faith. These qualities lead to greater understanding in

knowing that this process really works and that you can transform your life (Figure 20).

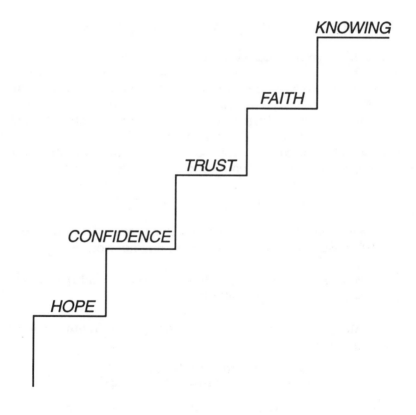

OTHER STEPS TO TRANSFORMATION

(based on the solid foundation
of mind guided by Spirit in applying
the Universal Laws)

FIGURE 20

Progression from doubt and fear to hope, to confidence, to trust, to faith is a normal sequence. Yet we, as individuals, are often at different points for each aspect of our lives, depending upon our previous development. We may, for example, have great faith in our ability to perform our job and at the same time have very little confidence in ourselves in other situations. We need to work at raising our consciousness in each area in which we have difficulty. You do not need to search for these. Since life is consciousness, it will bring to you opportunities in the areas in which you need to grow. These may appear as financial problems, difficulties in relationships, challenges to your beliefs, or other tests. Be thankful for them and seek the lesson each holds for you. As you begin to apply that lesson, you are taking a step toward transformation of that aspect of your life.

THE ALTERNATE PATH—THE LOW ROAD

If you base your belief system only on your intellect and the input of the world outside, the results will be uncertain. You can take this alternate path; the Universal Laws make no requirements of you. If you choose this path as we often do or have done at some point in our lives, it is all right. There is great opportunity for growth on the low road, for the resulting pain and confusion bring us many lessons which enlighten us and assist our transformation. It is the hard way, but it may eventually lead us to seek the better way.

NOTHING IS IMPOSSIBLE

To one invalid who asked, "Is it possible that I will be completely normal?" Cayce's source gave this revealing answer:

Nothing is impossible. This depends upon the faith and the expectancy of the body. (2968-3)

The statement reminds me of a placard posted in our engineering department:

The possible we do right away.
The impossible takes a little longer!

As we look at the tremendous scientific advances made in the last fifty years, that statement seems like fact. Science is built entirely on discovery and use of the scientific universal laws—and new laws continue to be discovered. Is anything truly impossible?

Our advances in other areas, particularly in our relationship to our fellow humans, have greatly lagged behind scientific discoveries. But, as we find and use the Universal Laws that apply in our relationships with self, others, and the Universe itself, our advances in these areas can be even more wonderful than those in the scientific world. NOTHING IS IMPOSSIBLE.

The key to the world of infinite possibilities is FAITH. In fact, each of the laws we have studied in this book is another way of stating that nothing is impossible! Jesus said it, too: "Everything is possible to one who has faith." (Mark 9:23, NEB)

We, as spiritual beings, have chosen to come into the earth with its conditions, in physical bodies, and with perfect patterns and guidance available for anything we need. It is within that context that nothing is impossible for us. The Universe imposes no limitations on us. The only restraints that exist are those we believe in, accept, or create for ourselves. We can dream the impossible dream and make it a reality in our lives, for nothing is impossible. These laws show us the way.

HIGHLIGHTS OF THIS CHAPTER

The law of faith is:

**WHATEVER YOU ASK IN PRAYER,
YOU WILL RECEIVE, IF YOU HAVE FAITH**

Faith is the ability to perceive that through the infinite power and wisdom of the Spirit within, working through the Universal Laws, nothing is impossible.

The law of faith is another key for transformation of your consciousness.

Chapter 20

Laws of Love

The Universal Laws, through which we can transform ourselves and our relations with others, are laws of love. The love on which they are based is not the kind of love that exists in the mass consciousness — the kind of love portrayed in contemporary media. The readings caution us:

> Do not confuse affection with love. Do not confuse passion with love. Love is of God, it is creative, it is all giving. (3545-1)

Cayce gave a series of readings for *A Search for God* on the subject of love. These provide an understanding of the kind of love needed in applying these laws:

> **Love is God. The whole law [Universal Law] is fulfilled in these three words. Mankind is urged to observe and to cultivate this attribute, for it is through love that physical life is perfected and the continuity of life realized. Life is Creative Force in action and is the expression of love.**
> **Love, divine love, is universal. It is found in the smile of a babe, which indeed is love undefiled, in the beauty of a song, and in a soul raised in praise to the Giver of Light. There is love manifested in the performance of duty when there is no thought of personal gain, in speaking encouraging words to those seeking an understanding, and in the activities of those doing their best with**

the talents entrusted to them . . .

Christ perfectly manifested the love of the Maker. His life and teachings are the inspiration for the regeneration of all mankind. As sons of God we can manifest God's love if we allow Him to have His way in our lives . . . Pure, undefiled love is so powerful that men may lay down their lives for others. Self is forgotten . . .

Love is the force that uplifts and inspires mankind. Children starve without it. Men and women wither and decay when it is lacking. It costs nothing, yet its value cannot be measured by material standards. It can lift a wretched human being from the miry clay of despair and set his feet upon the solid rock of respectability and service.[1]

During World War II my wife, Charlotte, was a nurse in a major children's hospital in Ohio. A baby was brought in who appeared to be very ill. The chief of staff examined the child but could find nothing wrong. Yet he knew the baby was dying. He sent for the mother, who was a very well-dressed, intelligent woman, but she was embittered by her husband's going to war and leaving her alone. The doctor told Charlotte, "This baby is starving for love. Teach that mother how to love that child!" Charlotte was an ideal choice for she has loved every child she ever saw. I know of no one who would know better how to love a child. She did as she was instructed. The mother listened and learned the need for love and learned how to love. The baby lived. Love was the answer!

Love is that dynamic force which brings into manifestation all things. It is the healing force, the cleansing force, and the force that blesses all things we touch. With our hearts filled with love we will see only goodness and purity in everybody and in everything.[2]

This quote describes the nature of love that is within you and that is referred to in the statement, "God is love." It is the kind of love you have been given as part of that first great gift you were given: "You were made in the image of the Creator." It is the nature of the love you can use in applying these laws of love. This is the kind of love by which you can transform yourself and your world, for the first law of love is:

LOVE TRANSFORMS

It is perhaps the simplest of all the laws. **It means that no matter what kind of a condition, situation, or relationship you are dealing with, when you bring love to that circumstance of life, it will change, it will be lifted, it will be transformed.**

I saw this work in the case of Dan, an attorney friend of mine who had a reputation as the roughest and toughest lawyer in town. Dan, however, was searching, and he joined a class to study the principles of love and Universal Laws which had been foreign to him. Intrigued, he began to ask the teacher whether love had a place in a court of law. He learned that love will transform, no matter where you apply it. He wanted to know how to do this in the courtroom. As he learned, he began to apply the law. To his amazement, he found that when he was loving toward the person on the witness stand, whom he would normally tear apart, he understood the person. He understood the individual's point of view instead of seeing the flaws in his or her logic. He was able to talk to that one in terms of that understanding and to make clear where the understanding was perhaps not accurate. Because his attitude was not as an adversary, these people didn't need to fight him. They could cooperate. He was not trying to destroy them; he was simply trying to elicit the truth.

In his pretrial work and negotiations with other attorneys, Dan found that some of the townspeople whom he had detested the most and had considered the worst in the legal community became wonderful people when he treated them lovingly. He was amazed at what they were able to work out creatively and constructively in the interest of their clients. The law works. "Love transforms."

Love transforms because it is the presence of God! It's not that God loves, but that **God is love.** The experience of love is the way in which you sense and touch the Presence within. As you accept the Presence within—the love within you—and focus it on aspects of your life, it transforms because it is pure creative force. It is the power of life available to you. It will transform anywhere, anytime, any condition, and any situation to which you apply it.

Let's use a modern hydroelectric installation as an analogy. The water held in the reservoir behind a huge dam is stored energy; love is also a tremendous store of energy available to us and within us. The stored water makes the reservoir a beautiful place to be and to enjoy. However, the reservoir's full potential isn't realized until the water is released through the dam's gates, flows through turbines which drive the generators to produce electricity, which in turn flows through transmission lines. Then power, heat, and light for homes and industry are provided. The water discharged from the turbines also forms a river which provides recreation, fishing, and irrigation for crops. It is transforming because it gives life to the land and those dependent on it. Note the continual flow involved.

You similarly have within you a reservoir of love in which you can find peace and beauty. Your full potential, however, isn't realized until you let it flow outward, generating creativity, healing, peace, beauty, and joy, transforming your life and the lives of those you touch.

You are the equivalent of the gates of the dam that control the flow of the water. You can decide whether to start it, stop it, or you can open the gates and let it flow.

You also are the turbines and the generators. Through the flow of love within, you generate and transmit that energy to whomever and whatever you choose.

You also are the river that carries the water for irrigation and that gives life to the land, as you share yourself, your talents, your life, and your abundance with others.

The key to the process of opening the gates is for you to recognize and to love that source of love within. As you do, you are able to open yourself and to increase the flow through you to the world.

This is a key. If you don't give attention to the source of love within you—the Spirit within—it is as if it didn't exist, because it makes no demands on you. Yet it is the greatest power of the Universe, in infinite supply within you, waiting for you to release it and let it flow. When you make the choice to open the gate and release that supply, you begin by accepting the love which is the God Presence within. As you do this, you naturally come to love yourself. That inevitably results in your loving others as you work out the negative patterns that have kept you from doing so.

In the analogy of the dam, the negative patterns are the equivalent of trash blocking the gates to prevent the flow of water. As the trash has to be removed from the gates, you need to remove the negative patterns from your consciousness. You can do this by a simple process involving the transforming power of love.

THE SECOND LAW OF LOVE

This second law involves a process of releasing. Very simply, the law is GIVING. For clarity we can express the second law of love more fully as:[3]

TRUE GIVING MANIFESTS LOVE

There are many wonderful ways in which you can give. There are more than twenty fruits of the Spirit that you can manifest. We so often think of giving in financial terms, yet much of what you can contribute is far more personal and, therefore, more valuable. "Love is the giving out of that within self." (262-44)

The readings often mention that one of the greatest gifts you can give is a smile. Perhaps that's because a smile can come from all three levels of your being. Given from the heart, it carries a spiritual lift; given with the mind attuned, it can carry thoughts of love which carry through to the physical, making your smile a three-way gift of love.

Your contribution can be done from any one, two, or all three levels. For example, on the spiritual level, you can give through prayer or the spirit which you hold toward others. On the mental level, you can give thoughts, ideas, support, or encouragement. On the physical level, you can give your time, effort, or possessions.

TRUE GIVING

The purpose for which you give is vital. The readings warn that giving with hope of reward or pay is in direct opposition to this law of love. To truly give in accord with the law of love, the giving must be done without any hint or feeling expressed, manifested, shown, or desired for reward. To give with such a desire for reward has nothing to do with love that is transforming; it is not the kind of true giving that this law of love requires. To the degree we give for the purpose of personal gain or glory, we have not truly given (we are still holding something to ourselves).

If even filial or marital or soul love seeks the exalting of self, then it is not fulfilling its purpose from the spiritual import. God is love! (1579-1)

The ideal is true giving with no strings of any sort attached. But we, as souls, learning how to love and trying to express our love, often give with strings attached. That is far better than not giving at all. It's like a baby's first steps—not perfect, but beautiful because of the potential. To the degree you truly and unselfishly give, you bring the transforming power of love to any situation, condition, or relationship.

UNCONDITIONAL LOVE

When we give without strings, we are expressing unconditional love. When we love this way, we accept others just as they are, **not in spite of what they are.** This is the ultimate ideal in love. While we frequently may fall short of this ideal, to the degree that we can achieve it, we release the power of love within us to transform, to heal, and to bring good in all its forms to ourselves and to others. The laws of giving will help you to understand better this process.

THE LAWS OF GIVING

The first of the laws of giving is from the law of cause and effect:

. . . AS YOU GIVE . . .
SO IT IS MEASURED TO YOU AGAIN.
(1532-1)AR

When you apply this law with love, it has far-reaching effects. You can start a cycle of perfection simply by loving others. As you focus on loving them, you give to them the best that is within you, and they or others begin to feel the potential you have expressed; then, they are inspired to manifest the best that is within them. As you apply this law by giving with love—because you love—you transform your relationships with others and also those of the world about you.[4]

A startling practical example of this law is revealed in this Cayce comment made to a good cook:

The ability to be a good cook arises from those activities, under whatever may be the environ, and you have recipes all your own. Keep them. And give them away if you would keep them. For, remember, **you can never lose anything that really belongs to you, and you can't keep that which belongs to someone else.** No matter if this is spiritual, mental or material, the law is the same. (3654-1) [Author's emphasis]

The reading says that by giving something to someone else, it

becomes your own. How different from the concepts of this materi-
alistic world!

Transforming self may seem to be a far cry from cooks and their
recipes, but it really isn't. You have talents and abilities, and knowledge and experience. As you add love of self and others to your
consciousness, you create the desire in yourself to give and to be
helpful and constructive, for self and for others. As you give your
talents, abilities, knowledge, and experience (your recipes) in service to others, they really become yours "For only that you give
away do you possess." (1786-2)AR

Through true giving we express our love to others. Each of us, in
our own way, is giving our gift, our creation, a part of self, so that
others, through us, might have access to and come to realize the
transforming power of love. True giving, then, is indeed the way of
the Christ. It is a way in which each one of us can follow His example and become more truly gods and goddesses in accord with our
soul's purpose.

GREATER UNDERSTANDING

Another law of giving shows that something else is gained by the
act of true giving:

. . . AS YOU GIVE YOU GAIN IN UNDERSTANDING.
(1472-10)AR

We have learned that when we start with Spirit, there is always
an increase. Since you are starting with love, one form of the increase occurs in understanding, because by manifesting love you
bring greater understanding to others. You have sown seeds of
understanding and by the law "as you sow so shall you reap,"
greater understanding will come to you.

It was this law of giving which my friend Dan, the attorney, put
to work when he began to be loving to the witnesses in the courtroom. He gained greater understanding, he was transformed, and,
since he was changed, the situation also was transformed in a way
that was beneficial for Dan and the witnesses.

COMPLYING WITH THE LAWS OF LOVE

A teaching that applies to the laws of love is the commandment
Jesus gave which was one of His unique contributions to the world:

Love one another. He knew that the inherent nature of love is to transform, so His teaching tells us how to put the law of love into action.[5]

The readings leave no doubt that the application of the "be-attitudes" like peace, joy, and kindness provides another way to comply with the law of love. I have previously listed these seeds of the spirit and also recommended them as spiritual and mental ideals. To live them in your life is to give in the highest way because they are aspects of love. As you adopt any one of them as the attitude by which you live, you will bring love and its transforming power into your life as well as into the lives of others.[6]

When you begin to apply the fruits of the Spirit or begin to give as a result of your love for another, you not only comply with the law of love, but you put into effect other laws. It is important that your giving be in accord with other Universal Laws.

For example, we have discussed how important it is to give only in accord with the laws of self. This doesn't limit your giving, but insures that you give with equal respect and consideration for self and others. This need for balance was pointed out in a Cayce reading for a mother who was having problems because she was giving too much:

> In the home and the activities, those relationships—be true to your own self and you will not be false to any. **The law of love is giving, not overtaxing body or mind but in patience.** For He is mindful of you. (303-24)AR [Author's emphasis]

The opposite advice was given in a reading for another woman who was concerned with material things and selfish desires:

> Let your daily thought and prayer be:
> "LORD, when I pray let it be for others! LORD, when I go to play or when I go to do this or that, may the thought ever be for others!" . . . He . . . has given you the opportunity that you may remind others of *His* love! (1315-10)AR

The two readings represent the extremes to which individuals go in giving—from giving all to giving nothing; from those who are completely self-denying to those who live only for the selfish ego-self. Both individuals were ignoring the laws of self and demonstrating forms of selfishness. The readings gave advice to each to bring them in accord with the laws of self. Both answers involved bringing love to the situation, one advising more love for self through patience, the other more love for others through giving others time, thought, and effort. Love is the answer, but how you use it and to whom you apply it is critical.

PRACTICAL APPLICATION OF
LOVE TO YOUR PROBLEMS

You can solve any difficulty in your life by applying the power of love to it, for "love transforms." Just as you created the situation through the misuse of the Universal Laws, so you can transform the situation by proper use of the laws, particularly the law of love.

You know the law of choice: "Life is the experience of your choices." From that law, you know that any difficult situation brings the message that you are at cause and have made choices that aren't in accord with your purpose or the purpose of the Universe. You've made such choices as a result of a negative pattern or negative beliefs within you. So each difficult experience is a wonderful opportunity for self-transformation. It contains and is showing you the pattern that has created the problem so that you can bring love to it. As you do, love will eliminate the pattern or change the belief, and so transform that aspect of you. The undesirable condition will no longer have reason to exist, so it will be resolved. You can achieve this by a three-step process based on the Universal Laws.

THREE STEPS FOR SELF-TRANSFORMATION

The three basic steps are:[7]

1. **Find the message.**
2. **Find the feeling.**
3. **Bring love to it.**

Let's go through the three steps using a real-life experience so that I can explain the reasons for each step. For practice, you may choose some recent incident that upset you, but not the most difficult one you are facing.

STEP ONE: FIND THE MESSAGE
THE EXPERIENCE HAS FOR YOU

To find the message, you do not have to know when or how you set the laws in operation or why you did it, or which laws were involved. Those questions are not important. What you do need to know is, What is the message this experience is bringing to you? The message you need to find is contained in the experience itself. You can discover it by looking closely at what occurred:

Recall the experience, go carefully through it in your mind, remembering your thoughts about it as it manifested. What form did it take? Was it a financial setback? A personal criticism? What was its nature? Note the sequence of events. Now describe the experience in ten or fifteen words or fewer. Write it down. This experience is making a comment to you by its nature, form, and sequence. Your brief summary will probably be a statement of the message in which you can find the lesson the experience holds for you.

For example, a woman wrote for advice to Ann Landers, complaining that her husband always gave her birthday gifts like automobile tires or appliances that he wanted. She might have summarized the situation as "My husband gives me selfish gifts." Since the world reflects to us our own consciousness (the fault we see in others is a reflecion of a fault within self), the experience was bringing her the message that she gives out to others in a selfish manner—with strings attached—so that she could benefit from her own actions. Possibly she was putting herself and her wants before those of others in her family. The laws of self require equal consideration for others. Selfishness is the negative pattern she needs to eliminate to resolve the situation.

This first step of writing a brief description of the experience will help you spot the negative pattern or belief within you that you are dealing with and tell you what aspect of your life it applies to. In the above case the negative pattern revealed was selfishness—in the giving aspect of her life.

When you have found the pattern, do not judge yourself for it. Accept it as if you were in school and the teacher gave you an interesting assignment.

Take time now to complete Step One on the experience you have chosen.

STEP TWO: FIND THE FEELING

Sit for a few minutes in a quiet place. Get in a relaxed or meditative state, close your eyes, mentally go over your body from head to toes, relaxing the muscles and tensions in each part. Take several deep breaths, relax, and release the tensions within mind and body as you breathe out. Now bring the incident to mind and go through it, visualize it or experience it in your mind. As you do this, note how you felt then and experience those feelings again. Notice what it feels like in your body when you have those feelings. **Hold those feelings that you are experiencing. Do not attempt to name them or analyze them. Just feel them, hold them.**

STEP THREE: BRING LOVE TO IT

Now stand aside as though you are looking at yourself, at this person you are who has these feelings. Realize that this person — you — is trying to grow and to learn. Look at the person you are and love that person. Think, say, and feel, "I love you just the way you are." Let your love be without conditions — totally loving, totally giving. Let yourself feel that love. Tell yourself: "You don't need to change, you are lovable even when you feel that way. I love you." Say it sincerely, feel it. Put your arms around that person, hold yourself close. Feel the warmth and the peace of that love. Feel what it feels like to love and to be loved. Hold that love. When it feels right, take a deep breath and release it, continuing to feel what it feels like to love. When it feels comfortable to do so, open your eyes. Be aware then of any change in that part of you that was carrying the negative emotion; be aware of your feelings now.

This third step brings transformation, as you accept yourself just as you are and love yourself just as you are. That lifts you to a higher consciousness — a healing consciousness.

In doing these three steps you have accepted responsibility for the experience, found the lesson, acknowledged your feelings, and accepted them. Acceptance is one form of love. Then you reinforced that acceptance by bringing love to the person you are, without any requirements or judgments. Thus you applied the law of love. "Love transforms."

This process will be successful to the degree that you can accept your responsibility for the situation, recognize and accept the lesson, respect and accept your feelings, and bring love to them unconditionally. Vital to Step Three is the release of any criticism, expectation, or judgment of self or of what you should have done or not done. In other words, accepting and loving yourself just as you are, a child of God. You may need to repeat this process several times for a given condition until you learn how to accomplish it effectively.

This is a simple process, but the Universal Laws are simple. The process works. It is basic to much of your transformation. It works because it transforms your consciousness, which is the cause, the creator of the difficulty.

You can use these three steps anywhere and anytime. Once you've used them a few times, they will come naturally and easily to you. The process can be used individually, in groups, or to help a friend. You only need to be willing to try it with some degree of expectancy and faith that in some way you will be helped.

There is no single way in which the difficult situation will be resolved once you have eliminated the negative pattern by the transforming power of love. Based on my experience, I can't predict just how it will be resolved. Sometimes the situation no longer occurs or I am no longer aware of it. If I am aware, it no longer disturbs me, or something unexpected happens that changes the existing conditions. Regardless of how it happens, you can know, based on the Universal Law "love transforms," that the situation will be resolved as soon as you have effectively applied the law.

There are other ways we can transform our lives because there are other higher Universal Laws of love, mercy, grace, forgiveness, and oneness. To resolve some of the more complex situations of life may require the understanding and application of those laws, particularly if you are misapplying them. But this three-step process using the power of love to transform the old nonloving or limiting patterns within you is a basic one that is extremely important to effective self-transformation.

HIGHLIGHTS OF THIS CHAPTER

The first law of love is:

LOVE TRANSFORMS

The second law of love is:

TRUE GIVING MANIFESTS LOVE

The laws of giving are:

AS YOU GIVE SO IT IS MEASURED TO YOU AGAIN

AS YOU GIVE YOU GAIN IN UNDERSTANDING

The three steps for transformation by the laws of love are:

ONE: **FIND THE MESSAGE THE EXPERIENCE HAS FOR**
            YOU

TWO: **FIND THE FEELING**

THREE: **BRING LOVE TO IT**

PROGRESS ON THE PATH OF UNIVERSAL LAW

We have come so far (Figure 21) that our view now includes only the higher Universal Laws, beginning with the laws of self. We have progressed a long way on the path—but we've further yet to go!

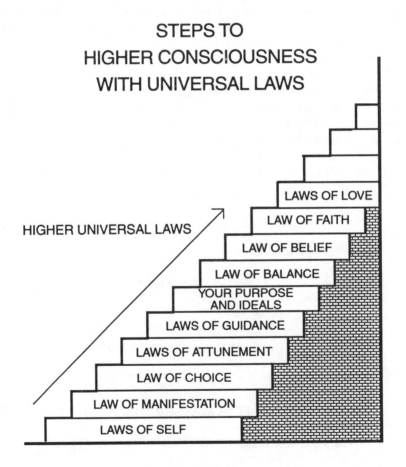

STEPS TO HIGHER CONSCIOUSNESS WITH UNIVERSAL LAWS

HIGHER UNIVERSAL LAWS

LAWS OF LOVE
LAW OF FAITH
LAW OF BELIEF
LAW OF BALANCE
YOUR PURPOSE AND IDEALS
LAWS OF GUIDANCE
LAWS OF ATTUNEMENT
LAW OF CHOICE
LAW OF MANIFESTATION
LAWS OF SELF

FIGURE 21

Chapter 21

Be the Law

YOUR WORK

I began Part III of this book by pointing out that it would present to you higher laws for your transformation. You have now studied these laws. They are the principles by which you can come to know yourself, can understand much of the meaning and purpose of life, and can help you begin the process of self-transformation. However, your work with studying these laws has just begun. It is merely the first of three necessary steps in utilizing the laws for transformation. The three steps are:

1. **Learn the *law* . . .**

2. **live the law;**

3. **be the law . . .** (2185-1)

LEARN THE LAW

Do not let this phrase intimidate you. It does not mean you must memorize or be able to quote the laws. It means: know that there are laws! Knowing this, you have already taken steps to incorporate the principles into your life by setting your purposes and ideals in accord with the laws. You have further learned the laws in that you know that through their operation, you are responsible for your life and your destiny. You have learned that the purpose of the laws is love and that as you "stand aside and watch yourself go by" you can gradually bring yourself to a higher state of consciousness where you use the laws in the highest way—that, as you do, you apply them for the greatest good for yourself and others. You have, through your study of this book, already learned many of the laws— all that you need to begin the process of self-transformation. To truly make the laws a part of your consciousness—if you have not already done so—you need to take the next step: to apply and live these laws.

LIVE THE LAW

When you begin to work with a law, look for opportunities to use it; usually they will come where and when you least expect. When they come, apply the law in the highest way you can conceive. That is to say: act in accord with your purposes and ideals. If you have any questions, seek guidance within on what to do, then do it. So live it day by day:

For the law of the Lord is not as a precept but is a living thing . . . (262-109)

These are unchangeable laws. And as the material universe is governed by and rests upon laws, so must each soul, each entity magnify same in the daily experiences; not merely the knowledge that such exists, but—existing—make them a part of your daily life . . . (1688-6)AR

To understand better how you can live the law, a simple example of dealing with a man-made law—not a Universal Law—may be helpful.

Several years ago, at the end of a long automobile trip which had been made at speeds considerably in excess of the speed limits, I found myself completely worn out. When I considered the causes behind the painfully obvious effect, it became clear that, in exceeding the speed limits, continual tensions were created by the need to decide how fast to drive, how to avoid detection, and how to handle the greater risks and demands involved with the high speeds. The solution to the problem was obviously to drive within the speed limits—apply the law! When I applied the law on my next trip by staying within the speed limits, I found that the tension, fatigue, and fears were eliminated. I was no longer fighting the law—I was complying with it.

You can live the Universal Laws in accord with their inherent purpose by getting in flow with the purpose of the Universe. This is where inner guidance is required, particularly in finding your purpose and setting your ideals so that you will be able to comply with the Universal Laws in the highest way you can. The choice to comply or not comply with the laws is always yours. How you choose will make a great difference in your life:

> *Rather* **does man—by** *his compliance* **with divine [Universal] law—bring** *order* **out of chaos; or, by his** *disregard* **of the associations [guidance] and laws of divine influence, bring chaos and** *destructive* **forces into his experience.**
>
> (416-7)

The great need for application of the laws is clear in this excerpt:

> . . . how, when and in what way does an individual become aware of the laws pertaining to the construction of a sentence in English? How, where, when, in what manner does an individual learn the rule of spelling a word? By the meditating upon same, by seeing, visualizing, acting. And then the *awareness* of same is manifested by the manner in which the individual puts same into practice in conjunction or association with its fellow man. The knowledge may be existent, the awareness in self may be present; but if the individual does not apply same in its associations—or if it uses some other manner, some other way of expression than that it has set as the rule or the standard [ideal]—it becomes of none effect.
>
> (272-9)

Furthermore, only in application is found the true meaning of all laws. The rewards for applying and complying with the laws are great:

> . . . **in compliance with laws all things become possible with one complying to such laws** . . . (900-65)

" . . . in compliance with laws all things become possible"! Isn't that wonderful! This is a state of true freedom in which there are no limits. We have long regarded freedom as being free of something. But freedom, in its broadest sense, is a much greater state in which all things are possible to you. The key to true freedom is living the

Universal Laws in the highest way. To achieve this freedom requires attunement to your Higher Self for guidance as to how you can apply the laws in the best way you are capable of doing.

The choice is yours to make! The key to whether you choose to comply with and live the laws or defy them is your own will. In other words, whether or not you ever achieve true freedom depends only on you—what do you will to choose?

When you apply the laws in your daily life, there is another great benefit—the Creative Force works with you:

> . . . in the application of that *you know* does there come the knowledge, the understanding of what, of where, of how, the next step, the next activity, is to be taken. (683-1)

BE THE LAW

As you apply the law, you become the law. In my example, as I applied the speed limit laws and began to see and understand the benefits derived, my intent and purpose gradually became to always drive within the limits. Since this is also the intent and purpose of those laws, in a sense I became the law as far as my life was concerned, perhaps even being an example to others.

As you recognize the Universal Laws and realize they are a vital part of your life and apply them in accord with your ideals and purposes, you become the law. An interesting excerpt explains how Jesus did it and how we can, too:

> . . . as He applied the law He made Himself equal with the law, by becoming the law. No doubt, no fear, no animosity, no self—but selfless in God's purpose. This overcomes the law as related to all phases of materiality . . . (2533-7)

Thus, to "be the law" is far more than just complying with a law. It involves making yourself one with the purpose of the Universe, which is a selfless purpose. As previously explained, to make the transition from a selfish base to selflessness requires establishing your purpose and your ideals, utilizing your inner guidance, and applying the laws of self. As you do this, you can release the fears, doubts, and animosities of your life because you are eliminating the selfish self which requires such. Thus, you can become one with the purpose of the Universe, which is to say, you have overcome the necessity for the law, you have mastered the law, you have become the law, you *are* the law.

We are urged by Cayce to "be the law" for some very good reasons:

> *Be* **rather the law, than** *within* **the law, or conforming to a law.** *Be* **a law. In this the entity may gain most in the present experience. In this may the entity make the life** *most* **worthwhile. In this may the entity aid others more, in understanding themselves.** (1729-1)

Finally, as you become the law, you fulfill the law. Fulfilling any law in the highest way you can is always a manifestation of love, for the law is love. And love is always the answer for "love transforms."

SO:
LEARN THE LAW
LIVE THE LAW
BE THE LAW
and you will
FULFILL THE LAW,
you will
TRANSFORM YOUR LIFE

This is the work of self-transformation. This is, I believe, my work in this world. It may be your work also, for it is in accord with the purpose of the Universe and with our purpose for being. I believe there is no higher calling! There is no work more fulfilling!

The laws are simple, but not always easy to apply. After all, Jesus told us to do it 2,000 years ago. If it were easy, we would have done it. But you and I are blessed in this age with the heritage of 2,000 years of learning difficult lessons. Now we have an openness and understanding of ourselves and a consciousness that is open to the laws. We can do it now! This is the opportunity of the ages!

THE OPPORTUNITY OF THE AGES

The Universal Laws give each of us an opportunity to make a difference in the world now and in what the world will become, perhaps even to prevent its ultimate destruction. We have, through the ages, tried to rule the world with force and power. We have, in this century, put our greatest minds to work in science and have made great advances in material things. In doing so, we have brought upon ourselves greater problems, until our world seems to teeter on the brink of disaster in many areas.

The Universal Laws plainly show us a better way. They give us the keys to transform first ourselves and, thereby, the world. I believe they can and will be the keys to transformation of the world, as we individually learn them, live them, and become them. They are so fundamental to our beings that we sense their rightness, their magnificence, and their potential, even though at this point we may not fully understand the whole picture. That understanding will become clearer for us as we each research and prove the validity of the Universal Laws by living them. As we live them, we see our world in a new light.

That light enables us to see that the Universal Laws, bit by bit and piece by piece, build the picture of a universe of divine order. The laws show us that our lives, just as they are now, are in divine order, for there is nothing by chance. All that happens has a cause and the results have purpose. You come to realize that no matter what is happening in the world or in your own universe, it is the result of the operation of Universal Laws. What happens is in accord with the purpose of the Universe, for the Universal Laws are so constituted to always work toward the greater good for the individual and for all. You begin to see that a divine order and purpose exist. You come to see that humankind cannot circumvent that order and purpose, no matter how hard it may try or how ignorant or devious it may be. By Universal Law even their worst creations eventually bring the lessons for the growth of consciousness of those involved.

It is fascinating to note that science is rapidly concluding that certain situations, such as development of weather patterns, once considered as unpredictable chaotic conditions, have predictable patterns. That means that such conditions are in accord with universal laws. It means that there is order even in chaos. It is just a little harder to see; it takes a higher viewpoint to discover it—one beyond the common assumptions and beliefs. To see the order in what looks like chaos requires the understanding that it is a Universe of order and the willingness to seek for and find the order in it.

You may remember the mirror principle: that all you see in the world is a reflection of yourself. Since the Universal Laws are the basis of the order in the universe, as you make them a part of your life you can come to perceive that order. You will see it in every event of your life if you ask to be shown and become willing to accept a higher point of view.

Since Universal Laws are the keys to the wonderful divinely ordered world existing all around us and within us, they are the stepping-stones to the tremendous opportunities which are ours as we choose to accept that possibility and open our awareness to it. Jesus said it by stating that "those who have ears to hear, let them hear." (Matthew 13:43) You do not have to have paranormal powers or great knowledge or experience or training. This growth in consciousness is available to each of us, here and now, as we learn and live and become the Law.

I believe the Universal Laws offer a potential to each of us and to the world that eventually all can come to understand and live. That is the potential to fulfill our purpose and to bring peace, wholeness, and contentment for all. As you and I make the Universal Laws the basis of our lives, as we learn them, live them, and become them, we can achieve that potential for ourselves. At the same time, by those results, we become examples and so inspire others to do the same. By this simple process we can each become a savior to the world, much as Jesus did during His time on earth.

Thousands of years ago, long before the time of Jesus, this ancient teaching was given. It is as true today as it ever has been. It applies for you and for me here and now:

> **Blessed is the man that walketh not in the counsel of the ungodly, nor standeth in the way of sinners, nor sitteth in the seat of the scornful.**
>
> **But his delight is in the law of the Lord; and in his law doth he meditate day and night.**
>
> **And he shall be like a tree planted by the rivers of water, that bringeth forth his fruit in his season; his leaf also shall not wither; and whatsoever he doeth shall prosper.**
> **Psalm 1:1-3, KJV**

It is my prayer that you, if you choose, may become like that tree planted by the river, that you shall bring forth the fruit of your purpose on the earth, that your life shall be a vibrant, healthy, joyous one, and that all you do shall indeed prosper in the highest sense. This can be your life. You can make it so through the Universal Laws.

❖   ❖   ❖

Notes

Chapter 1
How the Universal Laws Affect Your Life

NOTE: Unless otherwise noted the following references are quotations from the Edgar Cayce readings. For a description of the readings and the numbering system, see "Usage of the Edgar Cayce Readings" in the front of this book.

1. "For, as the entity experiences at times, there must be a law to *everything*—spirit, mental, material. To be sure, there *is*; but it is guided, guarded, watched over, and kept in accord with that which is the principle, the spirit, the *soul* of the First Cause." (1885-2)

2. "*Rather* does man—by *his compliance* with divine laws—bring *order* out of chaos; or, by his *disregard* of the associations and laws of divine influence, bring chaos and *destructive* forces into his experience." (416-7)

3. This statement might be challenged, pointing out the weightlessness experienced by astronauts in space. That is really a condition of freefall, and it is no different than the weightlessness experienced during a fall off a cliff. The point of the statement is not that the effects of gravity are always the same—obviously they are not; on the moon, for example, gravity is much less—but that the law of gravity applies consistently. The author recognizes that the subject of gravity is indeed a complex one, in view of Einstein's general theory of relativity. Reference: *Einstein's Universe*, by Nigel Calder, "Weightlessness," Ch. 6, Penguin Books, New York, N.Y., 1980.

4. "These laws are unfailing, in spiritual, in mental and in material aspects. These change not. They are unchangeable laws." (3409-1)P

"Then, what meaneth these laws? They are not merely statements or ideas, but are immutable, unchangeable, eternal." (2524-3)P

Universal Law and Its Relationship to Higher Dimensions (unpublished), by J.A. Vanderwert, Rt. 1, Alto, Michigan.

5. This is an Edgar Cayce reading number. Its significance and the various ways the readings are used are given in the section, "Usage of the Edgar Cayce Readings," in the front of this book.

6. "With the perfect understanding of any law, the law may be made a part of the entity, and as the development through the physical plane is to gain the understanding of all Universal Laws, the knowledge thus attained and made a part of the entity, brings the development . . . " (900-25)

Chapter 2
Like Begets

1. See reading 327-5.

2. "If you would have patience shown you, show patience to others." (1587-1)

See *A Search for God,* Book I, Ch. 7, for a wonderful presentation on "Patience." *A Search for God,* Books I and II, are basic texts on living in accord with the philosophy expressed in the Cayce readings. These books are used by the Search for God study groups throughout the world. (A.R.E. Press, P.O. Box 656, Virginia Beach, VA 23451-0656.)

3. Bruce McArthur, "Universal Laws," *The A.R.E. Journal,* A.R.E. Press, Virginia Beach, Va., November 1977, January 1978, March 1978, July 1978, September 1978.

4. "Hence, Destiny is: 'As ye sow, so shall ye reap.' And like begets like!" (276-7)

5. *Metaphysics II*, Unity School of Christianity, Unity Village, MO 64065, p. 66.

6. Ernest Holmes, *The Science of Mind,* Dodd, Mead & Company, New York, N.Y.,1938, p. 306.

7. See readings 137-124, 270-31, 1688-6, 3376-2, 3544-1, and 5349-1.

8. *A Search for God,* Book I, *op. cit.* Chapter 11, 1942, 1970, p. 126.

9. *The A.R.E. Journal,* a publication presenting articles and information on the Cayce readings. Published by the Association for Research and Enlightenment, Inc., an open membership organization of persons interested in the Cayce philosophy and information. (A.R.E. Press, P.O. Box 656, Virginia Beach, VA 23451-0656)

10. Lao and Walter Russell, *Universal Law, Natural Science, and Living Philosophy,* University of Science and Philosophy, Swannanoa, Waynesboro, VA 22980, 1951.

11. *New English Bible.* Matthew 7:1, 2.

12. "You have the ability to judge things. It is well to judge things—it is bad to judge yourself or your fellow man. Whatever the activities may be, whether pertaining to a washing machine or a flying machine, it is well to judge its abilities to serve man." (3544-1)AR

13. Dr. Robert Anthony, *Total Self-Confidence,* New Thought Publications, San Diego, Calif., 1979, p. 41.

14. David McArthur, *Unconditional Love, What a Concept!* (tape), Unity Church, South 2900 Bernard, Spokane, WA 99203.

15. *New English Bible.* Matthew 7:3-5.

16. *New English Bible,* Matthew 5:45. See also Matthew 5:44-56 and reading 254-87.

"No man has the right to find fault with his brother." (257-123)

" . . . find not fault in your friend nor in your enemy; for, has not He, the Father, allowed the tares and the wheat to grow up together?" (440-4)AR

17. "So does it behoove every soul to so live and so act, in its contacts with its fellow man in its business and commercial life, that it will not be afraid to stand on the corner and watch self pass by—in relationship to its activities with its fellow man." (531-1)

"First, as has been indicated, analyze yourself. Watch yourself pass by. Know what are your motivative forces." (1575-1)AR

"Begin in the beginning. Learn your relationships with God. Stand oft and look yourself in the mirror and see if you see an image of the God you worship. If you don't, change it. Change your disposition, smile more. Don't hate anyone. Don't begrudge anyone. And you will find life different." (3544-1)AR

18. "Hence like begets like, and man—or the *being* itself—is the pilot, director and keeper of self." (900-363)

Chapter 3
Laws of Increase

1. "And as has been given, the seed you sow multiply in the lives of others and return to you some thirty, some sixty, some an hundredfold. For *these* are the ways of life, these are the manifestations of the spirit of justice and truth and mercy." (1464-2)

2. " 'As you sow, so shall you reap.' Each thought, as things, has its seed, and if planted, or when sown in one or another ground, brings its own fruit . . . " (288-29)AR

"Thoughts are deeds and may become crimes or miracles in their application." *A Search for God,* Book I, "Cooperation," Ch. 1, A.R.E. Press, P.O. Box 656, Virginia Beach, VA, 23451-0656, 1942, 1970, p. 26.

3. Frank C. Laubach, *Prayer: The Mightiest Force in the World,* Fleming H. Revell Co., Old Tappan, N.J., 1946, pp. 111, 114-115.

4. "For the law is—as from the beginning—that what you sow you shall reap. The seed, the fruit of every act, of every deed—yea, of every thought is within its own self; unseen, save by the spiritual import that is put in same. Hence the spirit, the truth, the 'vitale' that is expressed within every activity must bring its own reward." (470-11)AR

"In the seed is the fruit of that *you sow,* whether it is envy and doubt, whether it is fear and trembling, or faith and hope and patience and long-suffering and gentleness and kindness. The *seed* are there, and you must meet same in your own self." (991-1)AR

5. See reading 3098-2.

6. *A Search for God,* Book II, "Destiny of the Soul," Ch. 7, A.R.E. Press, P.O. Box 656, Virginia Beach, VA, 23451-0656, 1950, 1978, p. 78.

7. See reading 3084-1.

8. "And remember you'll be back again! What do you want it to look like?

You have a greater opportunity at the present time than you will have at any other period of this particular sojourn. So you'd better be up and doing, keeping self in accord with God's laws. For remember, God is not mocked and whatsoever a man sows that must he also reap, spiritually, mentally and materially. For the law of the Lord is perfect. It will convert the soul if you seek to know that law in your experience." (4047-2)AR

9. See reading 3198-3.

10. " . . . if you would create confidence in yourself, *find and have* confidence in others . . . " (2419-1)AR

11. Charles Fillmore, *Dynamics for Living*, Unity School of Christianity, Unity Village, Mo., 1967, p. 126.

12. "You cannot hate, or doubt, or fear those things about self, or those things that would be used by others, and expect the law of love to be effective in you. For, the condemnation of self in others falls on self! And, as the entity will and does find, as the psalmist gave, 'That which I hated has come upon me.' " (3078-1)AR

13. "There must be ever the *one* answer, that there *is* the relation between the Maker and that made. There *is* the care *of* the Maker for that created. There is the duty due of the created *to* the Creator . . . The will of the one must become the will of the other, and *in* that may be found the answer to *all* questions as disturb; for does not the Father take care of all? Then why *worry*? Why be afraid? For 'He that is on the Lord's side, *who* may be against them?' Being one that trusts , know in whom you have believed, and know that He is able to keep that committed unto Him against *any* day, *any* time, *any* circumstance, *any* condition. (2502-1)AR

14. See footnote #13 above.

15. "For the application in self, the *try*, the effort, the energy expended in the proper direction, is all that is required of you. God gives the increase." (601-11)AR

16. "What you sow, you reap, unless you have passed from the carnal or karmic law to the law of grace.

"Then know that whatever exists is for a purpose, for He having overcome the world may aid you in overcoming the world." (5075-1)AR

17. Cf. Galatians 5:22.

"Patience, love, kindness, gentleness, long-suffering, brotherly love. There is no law against any of these. For they are the law of consistency in the search for peace. For they of themselves bring peace, and they are what He gave into the world with the offering of Himself to be the mediator between man and God." (3175-1)

18. "And it is mercy and grace and love you seek . . . *these* things *sow* in the lives, in the hearts, in the minds of others." (262-109)AR

Chapter 4
Laws of Attraction

1. For those who remember from physics that opposite poles attract, this reference note explains this seeming dichotomy with the law "like attracts like":

"Like attracts like" can be considered the master law of attraction. A second law of attraction applies to cases in which a search for balance exists: "As you seek, you attract and are attracted to that which will fulfill your search." The "search" of a magnetic pole is for balance which can be provided by an opposite pole. The imbalance of both poles attracts. That is: "like attracts like."

The law is referring not to the particular designation of the poles involved but to the nature of their condition or "search" and its fulfillment. Therefore, the laws of attraction and the way in which magnets operate are in accord.

2. Edgar Cayce, *Auras*, A.R.E. Press, P.O. Box 656, Virginia Beach, VA 23451-0656, 1973, pp. 5-6, 15.

3. " . . . those of like nature are attracted one to another, or as of a magnetic nature is attracted by the elements as constitute or make those same conditions." (900-387)

4. Charles Fillmore, *Mysteries of John*, 12th ed., Unity School of Christianity, Unity Village, MO 64065, 1985, pp. 30-31.

5. "Like begets like, whether in the mental, spiritual or physical realm." (317-7)

6. "In astrological aspects there are those influences to which and in which each entity may gain knowledge. The natural attraction, law of attraction, or law of repulsion, becomes manifest. For, separated from the body, the mind and the soul are drawn to that influence manifested; just as in the material world those that are thinking along the same lines, or who are desirous of individual achievement, are drawn to those sources from which help or stimulating influences may be had." (2410-1)

7. *"(Q) How can I best draw people of the right vibration to me?*

"(A) By the correct vibration in self. Like begets like. Toned to a tone brings the proper tone from the perfect radiation of such. Each entity *radiates* that tone, that reflection of the concept of its creative force. Each entity, each atom of the entity radiates that vibration to which it attunes itself. Each entity contacts, each entity brings that about itself by putting into action laws, those conditions, those individuals, those vibrations that are necessary for its own development." (2842-2)

8. See reading 2021-1. Also see Al Miner, "Universal Laws," Voyager Project, ETA Foundation, Inc., P.O. Box 4897, Santa Rosa Beach, FL 32459.

9. Column, Charly Heavenrich, *Principle Supporter*, Tucson, Ariz., April/May1988.

Arnold Patent, *You Can Have It All*, Celebration Publishing Company, Rt. 3, Box 365AA, Sylva, NC 28779, 1984, pp. 35-38.

10. See readings 3078-1, 3198-3, and 3691-1.

11. See reading 5233-1.

12. See readings 3706-2 and 3796-2.

13. Perry W. Buffington, Ph.D., *Do Opposites Really Attract?* Delta Airlines Inflight Magazine, Vol. 17, No. 2, Halsey Publishing Company, North Miami, Florida, 1988.

14. See reading 212-1.

15. Emmet Fox, *Life Is Consciousness*, Unity School of Christianity, Unity Village, MO 64065.

16. See reading 212-1.

17. See readings 254-17 and 3063-1.

18. See reading 1722-1.

Chapter 5
The Power of Expectancy

1. "For, that you really expect you receive. Not that you suspect, but expect. There's quite a difference in 'expect' and 'suspect,' though to many they mean the same thing." (3006-1)AR

"But this should be done systematically, *expectantly;* not doubting." (3049-1)AR

Author's Note: I have in the past referred to "what you really expect you receive" as the law of expectancy but have not found verification for that in the Cayce readings. The problem is that we cannot accurately define "really expect" in a way that we could be sure that the "law" would always work. Therefore, I no longer consider it a law.

2. "(Q) Any further advice for my better well-being?
"(A) Keep the mental attitudes in the way that is known by the body; that he that expects — and acts in an expectant manner, consistent with the mental and physical activities — will be rewarded." (532-2)

3. "As you sow, so shall you reap — this again becomes the foundation of what self, as well as others, may expect. If you would have friends, show yourself friendly; if you would have love, love you one another; like begets like. These are unchangeable laws. They do not alter. Man alters them only in the application by his purpose — as to whether it is to satisfy the ego or the animal, or the flesh, or the mind." (2174-2)AR

4. "Keep the body-mind, keep the mind, in creative and constructive influences. The best of this is found in: Don't condemn others, or don't belittle self. See the best in everything. Be more, or more often, the optimist than the pessimist. Know that all the power there is of body, of mind, of soul, lies within self, and God is not a respecter of persons. And if self keeps attuned to Him, who may surpass thee?" (2981-2)

5. *Daily Word,* Daily Word, P.O. Box DW, Unity Village, MO 64065.

6. Tuesday, April 22, 1980. *Daily Word, ibid.*

Chapter 6
Laws of Cause and Effect

1. "For, nothing — as is known in a causation world — happens of itself or without cause." (1998-1)

2. "For the entity came not merely by chance. For, the earth is a causation world, for in the earth, cause and effect are as the natural law." (3645-1)

3. "Causes and effects are *evident* in a material world. While one follows the other, they are as interlocking as day and night." (343-2)

4. "Three Initiates," *The Kyballion,* Yogi Publication Society, P.O. Box 1268, Homewood, IL 60430, 1912, p. 38.

5. See readings 270-15, 1796-1, 1859-1, 2533-1, 2620-2, 3474-1, 3645-1, and 5259-1.

6. See readings 263-18, 270-15, 1102-5, 1302-2, 1432-1, 1754-1, 2753-

2, 2823-3, and 5155-1.

7. "Nothing happens by chance, nothing is as good luck, as commonly called, for the cause must be present to produce that which is real, see?" (136-12) See also readings 333-5 and 3684-1.

8. "For, it is not by chance that each entity enters, but that the entity—as a part of the whole—may fill that place which no other soul may fill so well." (2533-1) See also reading 1102-5.

9. "No association or experience is by chance, but is the outgrowth of a law—spiritual, mental or material." (2753-2)

"As has been indicated through these channels, there is never a chance meeting, or any association, that hasn't its meaning or purpose in the development of an individual entity or soul." (1648-2)

10. Arnold Patent, *You Can Have It All*, Celebration Publishing Company, Rt. 3, Box 365AA, Sylva, NC 28779, 1984, p. 69.

11. "Now: There is set before you, then, the problem of making the choice as to whether the endeavors of self are to be in line with the preparations you have made or not. And the choice as to whether in this place, that place or the other, must be made within self. This does not mean that you are to be guided by circumstance, by 'hit or miss,' but rather as you will and are being directed within your inner self. Do that.

"These should be the answers ever. That choices are made by counsel here or counsel there only makes for confusion within self, oft. Rather meet within your own self your Maker, and let the guide come *there* as to what you shall do." (333-6)AR

12. Edgar Cayce, *Auras*, A.R.E. Press, P.O. Box 656, Virginia Beach, VA 23451-0656, 1973, p. 8.

13. Arnold Patent, *op. cit.*, p. 41.

14. See reading 1424-1.

15. Dr. Emmet Fox, *Power Through Constructive Thinking*, Harper & Row, San Francisco, Calif., 1990, p. 265.

16. *Study Group Readings*, Vol. 7, Edgar Cayce Library Series, A.R.E., P.O. Box 595, Virginia Beach, VA 23451-0595, 1977, p. 329.

Chapter 7
Unique Characteristics of the Universal Laws

1. See readings 270-18 and 816-3.

Chapter 8
Using the Laws to Create Your Destiny

1. See readings 256-5 and 281-6. Also see Eric Butterworth, *Discover the Power Within You*, Harper and Row, New York, N.Y., 1968, pp. 135-136.

2. See readings 262-83 and 1436-1.

" . . . cause and effect to many are the same as karmic. Yet, karmic is that brought over, while cause and effect may exist in the one material experience only." (2981-2)

3. Mary Ann Woodward, *Edgar Cayce's Story of Karma*, Berkley Pub-

lishing Group, New York, N.Y., 1984, Ch. 2.

4. Arnold Patent, *You Can Have It All*, Celebration Publishing Company, Rt. 3, Box 365AA, Sylva, NC 28779, 1984, pp. 41-42.

5. See reading 903-23.

6. "Yet, it is a fact that a life experience is a manifestation of divinity. And the mind of an entity is the builder. Then as the entity sets itself to do or to accomplish that which is of a creative influence or force, it comes under the interpretation of the law **between karma and grace. No longer is the entity then under the law of cause and effect,** or karma, but rather in grace it may go on to the higher calling as set in Him." (2800-2) [Author's emphasis]

7. See reading 2319-1 and John 9:1-4.

8. *Pioneer Press Dispatch*, St. Paul, Minn., May 8, 1988.

Grace Layton Sandness, *Brimming Over*, Mini World Publications, Minneapolis, MN 55369, 1979.

9. See reading 257-126.

10. Linda Gerber Quest, Ph.D., *The Politics of Hope*, A.R.E. Press, P.O. Box 656, Virginia Beach, VA 23451-0656, 1969, pp. 34-35.

Chapter 9
The Master Law for Your Transformation

1. *Edgar Cayce Reader, Volume I*, Warner Books, New York, N.Y., 1969, p. 31.

2. See readings 262-19, 282-4, 323-2, 423-2, 1538-1, 1554-6, and 1564-1.

3. See readings 262-8, 262-19, 262-81, 520-4, 900-323, and 3574-2.

4. See readings 254-80 and 333-6.

"But know that the truth is applicable in every experience of the entity's life, whether as a shoestring vendor or a seller of such, of a director of some great financial institution, or even a leader or ruler over many peoples." (3063-1)

5. See readings 849-17 and 1538-1.

6. See readings 900-302, 2537-1, and 4047-2.

7. *Alcoholics Anonymous*, 3rd ed., Alcoholics Anonymous World Services, Inc., New York, N.Y., 1976.

8. "Then when you quote as to what this or that author says, or this or that man has experienced, do not give same as if they were an authority— but that the experience has been in such and such a manner; as you in your experience have become aware of that truth that is *all truth*—that God *is!* And they that would know Him must seek Him, not in heavens, nor in the uttermost parts of the earth, but Lo, within your own self! For *there* the temple of your soul abides, and there *He* has promised to meet you. And there the covenant is made. And there the choice is taken." (1152-4)AR See also readings 262-52 and 1745-1.

9. See readings 336-6, 1580-1, and 4038-1.

"There are many phases of the approach to individuals. Every individual's troubles to him are the most important in his experience. Truth itself meets all such conditions, for it takes the individual where the individual is, meeting the individual problems in the individual's experi-

ence; else that which is truth becomes false to *that* individual." (254-80)
10. See readings 3004-1 and 5030-1.

"Truth," Circulating File, A.R.E. Press, P.O. Box 656, Virginia Beach, VA 23451-0656.
11. See readings 1219-1 and 1257-1.
12. Eric Butterworth, *Discover the Power Within You,* Harper & Row, New York, N.Y., 1968, p. 146.

Chapter 10
Why You Are Here

1. Eric Butterworth, *Discover the Power Within You,* Harper & Row, New York, N.Y., 1968, Ch. 4.
2. *A Search for God,* Book II, "Spirit," Ch. 12, A.R.E. Press, P.O. Box 656, Virginia Beach, VA 23451-0656, 1950, 1978, p. 117.
3. *A Search for God,* Book II, *ibid.*
Soul Development, Vol. 15, Edgar Cayce Library Series, A.R.E., P.O. Box 595, Virginia Beach, VA 23451-0595, 1986.
4. "Many say that you have no consciousness of having a soul—yet the very fact that you hope, that you have a desire for better things, the very fact that you are able to be sorry or glad, indicates an activity of the mind that takes hold upon something that is not temporal in its nature—something that passes not away with the last breath that is drawn but that takes hold upon the very sources of its beginning—the *soul*—that which was made in the image of your Maker—not your body, no—not your mind, but your *soul* was in the image of your Creator." (281-41)AR

"Each soul is a portion of the Divine. Motivating that soul-body is the spirit of divinity. The soul is a companion of, a motivative influence in, the activities of an entity throughout its experiences in whatever sphere of consciousness it may attain perception." (1096-4)
5. See readings 585-1, 622-6, 900-59, 2174-2, 3241-1, and 5118-1.
Jesus the Pattern, Vol. 10, Edgar Cayce Library Series, A.R.E., P.O. Box 595, Virginia Beach, VA 23451-0595, 1980.
Mind, Vol. 20, Edgar Cayce Library Series, A.R.E., P.O. Box 595, Virginia Beach, VA 23451-0595, 1986.
6. "For, the soul is equal with the universal consciousness or purpose, or God-consciousness—as it may be termed, and thus is a part of all it has experienced; having an influence upon, and being influenced by all of these, according to the will of the entity." (3062-2)

" . . . God, the Creative Force, in creating souls—with the attributes of the 'over-soul,' or the One—endowed each soul with *free will,* in its movement through time and space—being endowed then with a consciousness in whatever dimension of manifestation the soul moves in that period of expression." (815-7)

See also readings 262-79, 826-8, 900-20, 1440-1, and 3929-1.
7. "As has been experienced in the mental self, there is as much reason to dwell upon the thought from whence the soul came, as it is upon whence the soul goes . For, if the soul is eternal, it always has been—if it is always to be. And that is the basis, or the thought of Creative Force, or God. He ever was, He ever will be. And individuals, as His children, are a

part of that consciousness. And it is for that purpose that He came into the earth; that we, as soul-entities, might know ourselves to be ourselves, and yet one with Him; as He, the Master, the Christ, knew Himself to be Himself and yet one with the Father." (3003-1) See also readings 900-340 and 1435-1.

8. "Yet, know that no urge, no sign, no emotion—whether of a latent mental nature or of a material or emotional nature finding expression in the body—surpasses that birthright, *will*—the factor which makes the human soul, the human individual, *different* from all other creatures in the earth, from all manifestations of God's activity!

"For he, man, has been made just a little lower than the angels; with all the abilities to become *one with Him!* Not the whole, nor yet lost in the individuality of the whole, but becoming more and more personal in *all* of its consciousnesses of the application of the individuality of Creative Forces, thus more and more at-onement with Him—yet conscious of being himself." (2172-1)

9. "As to those things that are constructive as to colors, as to stones, as to numbers, as to signposts for the entity, all of these have their welcome as it were in the experience.

"But *will*—as in compliance with Creative Forces, or God—is the greater influence in the experience of every soul.

"As was given, these are signs—which man with his mental self is to use and not abuse." (1397-1)

10. Eula Allen, *Before the Beginning, The River of Time, You Are Forever,* Creation Trilogy, A.R.E. Press, P.O. Box 656, Virginia Beach, VA 23451-0656, 1979, 1976, 1979.

Robert Krajenke, *From the Birth of Souls to the Death of Moses,* A.R.E. Press, P.O. Box 656, Virginia Beach, VA 23451-0656, 1973.

Glenn Sanderfur, *Lives of the Master,* A.R.E. Press, P.O. Box 656, Virginia Beach, VA 23451-0656, 1988, p. 10.

11. Eric Butterworth, *op. cit.,* "Prologue," p. xiii.

12. See readings 1826-11, 5749-3, 2549-1, 518-2, 3003-1, 416-18, 3083-1, and 2533-1.

13. See reading 5744-14.

Chapter 11
Laws of Self

1. "Know Yourself," Circulating File, A.R.E. Press, P.O. Box 656, Virginia Beach, VA 23451-0656.

2. See readings 352-1, 2545-1, 3253-2, 3795-1, and 4162-2.

3. Raynor Johnson, *The Situation of Modern Man,* A.R.E. Press, P.O. Box 656, Virginia Beach, VA 23451-0656, p. 4.

4. Sources of information on laws of self:

The Cayce readings give many references which, at first glance seem contradictory regarding service to others versus consideration for self. This does not mean that some are wrong and some are right, but because they are taken from readings for different individuals they represent the specific suggestions required in each case. Cayce did not offer a specific law of self to which all these could be related, nor was I (the author) able to derive or conceive a law which could be said to cover the wide range of statements made on this subject in the readings. Not only that, but I realized that Cayce in his own life had great difficulty with this, for his inability to balance the demands from others with his own needs eventually resulted in his death. I wondered how significant that was relative to the lack of a defined law in the readings on these factors. Could his own weakness or prejudice in this area have blocked a clear understanding and transmission of full information on that subject?

Yet it was evident to me there had to be basic laws of self that would express the fundamental relationship of self to others, defining the priority involved. I had noted that some modern-day psychics had made statements regarding laws of self. Consequently I researched both published and unpublished works of several other psychics (Al Miner, Joshua Setliff, Mary-Margaret Moore)* regarding this law. Their views were most helpful in developing the chapter on the Law of Self.

The material from them is not basically in conflict with the Cayce philosophy, but rather has helped me to understand the Cayce readings more clearly. This further explanation has given me a better understanding of the relationship of self to others, having a much different emphasis than some of the Cayce readings on this subject. I believe this is understandable and necessary because today we are much more open to a broader view of life and relationships. Cayce died more than forty-five years ago, before the major changes in outlook of the Sixties. He was indeed a forerunner, a prophet, emphasizing the great need of service to others in the strongest manner he could to begin to awaken people to the fact that there was a better way, a higher way.** Now it is hoped that we are beginning to understand and are ready to look more fully at the higher perspective as expressed by the laws of self.

*Bartholomew, *Reflections of an Elder Brother,* High Mesa Press, P.O. Box 2267, Taos, NM 87571, 1989.

*Joshua Setliff, "Universal Law" (unpublished), Psychical Research and Development Foundation, P.O. Box 4305, Virginia Beach, VA 23454.

*Al Miner, *Universal Laws,* ETA Foundation, Inc., P.O. Box 4897, Santa Rosa, FL 32459.

**Richard H. Drummond, Ph.D., *Unto the Churches,* A.R.E. Press, P.O. Box 656, Virginia Beach, VA 23451-0656, 1978, pp. 25-42.

5. See footnote #4.

6. See reading 900-59.

7. See readings 254-17, 264-55, 708-1, 721-1, 1599-1, 1620-1, 1709-1, 1709-7, 2725-1, 3063-1, and 5673-1.

8. See reading 4735-1.

9. See reading 1264-1.

10. See readings 262-114, 1264-1, 2803-2, and 3292-1.

11. "First find self. Let nothing deter you from putting the first things first . . . " (2780-3)AR

12. Brother Lawrence, *The Practice of the Presence of God,* Fleming H. Revell Co., Westwood, N.J., 1980.

13. See reading 364-7.

Chapter 12
Consciously Creating Results
with the Master Law of Manifestation

1. "Awaken that within self to the abilities, to the qualities that the body may experience through the activity of the spiritual forces within self, that will give the reactions and make the effects as may be created in the physical; for the spiritual is the life, the mental is the builder, and the physical or material is the result." (4722-1)

2. " . . . Spirit, this is the beginning and the end of all matters that pertain to the individual development in the material experiences.

"For as the individual entity, or soul, is Spirit, so its end—or at the beginning and the end—is Spirit." (262-113)

3. Herbert Bruce Puryear, *The Edgar Cayce Primer*, Bantam Books, New York, N.Y., 1982, p. 107.

4. Grady Claire Porter, Glenda Lippmann, *Conversations with JC*, High View Publishing, Rt. 3, Box 365AA, Sylva, NC 28779, 1985, "Morning Meditation," March 4, 1984.

5. See readings 262-78 and 2174-2.

6. *A Search for God*, Book II, "Spirit," Ch. 12, A.R.E. Press, P.O. Box 656, Virginia Beach, VA 23451-0656, 1950, 1978.

7. "Economic Healing," Parts I and II, Circulating File, A.R.E. Press, P.O. Box 656, Virginia Beach, VA 23451-0656.

8. Mark Thurston, *Discovering Your Soul's Purpose*, A.R.E. Press, P.O. Box 656, Virginia Beach, VA 23451-0656, 1984, p. 137.

9. "For the entity likes to be well-spoken of. Then speak well of everyone else and everyone will look and find that in you to speak well of. Then, you have to live it, and it is the spirit of truth, peace, harmony, patience, gentleness, kindness. For like begets like, spiritually, mentally, materially. It is the unchangeable law." (5349-1) See also reading 288-36.

10. "(Q) How may the material activities and the spiritual purpose be coordinated?

"(A) That in the material world is a shadow of that in the celestial or spiritual world. Then, the material manifestations of spiritual impulse or activity must be in keeping or in attune with that which has its inception in *spiritual* things. For, the *mind* of man *is* the builder; and if the beginning is in spiritual life, and the mental body sees, acts upon, is motivated only by the spiritual, then the physical result will be in keeping with that you have sown." (524-2)AR

Chapter 13
Making the Right Choices for Your Life

1. See readings 288-37, 294-183, and 524-2.
Soul Development, Vol. 21, Edgar Cayce Library Series, A.R.E., P.O. Box 595, Virginia Beach, VA 23451-0595, 1986.

2. See readings 262-80 and 454-1.

3. Exodus 19:5. See also readings 257-87, 440-4, and 1151-17.

4. Matthew 6:33.

5. Everett Irion, *Vibrations*, Ch. 6, A.R.E. Press, P.O. Box 656, Virginia Beach, VA 23451-0656, 1979.

See also readings 254-95, 262-52, 281-4, 900-22, 2842-2, and 5756-4.

Chapter 14
All the Answers

1. Montgomery, Ruth, *A Search for the Truth*, William Morrow & Company, New York, N.Y., 1967.

2. (1) 264-45, (2) 873-1, 3488-1, 5752-5, (3) 877-7, 2174-3, (4) 262-109, 2454-4, 3376-2, (5) "Use That at Hand," Circulating File, A.R.E. Press, P.O. Box 656, Virginia Beach, VA 23451-0656, (6) 696-3, 991-1, (7) see Ch. 10.

3. See reading 352-1.

4. (1) 2072-4, (2) 262-5, (3) 267-1.

5. (1) 1776-1, (2) 264-45, (3) 1456-1, (4) 1456-1, (5) 254 series.

6. See reading 5752-5.

7. See reading 333-6.

8. See reading 1158-9.

9. *A Search for God*, Book I, A.R.E. Press, P.O. Box 656, Virginia Beach, VA 23451-0656, 1942, 1970, p. 36.

10. Crum, Jesse K., *The Art of Inner Listening*, Quest Books, Wheaton, Ill., 1975.

The Impersonal Life, Sun Publishing Co., Tonawonda, NY 14150, 1941, p. 151.

11. *A.R.E. Meditation Course*, A.R.E. Press, P.O. Box 656, Virginia Beach, VA 23451-0656, 1978.

Herbert B. Puryear and Mark Thurston, *Meditation and the Mind of Man*, A.R.E. Press, P.O. Box 656, Virginia Beach, VA 23451-0656, 1975.

Meditation, Parts I and II, Vols. 2 and 3, Edgar Cayce Library Series, A.R.E., P.O. Box 595, Virginia Beach, VA 23451-0595, 1974, 1975.

12. *Handbook for A.R.E. Study Groups* (out of print) and *Edgar Cayce and Group Dynamics*, A.R.E. Press, P.O. Box 656, Virginia Beach, VA 23451-0656.

13. *Handbook for A.R.E. Study Groups*, ibid., pp. 2-3.

14. Arnold M. Patent, *You Can Have It All* (1984) and *Death, Taxes, and Other Illusions* (1989), Celebration Publishing Company, Rt. 3, Box 365AA, Sylva, NC 28779.

Chapter 15
Finding Your Life's Purpose

1. Based in part on the purpose statement exercise developed by Arnold Patent and on the article prepared by Melva and Jesse Johnson in *Principle Supporter*, 2509 North Campbell Avenue, #355, Tucson, AZ 85719.

"Understanding the Purpose of Life," Circulating File, A.R.E. Press, P.O. Box 656, Virginia Beach, VA 23451-0656.

Arnold Patent, *You Can Have It All*, Celebration Publishing Company,

Rt. 3, Box 365AA, Sylva, NC 28779, 1984.

2. Patent, Arnold, *You Can Have It All, ibid.*, p. 35.

Chapter 16
Setting Your Ideals in Accord with Spirit

1. See reading 5118-1.

2. "Keep before the mental body that that will ever be *constructive* in its nature; for the mind *is* the builder, the spiritual or the ideal is the life. If the ideal is set in material things, these do rust, they do corrupt. If the ideal is set in heavenly things, in spiritual things, they grow brighter by use, they grow more harmonious by their age and attunement, and build in the material body, the material experience of the body, that which is *satisfying* in that it brings contentment." (912-1) See also readings 578-2, 1494-1, and 5000-1.

3. Herbert B. Puryear, Ph.D., Mark A. Thurston, Ph.D., *Meditation and the Mind of Man*, A.R.E. Press, P.O. Box 656, Virginia Beach, VA 23451-0656, 1975.

Carolyn DiPaolo, *Teaching for Wholeness*, A.R.E. Press, P.O. Box 656, Virginia Beach, VA 23451-0656, 1985.

Chapter 17
Bringing Balance to Your Life

1. See readings 257-180 and 1537-1.

2. Walter Russell, *The Messaage of the Divine Iliad*, University of Science and Philosophy, Swannanoa, Waynesboro, VA 22980, 1948, pp. 74-79.

3. Lao Russell, *God Will Work with You But Not for You*, University of Science and Philosophy, Swannanoa, Waynesboro, VA 22980, 1955, p. 130.

4. See readings 307-10 and 2533-3.

5. "And then, as must be seen, must be felt, must be experienced sooner or later the awareness, the consciousness that, only *spirit* is everlasting, then the promptings, the balance must be spiritual in its essence in dealing with or judging the mental attitudes, the social relationships, the material experiences.

"For unless they are such, how *can* they be *ever* lasting or constructive in the experience of any individual entity?

"For that which had a beginning has an end." (816-10)

6. See the 257 series of readings.

7. McArthur, David, "The Great Balancing Act" (tape), Unity Church, South 2900 Bernard, Spokane, WA 99203, Aug. 6, 1989.

8. See reading 340-29.

9. Annita Harlan (unpublished manuscript), Tucson, Arizona.

10. See reading 2691-1.

11. See reading 3605-1.

12. See reading 1925-2.

13. See reading 1315-10.

14. See reading 4406-1.

15. Sanaya Roman, *Living with Joy*, H.J. Kramer, Inc., P.O. Box 1082, Tiburon, Calif., 1986, pp. 123-124.

16. Riane Eisler, *The Chalice and the Blade*, Harper Collins, San Francisco, Calif., 1988.

17. "As has been so oft indicated to man, throughout his search for God, take time to be holy. This may imply and does apply to the general physical health as well as to the general physical, mental and spiritual being. For, holiness is oneness of the mental, spiritual *and* the material body." (303-32)

Chapter 18
Law of Belief

1. *American Heritage Dictionary*, Houghton Mifflin Co., Boston, 1973.

2. The Option Institute, R.D. #1, Box 174-A, Sheffield, MA 01257.

3. Eric Butterworth, *Dare to Dream* (tape), On the Air Series, Unity School of Christianity, Unity Village, MO 64065.

Chapter 19
Nothing Is Impossible

1. Charles Fillmore, *The Revealing Word*, Unity Books, Unity Village, MO 64065, p. 153.

Silent Unity, Unity Village, MO 64065. For information, phone 816-251-3580. For prayer, phone 816-246-5400 anytime, day or night.

2. Silent Unity, Unity Village, MO 64065.

3. *"(Q) Is the present trouble to be expected as an aftermath of future illnesses, or will it be eradicated after the present attack is over?*

"(A) . . . the applications . . . should *eradicate* the condition—and not to be expected to be returning! though if the body builds that consciousness that 'I've got a weakness or a tendency and must give way to it,' then if you look for that, and know you're going to have it, you'll certainly have it! for the mind builds it then, and it must be met! For remember, ever is the individual constantly—in the physical—meeting that it has builded in its mental *and* physical forces of its body!" (849-23)

4. Morgan, James Coyle, *Jesus and Mastership*, Oakbridge University Press, 6716 Eastside Drive N.E., Suite 50, Tacoma, WA 98422.

5. "As we have in correlation of conditions that assist in the building, the developing, in the physical body, the entity, the inmost being, the expectancy of the physical body must be awakened before the body, through its tissue, its vital forces, can emanate the necessary building, or eliminating forces, of the physical body, to rebuild or develop properly." (900-21)

Chapter 20
Laws of Love

1. *A Search for God*, Book I, "Love," Ch. 12, A.R.E. Press, P.O. Box 656, Virginia Beach, VA 23451-0656, 1942, 1970, pp. 135-136.

2. *A Search for God, ibid.*, p. 136.

3. *"That is the law of love.* Giving in action, without the force felt, expressed, manifested, shown, desired or reward for that given." (3744-4)

"What is love, then? *Giving—giving!* For God so loved the world as to give His only Son, that was manifested in the flesh that we through Him might have access to Him." (1992-1)

4. See reading 262-45.

5. See reading 2982-4.

"Be rather, then, in your associations in friendships, the impersonal: yet with the love of your fellow man so deep, so high, as to show forth *that* love that passes understanding. For *rest* rather in those promises that He has given, in 'A new commandment I give, that you love one another,' and thus *fulfill* the law of love. Love *is* law, law *is* love, to those that love *His* appearing." (694-2)AR

6 See reading 1156-1.

7. David McArthur, *The Laws of Consciousness* (tape series), Unity Church, South 2900 Bernard, Spokane, WA 99203, June 7, 1989.

SELECTED REFERENCES*

Ernest Holmes, *The Science of Mind,* Dodd, Mead & Company, New York, N.Y., 1938.

Raymond Holliwell, *Working with the Law,* School of Christian Philosophy, 1325 Boardwalk, Atlantic City, N.J., or 3121 North 60th Street, Phoenix, Ariz., 1984.

Margaret Pounders, *Laws of Love,* Unity Books, Unity Village, MO 64065, 1979.

John Price, *The Planetary Commission,* Quartus Foundation, P.O. Box 26683, Austin, TX 78755, 1984.

Arnold M. Patent, *Death, Taxes, and Other Illusions,* Celebration Publishing, Rt. 3, Box 365AA, Sylva, NC 28779, 1989.

David Spangler, *The Laws of Manifestation,* Findhorn Foundation, Scotland, 1975.

George Winslow Plummer, *Consciously Creating Circumstances,* Society of Rosicrucians, 10 East Chestnut Street, Kingston, NY 12401, 1992.

I Come as a Brother: Bartholomew, ed. by Mary-Margaret Moore, High Mesa Press, P.O. Box 2267, Taos, NM 87571, 1986.

Eric Butterworth, *MetaMorality,* Unity Books, Unity Village, MO 64065, 1988.

Dr. Venice Bloodworth, *Key to Yourself,* DeVorss & Co., Marina del Rey, Calif., 1986.

*See Notes for additional references.

LIST OF UNIVERSAL LAWS
(in the order in which they are presented)

What Is A.R.E.?

The Association for Research and Enlightenment, Inc. (A.R.E.®), is the international headquarters for the work of Edgar Cayce (1877-1945), who is considered the best-documented psychic of the twentieth century. Founded in 1931, the A.R.E. consists of a community of people from all walks of life and spiritual traditions, who have found meaningful and life-transformative insights from the readings of Edgar Cayce.

Although A.R.E. headquarters is located in Virginia Beach, Virginia—where visitors are always welcome—the A.R.E. community is a global network of individuals who offer conferences, educational activities, and fellowship around the world. People of every age are invited to participate in programs that focus on such topics as holistic health, dreams, reincarnation, ESP, the power of the mind, meditation, and personal spirituality.

In addition to study groups and various activities, the A.R.E. offers membership benefits and services, a bimonthly magazine, a newsletter, extracts from the Cayce readings, conferences, international tours, a massage school curriculum, an impressive volunteer network, a retreat-type camp for children and adults, and A.R.E. contacts around the world. A.R.E. also maintains an affiliation with Atlantic University, which offers a master's degree program in Transpersonal Studies.

For additional information about A.R.E. activities hosted near you, please contact:

A.R.E.
67th St. and Atlantic Ave.
P.O. Box 595
Virginia Beach, VA 23451-0595
(804) 428-3588

A.R.E. Press

A.R.E. Press is a publisher and distributor of books, audiotapes, and videos that offer guidance for a more fulfilling life. Our products are based on, or are compatible with, the concepts in the psychic readings of Edgar Cayce.

We especially seek to create products which carry forward the inspirational story of individuals who have made practical application of the Cayce legacy.

For a free catalog, please write to A.R.E. Press at the address below or call toll free 1-800-723-1112. For any other information, please call 804-428-3588.

A.R.E. Press
Sixty-Eighth & Atlantic Avenue
P.O. Box 656
Virginia Beach, VA 23451-0656